Bromo-Seltzer King

ALSO BY BOB LUKE

Integrating the Orioles: Baseball and Race in Baltimore (McFarland, 2016)

Dean of Umpires: A Biography of Bill McGowan, 1896–1954 (McFarland, 2005)

Bromo-Seltzer King

*The Opulent Life of
Captain Isaac "Ike" Emerson,
1859–1931*

Bob Luke

McFarland & Company, Inc., Publishers
Jefferson, North Carolina

ISBN (print) 978-1-4766-7482-7
ISBN (ebook) 978-1-4766-3687-0

LIBRARY OF CONGRESS AND BRITISH LIBRARY
CATALOGUING DATA ARE AVAILABLE

© 2020 Bob Luke. All rights reserved

No part of this book may be reproduced or transmitted in any form or by any means, electronic or mechanical, including photocopying or recording, or by any information storage and retrieval system, without permission in writing from the publisher.

On the cover: Isaac Edward Emerson at about age 60 (courtesy of Andrew Murray); a night view of Emerson's Bromo-Seltzer Tower circa 1920 with the twinkling lights at the very top; detail of Bromo-Seltzer advertisement from 1908

Printed in the United States of America

McFarland & Company, Inc., Publishers
Box 611, Jefferson, North Carolina 28640
www.mcfarlandpub.com

For Judy

Acknowledgments

Thanks are due to many people for their help along the way. John H. Emerson, great-nephew of Isaac and the Emerson family historian, for a hospitable visit at his home in Cary, North Carolina, and for his stories about the Emersons, and to his wife Joyce, who introduced me to a traditional southern dish, Brunswick Stew.

Matt Balding, Arcadia's manager and the son of Lucille Pate, who owned Arcadia in 2018 and was the daughter of Isaac's grandson, George Vanderbilt II, for a tour of Arcadia, its grounds and buildings; sharing his stories of the Captain and the area, and inviting me to a Southern lunch with his mother in the "Big House."

Andrew Murray, a great-great-nephew of Isaac, for lunch at Baltimore's Maryland Club where he, in addition to sharing stories about the Emersons, showed me the oil painting hanging over the club's bar that Emerson brought back from Europe. Many of the photographs in this book come from Andy.

Dr. Lee Brockington, Senior Interpreter at Hobcaw Barony, the restored estate of Bernard Baruch, who was a neighbor of Emerson, for spending a morning at Hobcaw describing the history of the "lowcountry" and Emerson's relationship to it.

Glenn Lazarus, who after a distinguished military career, serves as a volunteer in the genealogy section of Chatham Community Library, for providing the information about Emerson's ancestors in the early days of North Carolina.

Gil Sanders, retired correspondent for several Baltimore newspapers, for providing copies of articles he had written about various Emerson endeavors.

People at a number of organizations gave extensively of their time and expertise, including Tracy Adams in the Portsmouth, New Hampshire, Clerk's Office; Anne Bennett at the College of Charleston Library; Jessica Kincaid at the Wilson Special Collections Division of the Wilson Library at Emerson's alma mater, the University of North Carolina at

Chapel Hill; Thomas Mann, Senior Reference Librarian Emeritus at the Library of Congress; Dr. Norman Needleman, President of the Tower Corporation; Susan Newrock at the Charleston Historical Society; Shirley Eastham, President, Narragansett Historical Society; Kay Peterson at the Smithsonian's Museum of American History's Archives Center; John Swann, Ph.D., Historian for the U.S. Food and Drug Administration; and Tammi Prysiazny and Shawn Ward, manager and grounds superintendent at Baltimore's Green Mount Cemetery.

A large bouquet of appreciation is due Katherine Chaddock for taking time out from her writing to read and critique an earlier draft.

Paul Dickson and Robert J. Brugger offered much-appreciated ideas and support.

My wife, Judith Wentworth, as always, has been a constant fountain of support for her sometimes overly engaged husband.

All errors are mine alone.

Table of Contents

Acknowledgments vii
Preface 1
Introduction 3
1—Arriving in Baltimore 7
2—Inventing Bromo-Seltzer 16
3—Leading the Naval Reserves 26
4—Breaking In 40
5—Separation Strains 47
6—Problems with the Nostrum 60
7—Arcadia 69
8—Coping with Marital Strife 78
9—Politics, Buildings and Jim Crow 93
10—Vanderbilts 101
11—Fresh Starts 115
12—Building, Divorcing and Marrying 124
13—New Projects 137
14—Those Marrying and Unmarrying Emersons 148
15—Changes Come to Bromo-Seltzer 158
Epilogue 167
Chapter Notes 169
Bibliography 189
Index 193

Preface

Isaac Edward Emerson was a force to be reckoned with. A man of boundless energy, intelligence, and ambition, he invented and marketed Bromo-Seltzer, the leading patent medicine for headache and upset stomachs during the Gilded Age. Bromo-Seltzer made him a millionaire many times over. His wealth enabled him to indulge in globetrotting while collecting yachts, horses, fast cars, buildings, and expansive estates. With wealth also came the social prestige that he routinely courted. He rubbed elbows with other entrepreneurs, presidents, presidents-to-be, governors, senators, and mayors. His philanthropic efforts showed that he never forgot his and his family's roots in North Carolina. He was a patriot, using his own resources to found and lead the Maryland Naval Reserves during the Spanish-American War.

Described by many as "eccentric," he marched to the tune of his own drummer in an upper class society where formality and discretion were publically professed but frequently honored in the breech. Edward Emerson Murray described his great-uncle as "being of the age, fancy, free, and a man who lived his life with the cup full!!"[1] Edward Murray's son, Andrew Murray, said Emerson suffered from the three worst afflictions a man could have, namely "slow horses, fast women, and bad whiskey."[2]

Following a bitter divorce from his first wife of 30 years, he married his daughter Margaret's best friend six weeks later. The national press covered it all in exquisite detail. He once spirited guests away from his South Carolina plantation in a private rail car to avoid a sheriff concerned that some did not have a hunting license. He made sure the finest wines and spirits flowed generously regardless of venue, aboard ship or at one of his estates—and regardless of the law of the land. He met Prohibition's (1920–1933) challenges in two ways. He imported 30 barrels of Scotch from Europe just before the onset of the 18th amendment. He also asked an employee to make regular flights from his Baltimore estate to the Coast Guard Station at Narragansett, Rhode Island, to purchase wine and spirits from a supply of dubious origin, no questions asked.³ Millions of other Americans also skirted Prohibition's strictures, much to Emerson's benefit.

His only surviving biological child, Margaret, was no stickler herself for the social customs of the upper classes, particularly as they applied to women. She attended prize fights, bred and raced thoroughbred horses, like her father was a crack shot, owned five estates, traveled from one to the other in her private rail car, and married four times, once to Alfred Gwynn Vanderbilt, who perished on the *Lusitania*.

Introduction

Isaac Edward Emerson (1858–1931) grew up and built the foundation of his Bromo-Seltzer fortune during the Gilded Age, a term coined by Mark Twain and Charles Dudley Warner in their 1873 book The Gilded Age: A Tale of Today. A cheap metal coated in gold is said to be gilded. The Gilded Age lasted from the end of the Civil War to about 1900. During that time, economic and population growth skyrocketed in America. Super-rich industrialists, variously called captains of industry or robber barons, depending on one's point of view, including such names as Rockefeller, Carnegie, Astor, and Vanderbilt, led the economic explosion. These men, and others like them, used their fortunes, wrought from railroads, oil, steel, and real estate, to build opulent mansions and hotels for themselves. Many favored the king of sports. They entertained the elite and those on the rise lavishly with parties covered in detail by the press. They also were philanthropists, founding public sector enterprises such as libraries, colleges, museums, opera houses, and charities.

New technologies such as the telephone, skyscraper, refrigerator, linotype machine, automobile, and electric light bulb made their appearance. Unions fought for the eight-hour work day and an end to child labor. By the end of the Gilded Age, whose demise was hastened by the Panic of 1893, which lasted until 1897, a modern industrial society had largely replaced regions of small communities. American was well on her way to becoming the world's most powerful nation. Left behind in the Gilded Age's wake were African Americans, who experienced the country's worst racism since the Civil War. Lynchings, segregation, and discrimination were the orders of the day.[1]

European immigrants, flocking to America to fill the multitude of unskilled jobs created by the industrialists, drove cities' populations to unprecedented heights. Chicago's increased four-fold from 1870 to 1900. Both New York and Baltimore saw a 60 percent increase during those two decades.[2] From 1880 to 1910 Baltimore's population nearly doubled to 558,485 people; a number that included more than 88,000 blacks.[3]

The number of over-the-counter patent medicines, including Bromo-Seltzer, also saw unprecedented growth during and after the Gilded Age. Emerson's invention gave relief from headaches, hangovers, and upset stomachs. His genius for advertising and surviving legal and medical challenges to his effervescent nostrum propelled his product to national and international prominence. Emerson founded the Emerson Drug Company in 1891 in Maryland to produce and sell his invention. In October of 1929, the same month that saw the start of The Great Depression, the company offered 56,000 shares for sale. The notice of sale listed branches in New York, Chicago, San Francisco, Los Angeles, New Orleans, and Toronto, Canada. Representatives of the company were listed as stationed in London, Paris, Sydney, Australia, Puerto Rico, Panama, and the Philippines. The formula also enjoyed sales in Spain, Japan, India, Greece, South America, Mexico, Jamaica, Newfoundland, New Zealand, and Alaska.[4] As was true of the British Empire at the time, it could also be said that the sun never set on Bromo-Seltzer.

Bromo-Seltzer, like many patent medicines, went from being an unregulated financial bonanza for its inventor, with sometimes harmful effects on users, to becoming a tightly regulated product as a result of actions by the Food and Drug Administration, the Federal Trade Commission, and the U.S. Supreme Court.

He was a joiner. His memberships included the Royal Yacht Club of Belgium, the New York and Maryland Yacht Clubs, the Societé Nautique de Nice, the Harford and Green Spring Valley Hunt Clubs, the Maryland Jockey Club, the Maryland Polo Club, the Point Judith Country Club, the Dunes Club (Narragansett, Rhode Island), the North Carolina Society of Baltimore, the Racquet Club, the American Pharmaceutical Association, the Maryland Pharmaceutical Association, and the New York Southern Society. He was a 32nd-degree Mason and a Shriner.[5]

He indulged himself with abandon. In addition to his yachts, he owned two mansions in Baltimore, one in Narragansett, and a 12,000-acre former rice plantation in South Carolina. Each was the site of parties, elegant dinners, and weddings all worthy of elaborate descriptions in newspapers' society pages. French automobiles and Rolls Royces graced his garages. He raced fast cars. An avid hunter, he downed many a duck and deer and won many bird shoots with his shotgun.

His many professional accomplishments included presiding over, in addition to the Emerson Drug Company which manufactured Bromo-Seltzer, the Citro Chemical Co. of America, and the Maryland Glass Corporation. The latter churned out Bromo-Seltzer's distinctive cobalt blue bottles. He served as a director of three banks: Drawers' and Mechanics', Century Trust Company, and the National Bank of Baltimore.[6]

The Bromo-Seltzer king gave generously to charities including his alma mater, University of North Carolina at Chapel Hill (UNC-CH), and to relatives. Dairy farming, sailing, various business interests, and horse racing occupied his later years.

He loved to build. Ten feet from his Baltimore mansion, he built an eight-story apartment building—the Emersonian—on the ground where he had earlier installed an expensive, sunken Italian garden. He first removed the plants and statues. The building not only blocked his ex-wife's once-spectacular view of Druid Hill Park and its lake, so the story goes, but its penthouse literally allowed him and his new wife to look down on his ex. Baltimore's most elegant hotel of its day, the Emerson Hotel, came into being after, according to local lore, the maître d' at the Belvedere Hotel upbraided him for shedding his dinner jacket on a hot summer evening. His hotel became the gathering place and watering hole for local and national political leaders, including Woodrow Wilson and Theodore Roosevelt, celebrities visiting Baltimore such as Joe Louis and Charles Lindbergh, and innumerable clubs, professional associations, industry groups, and tourists of all descriptions.

The Bromo-Seltzer Tower, Baltimore's tallest building from 1911 to 1923 and an advertising coup, was another favorite project. The 12 letters in Bromo-Seltzer replaced the usual numerals on the tower's oversized clock. All in the city were constantly reminded of the headache remedy. Ships on the Chesapeake Bay used the tower's lights as a navigation aid. In addition to the tower, postcards, sheet music, streetcar panels, incentive plans for druggists, and trademark cobalt blue bottles containing the nostrum combined to get the message out around the world.

The Gilded Age produced many men like Emerson. He socialized with many of them in Baltimore; Washington, D.C.; Palm Beach, Florida; South Carolina; New York City; Newport and Narragansett, Rhode Island; as well as in Europe. Largely forgotten today, he was one of Baltimore's and America's most prominent and colorful citizens, as famous in his day as Bill Gates is today.

He left a fortune of $20 million ($249 million in 2017 dollars) at the time of his death in 1931. I do not recall my first encounter with Emerson's story, but the more I learned about his life the more I thought him to be a compelling and complex character whose lifestyle mirrored that of the well-heeled upper class. He could be at times visionary, industrious, hard-driving, demanding, mean, and generous on his way to becoming filthy rich. Here is his story as I have come to know it.

1

Arriving in Baltimore

Had Isaac Emerson's great-great-great-grandfather, James Emerson, Sr., not escaped the hangman while the noose was being tightened around his neck, neither Emerson, one of the most colorful figures of the Gilded Age, nor his phenomenally successful patent medicine, Bromo-Seltzer, would have captured America's and the world's attention.

James Emerson, Sr., belonged to The Regulators, a loosely organized group of farmers angry at the British Crown's increasing intrusion into their lives with ever more rigid regulations and increasing taxes imposed from afar. Frustrated by seeing their entreaties for reform fall on the deaf ears of the Crown's Royal Governor, William Tyron, 1,100 of their number met a like number of Tyron's militiamen in the Battle of Alamance Creek on May 16, 1771, in Orange (now Alamance) County, North Carolina. Seventeen farmers and 20 militiamen died. Following a hastily arranged and conducted trial, Tyron sentenced Emerson and 11 others to hang. Soldiers cleared the area around the quickly erected wooden gallows, situated on top of a small hill overlooking the Eno River 20 miles east of Hillsborough, of trees and brush to give spectators a better view. They rounded up as many people as they could find, including relatives of the condemned men, and forced them to view the spectacle. Moments before the executions on June 19, Tyron ordered the nooses removed from the necks of six of the men, including Emerson.[1] The Regulators were heard from no more, but their resistance to the Crown presaged the soon-to-follow American Revolution sparked by similar grievances.

James later served as a private in The War for Independence with a company from Chatham County. For his service, he received a grant for 400 acres near the confluence of Rocky River and Tick Creek in 1780. A son, James Emerson, Jr., received a 200-acre grant on nearby Bear Creek in 1789.[2] One of his grandsons, John Emerson, farmed those acres and, with his wife, Asenath Hunt Stuart, raised a family of nine boys and six girls.

One of the boys, Robert Jehu Emerson, born on August 5, 1835, in

Chatham County, became Isaac's father on July 24, 1858.³ Isaac's mother, Cornelia Lewis Hudson Emerson, was the daughter of Col. Isaac Hudson of nearby Wake County.⁴ Isaac was likely named after his maternal grandfather. A brother, John Watson Emerson, joined the family, on October 22, 1860. A year and a half later Robert, at age 26, and six of his brothers enlisted as privates in the Confederate Army.⁵ Robert mustered in with a North Carolina Cavalry Regiment for a three-year tour where, according to his son John, he served as a courier.⁶

While his father and uncles were away at war, Isaac and John attended school with other children in a classroom fashioned from the Emerson's basement with their mother as their teacher. The one intrusion into their lives by the war came when a troop of Union Calvary scouts under Union General William T. Sherman's command called one evening late in the war. John remembered his mother inviting the officers to stay overnight in the house and offering the barn for the soldiers and horses. They departed the next morning without incident, but precautions had been taken. Cornelia, having heard Union soldiers were nearby, removed all the hams from the smokehouse and hid them. An African American farmhand led the Emerson horses into the woods after putting tar plasters, a painful but effective congestion remedy of the day similar to mustard plasters, on their backs so, should the troops see the horses, they would think their backs were sore and therefore of little value.⁷

The war finally came to an end in North Carolina when in Durham, on April 26, 1865, 17 days after Confederate General Robert E. Lee had surrendered to Union General Ulysses S. Grant at Appomattox, Virginia, Confederate General Joseph E. Johnston, vainly hoping to continue the fighting, surrendered nearly 90,000 troops from South Carolina, Florida, Georgia, and North Carolina to Sherman, Robert and his brothers likely among them.⁸

* * *

By 1866, after the births of daughters Anna Clark and Laura White, the family moved from their farm to the outskirts of nearby Chapel Hill, where Robert established a shingles and grist mill. The last Emerson child, Cornelia Lewis, was born there in 1870. The University of North Carolina at Chapel Hill (UNC-CH), the nation's first public college to award degrees and Chapel Hill's only major enterprise at the time, closed that year due to lack of funds and students, another causality of the war. The closure brought a lull to the town, leading John Emerson to describe it as "the deadest town in the United States."⁹

One evening, in an attempt to liven things up, the two brothers "borrowed" a horse-drawn hearse stored in a barn near the cemetery and pulled it into position on top of a hill near the cemetery's gate. They fashioned a "driver" out of old clothes and a top hat. They tied one end of a rope to the gate, held on to the other, hid behind the hearse, and waited for the young boy who worked at their father's mill to arrive. They had arranged for him to work late. They knew he cut through the cemetery on his way home. As the two saw him nearing the gate, John and Isaac yanked on the rope. The rusty gate opened with a loud squeak. Then they pushed the hearse down the hill, directly at the boy. He stopped, looked around frantically, screamed, and raced home.

The two youngsters were witnesses to, as well as perpetrators of, scary events. Public hangings were still not uncommon. The two boys witnessed a bungled hanging of three men convicted of robbery. The sheriff had made the ropes too long. They once stood in front of a row of closed stores as a group of white-robed, mounted Klu Klux Klansmen rode silently down Franklin Street, Chapel Hill's main artery, late one night.[10]

* * *

Emerson grew up in a culture dominated by white supremacy. Not only did the Klu Klux Klan enjoy wide popularity among whites, but by the 1890s many North Carolinians, Isaac's father among them, had exchanged their life-long allegiance with the Democratic Party for a growing populist sentiment. In a speech given in Durham on November 2, 1898, former Congressman A. M. Waddell decried the number of "negroes" holding public office and proclaimed, "We are threatened with an influx of negroes from all the southern states who look upon Eastern North Carolina as their paradise."[11] Waddell handed out a letter written by Robert Emerson decrying the fact that the party [Democratic] "has moved so far from her moorings until little else than republicanism, goldbugism, and negro supremacy can be seen in the nominations for office."[12] A week later, Waddell led a riot that overthrew the government of his home town of Wilmington, North Carolina. He called the uprising "perhaps the bloodiest race riot in North Carolina history." He served as the city's mayor until 1905.[13]

* * *

The Emerson family suffered a tragedy when Isaac's mother, Cornelia, died on January 31, 1873, leaving Robert with five children, ages 14 (Isaac) to 2½, (Cornelia). Less than six weeks later, Robert married 30-year-old Julia Booth, on February 10, 1874, at a ceremony in her home.[14]

All did not go well with the newly blended family. Before going into Chapel Hill for supplies one afternoon, Robert closed his mill and told his sons not to open it until he returned. Two of their step-mother's brothers arrived shortly with sacks of grain to be ground. They did not take "no" easily. An argument escalated into a fist fight. John picked up a piece of stove wood, gave it to Ike (Isaac's nickname) with the entreaty "kill 'em." Before Isaac could get a swing in, Julia, in full flight from the living quarters since the arguing began, grabbed the wood and Isaac. No blood was spilled, but living arrangements changed. Robert sent Isaac to live with his aunt and uncle, Mr. and Mrs. A. J. McDade, his mother's sister and her husband, in Chapel Hill near the university. John soon followed.[15]

Life with the McDades had a calming influence on the boys. Isaac was baptized by the Rev. Amzi Clarence Dixon, a recently ordained Baptist minister, along with 23 others in June of 1876.[16] In the fall, after the university had re-opened its doors in 1875, Isaac enrolled along with 42 other students in UNC-CH.[17] John took to splitting shingles at his father's mill for a year, giving some of his earnings to Isaac to help pay tuition. A year later, John enrolled in the Bingham School, a private academy offering education in the classics, in Mebane, North Carolina. He left the school a year later to seek his fortune in Texas.[18]

* * *

Isaac remained at UNC-CH, majoring in chemistry. He complemented his studies with two extra-curricular activities: membership in the Dialectic Society (a debate club),[19] and the Chapel Hill String Band which performed on campus and around town. The band is best remembered, not for its music, but for the fate of its oldest member, Alphonso Davis, age 33. A jury convicted Davis, a white man, along with three other men, one white and two black, of attacking a white woman in her home with an axe in an attempt to steal $1000 rumored to be hidden there. The judge sentenced Davis, his white compatriot, Henry Adams, and one of the black men, Lewis Carlton, to be hanged. Whites flooded Governor Thomas J. Jarvis' office, protesting the hanging of two white men based at least partially on contested testimony from African Americans. Four black prostitutes testified that Davis and Adams had been with them during the time of the robbery. Four other Chapel Hill citizens, all white, testified otherwise. The condemned men were hanged.[20]

To help meet tuition costs, Isaac worked as a teaching assistant at the university while he also became the druggist for two Chapel Hill physicians, Dr. A. B. Robertson and Dr. William Peter Mallet. He noticed that many of their patients complained of feeling ill after consuming large quantities of food and alcohol, a condition he no doubt found himself in at times. He experimented with a number of concoctions, several of which

A drug store located on Franklin Street in Chapel Hill, North Carolina, where Emerson worked during his college days and discovered the formula for Bromo-Seltzer. Courtesy of Andrew Murray.

were well received and started the young chemist on the road to wealth and notoriety.[21]

* * *

Isaac's appearance and attitude appealed to the fair sex and opened another route to notoriety for him. He stood five feet, eight-and-a-half inches tall. His blue eyes, dark brown hair, a broad and high forehead, and a florid complexion did not go unnoticed.[22] Historian James Vickers described him as "a handsome, well dressed, young fellow with a zest for life."[23]

His zest included a relationship during his second year at UNC-CH with the young and beautiful but divorced Emma Askew Dunn, four years his senior. She was the daughter of Col. William F. and Harriett Askew of nearby Raleigh, and the mother of two young daughters, Daisy and Lillie.[24] John warned his brother that he had best sever ties with Emma or leave town. Isaac, who had a stubborn streak in him, initially demurred on both counts.[25] He kept seeing Emma and took a position as an assistant to the university's chemistry professor in the summer of 1879.[26] The job could have been a promising start to a local career for the 21-year-old chemist had his relationship with Emma not created a scandal. His aunt disowned and disinherited him, calling Isaac her "wayward nephew."[27]

At the time, adultery by the woman was the only grounds for divorce in many parts of the South, which led to the prevailing attitude that any divorced woman was no better than "a fallen woman." For a man to court such a woman was one of the region's strongest taboos.[28] There is no written account of Emma being unfaithful to her husband, but their neighbors believed she had. They made life so miserable for the young lovers that Isaac, Emma, and her daughters finally pulled up stakes and headed north in the fall of 1879 to start a new life in Annapolis, Maryland.[29] The two were married on October 20, 1879, in Baltimore.[30] Since Isaac had left college after his junior year, he settled for a certificate of chemistry instead of a diploma.[31]

* * *

With the benefit of his studies in chemistry and the tutelage of established chemists, the newly-wed chemist opened his first drug store upon arriving in Annapolis. But after three years in Maryland's capital city, he decided to seek his future in the much larger city of Baltimore. In 1882, he moved his family 30 miles north to Baltimore. There he purchased and operated three small drug stores.[32] The source of funds used to buy and stock the stores is a matter of conjecture. He may have had help from Emma's family, whose father was considered "one of the leading manufacturers and businessmen of the state." The 1870 census shows William Askew to be a stock trader with a "personal estate" of $10,000 and real estate worth of $5,000; about $175,000 and $87,000 respectively in 2017. Isaac's father may have helped. The Raleigh–based newspaper, *News and Observer*, referred to Robert Emerson on November 9, 1895, as "one of Durham's prosperous farmers." The same article noted that Isaac had recently given him "a fine blooded horse."

Another possibility is the story of a rich man whose throbbing headache was quickly relieved by a dose of the effervescent salt that Emerson had named Bromo-Seltzer, after he had wandered into one of Isaac's "teeny" pharmacies. The man, according to an account in the *Charlotte Journal*, was so pleased that he offered to finance Isaac. The same story noted that "people of the old university town saw nothing special in him." His image with them would soon change.[33] Dr. Joe Schwarcz, in his book, *The Fly in the Ointment*, says Emma provided the financing but cites no source for his statement.[34]

Once in Baltimore, Emerson used a variety of terms to describe himself as a professional between 1882 and 1891. He chose "apothecary" for Baltimore's 1882 *City Directory* and alternated the use of "chemist" and "druggist" for the next several years. Always attentive to his professional image, he settled on "manufacturing chemist" in 1891 and used that title in succeeding years.[35]

An example of Emerson's work with oils. Owned by John H. Emerson. Courtesy of John H. Emerson.

The manufacturing chemist did not spend all his time in his drug stores. By age 30 in 1888, he had taken up oil painting with some success, winning a prize for one of his works from Baltimore's American Art School in June of that year.[36]

* * *

Baltimore's drug stores in Emerson's day were a far cry from those of today. You could not have lunch, buy a greeting card, or print favored photographs. The primary thing you could buy was nostrums for what ailed you or your child. Minor abrasions, cut fingers, skinned knees and the like were treated with iodine and a band aid under the pharmacist's supervision. Oil of clove was applied to an aching tooth. For stomach and headaches, the pharmacist would prepare powders and emulsions the old-fashioned way, with a mortar and pestle, or recommend one of the many patent medicines on his shelves. While the druggist worked, customers could pass the time with a cold bottle of Moxie or a bracing fizzing glass of celery phosphate.[37]

* * *

The Monument City presented two images of itself to a traveler from London. The southern part of the city consisted of what he described as "shabby little one and two-story dwellings largely inhabited by Negroes, pigs, chicken coops, and swarming children." The view, he concluded, "gave one the impression of the city as a dirty, dreary, ramshackle sort of place." The British observer had a more favorable opinion of Charles Street, which began in northern Baltimore. "It was," he wrote, "a fine street full of character. Black servants washed the large windows and swept the stone steps of fashionable townhouses all of which had a certain Southern aspect very picturesque to one coming from the more commonplace Northern towns."[38]

Whatever one's view of the city, Baltimore was on the move, adapting itself to the new age. Its harbor, gateway to the Chesapeake Bay which famed Baltimore writer H. L. Mencken, reflecting on his childhood, described as "the immense protein factory" from which residents "ate divinely," supported large shipping and cannery operations.[39] Enough grain and coal passed through the harbor by 1900 to make it the nation's third largest. New York City's port, thanks to the genius of Cornelius Vanderbilt, took first place. Bethlehem Steel opened its massive plant, covering 1,100 acres, in 1889. With industrialization came progress in the forms of more jobs, electric street cars replacing horse-drawn carriages, and gas and electric companies allowing people to forego the use of coal and wood to heat their homes and cook their food. The Baltimore and Ohio Railroad and steamship lines offered escapes to the mountains and seashore. By 1879, people could call one another on the telephone.[40]

The changes magnified the social divisiveness which had long characterized the city. The wealthy could continue to take advantage of the burgeoning products and services of the growing city. The minorities and the poor had it harder. Though the number of jobs had increased, most were unskilled, low-paying, and demanded long hours. Baltimore's first labor union, the Knights of Labor, formed in 1878, began the fight for higher wages, shorter hours, and better working conditions. Lack of waste treatment turned streets into open sewers. The refuse-polluted water supplies spread diseases such as smallpox, which killed 1,184 Baltimoreans in 1882 and 1883. White-owned stores, theaters, restaurants, and hospitals refused service to blacks, who were also barred from the better-paying jobs. Black and white children attended separate schools.[41] The city's phone books listed whites in the first section and "colored persons" in the second.[42] "No Irish Need Apply" appeared in many job ads. Jews found it hard to find adequate housing and jobs and to enroll in college.[43]

*   *   *

Emerson and his family experienced little of the city's racial and ethnic strife. Since arriving from Annapolis, they had lived in several rented houses in Druid Park, a fashionable neighborhood at the time noted for its wealthy residents and imposing homes. They were not untouched, however, by hardship. The couple's attempt to have a child of their own ended tragically. On July 5, 1883, their infant son, Ralph Waldo, named after the New England writer and poet, died at age nine months.[44] A year later, however, a blessed event occurred when daughter Margaret was born on June 17, 1884. She would become a close companion of her father and a famous and wealthy socialite in her own right.

2

Inventing Bromo-Seltzer

A year before Margaret's birth, Isaac had perfected Bromo-Seltzer through dint of trial and error, as was the case for most purveyors of patent medicine. Formal education of pharmacists in American lagged far behind programs in Europe, notably Germany, France, Great Britain, and Spain, where one could earn a Ph.D. in the subject. A few American medical schools sought to add pharmacy departments, the most successful at the turn of the 20th century being those at the Medical College of the State of South Carolina and the Medical College of Virginia. Eight state universities had started pharmacy programs by 1900.[1] None of these had been available to Emerson. UNC-CH didn't have a pharmacy school until 1897.[2] What formal training Emerson had in drugs and medicine came from his course work in chemistry and apprenticeships with local pharmacists.

The name Bromo-Seltzer came from the fizzing sound, similar to that made by seltzer water, produced when the effervescent granules were dissolved in water, and the presence of sodium bromide, a tranquilizer, as an ingredient in the nostrum's initial formulation.[3] Sales of the mixture put him on his way to fame and fortune. By 1890 at age 32, he could support his family in comfort as well as purchase a 162-acre farm outside of Durham for his sister Anna and her husband, Jack Pope, the first of many such real estate gifts he would bestow on family members.[4] By 1905, he had purchased a residence for each of his two other sisters, Laura White Emerson and Cornelia Lewis Emerson.[5]

* * *

Business became so brisk that by May of 1889, he had sold his drug stores to devote himself to the manufacture and distribution of Bromo-Seltzer.[6] That same year he applied for and received a trademark for a "granular effervescent salt" and registered the term "Bromo-Seltzer."[7] Two years later, at the age of 33, he founded the Emerson Drug Company with himself as president, John F. Waggaman as vice president, and Joseph F. Hindes, Jr., as secretary and treasurer.[8] In Hindes, whom Emerson first hired as a bookkeeper and soon promoted to secretary and treasurer, Emerson had a Baltimore native with many years' experience working for several large companies in the city. Waggaman, a successful Washington, D.C., real estate broker, became an equal partner with Emerson in return for a $10,000 investment to get the company off the ground. Emerson would buy Waggaman out in 1905.[9]

All went smoothly for the new company until May of 1893, when Waggaman asked Washington, D.C., businessman Edward C. Hall, whom Waggaman knew from his real estate dealings in the nation's capital, to invest $10,000 in the company. In return, Waggaman promised Hall a one-quarter interest in the company and a job as salesman for $100 a month. Hall agreed and left a lucrative job in Washington. Five months later, Waggaman fired him. Hall was stunned. Despite repeated pleas, Waggaman refused to give Hall any reasons for his action. Frustrated and angry, Hall sued Emerson and Waggaman in Circuit Court, only to see his case dismissed on December 2, 1893. Hall fared no better with the Maryland Court of Appeals, which ruled that Hall's interest in the company ended when he was fired.[10] Hall did not get his money back.

* * *

Hall's infusion of cash did allow Emerson and Waggaman to buy a seven-story building at 311 W. Fayette Street in Baltimore. There they, and the 20 men they hired, manufactured the "effervescent salt."[11] Emerson soon turned over day-to-day operation of the company, which now issued stock, to Waggaman and Hindes. Isaac set about creating an advertising campaign that would allow Bromo-Seltzer to become a dominant player throughout the world in the crowded field of patent medicines.

* * *

Patent medicines first arrived in America during the early 18th century, brought by settlers from England, where they were produced under "patents of royal favor" (hence the name) by those who provided medicines to the Royal Family. Some of the first such elixirs to arrive in America were Daffy's Elixir Salutis for "colic and griping," Dr. Bateman's Pectoral Drops, and John Hooper's Female Pills. Prior to the Civil War, patent medicines could be found everywhere. Postmasters, goldsmiths, grocers, tailors, and other local merchants gladly sold them while claiming they'd cure most any ailment, including venereal diseases, tuberculosis, colic in infants, indigestion and cancer. The concoctions did not enjoy the best of reputations. Some doctors and medical associations claimed they cured little if anything and caused alcohol and drug dependency. Morphine, opium, and cocaine, along with the spirits, comprised the bulk of ingredients in many elixirs.[12]

In addition to the group's unsavory reputation among physicians and many in the public, Emerson also had to contend with competing mixtures claiming to cure headache and other ailments, many in his home state of North Carolina. The Goose Grease Company in Greensboro, North Carolina, for example, offered Goose Grease Liniment to "cure all aches and pains." Some, convinced that an excess flow of blood caused headaches, tied a rag or bandana, often red and soaked in turpentine, camphor, or vinegar, tightly around their head. An ad for "Stanback Headache Powders" took up the entire side of a building in Spencer, North Carolina.[13] Wilson, North Carolina's newspaper, the *Wilson Mirror*, touted St. Jacob's Oil. "It cures," the paper shamelessly promised, "backaches, Headache, tooth ache and all aches Promptly."[14]

Similar ads appeared in the *Baltimore Sun*. One W. R. Read placed an ad in the paper on February 21, 1890, that read "Read's 3-Minute Headache cure and Read's Grand Duchess Cologne are splendid." On June 25, 1890, *Sun* readers of the classifieds saw "Drive Away Headaches, Regulate the liver and keep away all general ailments by using HANCE'S SARSAPARILLA BLOOD PILLS. They cure quickly." The *Washington Post* carried an ad on February 8, 1893, for "Dr. Franks' Grains of Health." "These little pills," the ad promised, "will quickly cure CONSTIPATION!, CONGESTION!, HEADACHE!."

The ingredients of some could prove fatal or habit-forming. Opium, cocaine, or morphine, present in many concoctions, could, and did on occasion, spell the doom of small children while creating addictions in adults.[15] The presence of alcohol in some no doubt helped boost sales, to the dismay and distain of Dr. Ashbel P. Grinnell, a New York physician. He maintained that people imbibed more alcohol through patent medicines than was dispensed legally save for beer and ale.[16]

Emerson enhanced Bromo-Seltzer's success by avoiding exaggerated promises. He limited the claims to curing headaches, stomach aches, and nervousness caused by "Over Brain Work, Alcoholic Excesses & etc." He also let customers know that his product "contains no antipyrine (a pain reliever of dubious repute), morphine or cocaine." He had removed cocaine after learning that it caused blue lips among some users and could be addictive.[17] He failed, however, to disclose the presence of antancilide in the formula and its potential poisonous effects.

While Emerson avoided making the sweeping curative claims of many of his competitors, his ambition took him a bit afield when he manufactured an effervescent salt as a cure for rheumatism and other ailments in 1899. An ad for the salt appeared in the *Baltimore Sun* on June 1, touting it as "A scientific combination of Lithia and other rheumatic components." The "agreeable salt" was for "Rheumatism, Lumbago, Gout, Kidney

Many ads for Bromo-Seltzer, in this case Ginger Mint Julep, appeared on moving vehicles. Here, an early version of the pickup truck, circa 1920, carries the message. Courtesy Andrew Murray.

Troubles." A similar ad appeared in the June 22 edition of the *Chicago Daily Tribune*, claiming the salt would "eliminate uric acid, the primary cause of rheumatism." The salt, evidently not as agreeable as advertised, did not take hold and was never heard from after 1899.

In another side-line, the Bromo-Seltzer king invented and marketed a carbonated soft drink consisting of ginger, mint, and seltzer which he named Ginger Mint Julep, not to be confused with a drink of a similar name which includes bourbon. While popular for awhile, it never came close to matching Bromo-Seltzer's popularity.

* * *

Bromo-Seltzer owed its success in large part to Emerson's talent for advertising, which took many forms. Even before forming his partnership with Waggaman, he began advertising in newspapers. The City Bulletin in *The Washington Post's* May 9, 1889, edition contained "Bromo-Seltzer cures sick headaches, nervous headaches, and neuralgia. Trial size .10 cents. At druggists." On May 25, 1889, sandwiched between a notice for a baseball game and a rare book sale, the following appeared in the *Baltimore Sun*: "Wanted-Everybody suffering with Headache to try BROMO SELTZER. Trial size 10 cents. At Drugstores." By 1893, such one-liners had reached across the country to the *Los Angeles Times* and the *San Francisco*

Before the automobile became popular, Emerson placed ads on horse-drawn vehicles such as this one. Notice the Bromo-Seltzer bottle and the lack of information about its contents. In those days, Emerson could get by with just the name of the product and its objective—"Cures Headaches." That would change as the years went by. Author's collection.

Chronicle.[18] As business picked up, Emerson expanded his advertising by placing ads on the sides of horse-drawn wagons and streetcars and in druggists' windows.

A New York barber placed a sign in his window that read "Bromo-Seltzer on draught."[19] Emerson and his agents promised druggists in Baltimore, Philadelphia, Washington and other cities stock in the Emerson Drug Company if they met certain sales goals. In 1899, for instance, a druggist who sold 25 dozen bottles at the full retail price of 50 cents a bottle would receive one share of stock. A druggist who sold 50 dozen would receive two shares, but two was the most a single druggist could acquire. Emerson didn't limit himself to English-language publications. This offer appeared in a German-language magazine published in Chicago.[20]

After purchasing the building on Fayette Street, he plastered "Bromo-Seltzer" in large white letters on the side of the building. A large sign, "Emerson Drug Co.," graced the front. The company stationery featured an etching of the office building and, in bold letters, "EMERSON DRUG COMPANY—MANUFACTURING CHEMISTS."

Readers of *The Fisherman & Farmer* in Edenton, North Carolina, were asked on February 20, 1891, "Does your head ache? Are you nervous?" They were assured that "Bromo-Seltzer is a guaranteed cure." 1891 also saw the first Bromo-Seltzer ads on sheet music. As family and friends gathered around the piano to sing "Over the Moonlit Sea," for instance, they would see a half-page ad for Bromo-Seltzer in large letters against a floral background. Offers to receive two sheet music compositions for two labels from ten cent bottles of Bromo-Seltzer appeared at the bottom of many ads.

The Emerson Drug Company distributed 12-page, pocket-size booklets that told a clever tale. In one, *How Schneider Got There*, a bartender gets elected to Congress by trading a dose of Bromo-Seltzer for a sufferer's vote. Mike O'Dooley receives a dose from Schneider, who advises the Irishman, "Here drink it while it fizz!" O'Dooley does and exclaims, "You've cured me head, begob, and yez kin hev me vote!" Other sufferers follow—an Italian man, Cholly Jones "who didn't like a German worth a cent," Yankees and Dutchmen, all of whom share O'Dooley's gratitude. Schneider concludes his tale with "I'm glad to tell it sir: I owe my station proud in life to glorious Bromo-Seltzer."[21]

Those in Chicago who had partied too hard the night before were advised by an ad in the *Chicago Daily Tribune* on May 4, 1892, that "Before breakfast Bromo-Seltzer Acts as a bracer-10c. a bottle." Many such ads appeared in the *Tribune* in the following year. "For that 'out-o'-sorts feeling,' Take Bromo-Seltzer" appeared at the bottom of an article about Chicago Lumbermen fighting "Tramp Contractors" on January 5. At the end of a piece describing a Michigan woman's body being exhumed ran the line "To quickly relieve neuralgic headache, use Bromo-Seltzer," on January 27. On March 3, the day before Grover Cleveland's second inauguration as president, Emerson ran, "Inaugural headaches promptly cured by Bromo-Seltzer. Trial bottle 10c," in *The Washington Post*. "With nerves unstrung and heads that ache, wise women Bromo-Seltzer take" appeared on October 7, 1893, just below an article recounting the prior day's events at the Chicago World's Fair. Two weeks later, "Before going to the World's Fair take Bromo Seltzer. It clears the head and invigorates" appeared again in the *Tribune*, this time just below a short article about the Fair noting that 2,000 people had left Toronto, Canada, for the Fair the day before, and that trained steers from Connecticut could be seen free of charge at the Stock Pavilion. The ads' contents and placements were not without purpose.

The Chicago World's Columbian Exposition, popularly known as the World's Fair, an event of unparalleled magnitude in America, provided an expansive platform for Emerson's advertising. Pavilions sponsored by 46 countries spread across 600 acres. Twenty-seven million people from all over the world attended the Fair from May to October of 1893.

Here is an example of the sheet music, with a large ad on the back page, which the Emerson Drug Company sent to users who mailed in a two-cent stamp and one "Bromo-Seltzer Wrapper." Music lovers had their choice of 77 selections; to acquire them all would require purchasing 77 bottles of Bromo. Author's collection.

THIS IS IT! TRY IT!
BROMO-SELTZER
FOR HEADACHES
MADE IN BALTIMORE.

EFFERVESCES EVERYWHERE.

BROMO - SELTZER "EDITION DeLUXE" SHEET MUSIC

INSTRUMENTAL	VOCAL
Angel's Serenade, Transcription.............Smith	Ave Maria, from "Cavalleria Rusticana"............Mascagni
Barcarolle (from Contes d'Hoffman).......Offenbach	Believe Me if all Those Endearing Young Charms, Stevenson
Bridal Chorus, "Lohengrin"..................Wagner	Come Back to Erin.........................Claribel
Brook (The).....................................Spindler	Daily Question, The.....................Meyer-Helmund
Ciribiribin, Valse..............................Pestalazza	Flowers that Bloom in the Spring (Mikado)........Sullivan
Consolation..................................Mendelssohn	Flower Song, from "Faust"..................Gounod
Edelweiss Glide..............................Vanderbeck	Good-Bye..Tosti
Farewell to the Piano........................Beethoven	Heart Bowed Down, "Bohemian Girl"...........Balfe
Flower Song..................................Lange	Home to Our Mountains, from "Il Trovatore"......Verdi
Garland of Roses, Waltz....................Streabbog	Killarney, Medium...........................Balfe
Humoresque....................................Dvorak	Massa's in the Cold, Cold Ground............Foster
Little Fairy, Waltzes.........................Streabbog	Oh, Fair Dove, Fond Dove...................Gatty
Longing for Home (Heimweh)................Jungmann	Old Black Joe...............................Foster
Maiden's Prayer..............................Badarzewska	Old Farm-House on the Hill..................Lerman
Melody in F,.................................Rubinstein	One Sweetly Solemn Thought...............Ambrose
Morning Prayer ....Streabbog	O Thou Sublime, Sweet Evening Star, from Tannhauser
Mountain Belle, Schottische..................Kinkel	Wagner
Orange Blossoms Waltzes....................Ludovic	Once Again I Would Gaze, "Faust"............Gounod
Prince Imperial Galop........................Coote	Palms (Medium)..............................Faure
Sack Waltz,..................................Metcalf	Pilgrim's Chorus, from "Tannhauser".........Wagner
Sextette from "Lucia".......................Bohm	Sally in Our Alley...........................Cary
Spring Song..................................Mendelssohn	Still as the Night............................Bohm
Traumerei and Romance.....................Schumann	The Wearing of the Green...................Glenney
Under the Double Eagle, March..............Wagner	Toreador Song, from "Carmen"...............Beitz
You and I Waltzes,...........................Claribel	When You and I Were Young, Maggie.......Butterfield
	Yankee Doodle...................Composer Unknown

The Exodus, Plantation Song, Words and Music by Carlos V. Cusachs.

Will send any one of the above pieces upon receipt of a two-cent stamp (to cover cost of mailing) and Bromo-Seltzer Wrapper. For two pieces, send two, two-cent stamps and Bromo-Seltzer Wrapper, and so on.

Address, MUSIC DEPARTMENT,

EMERSON DRUG CO., Bromo-Seltzer Tower Building, **Baltimore, Md.**

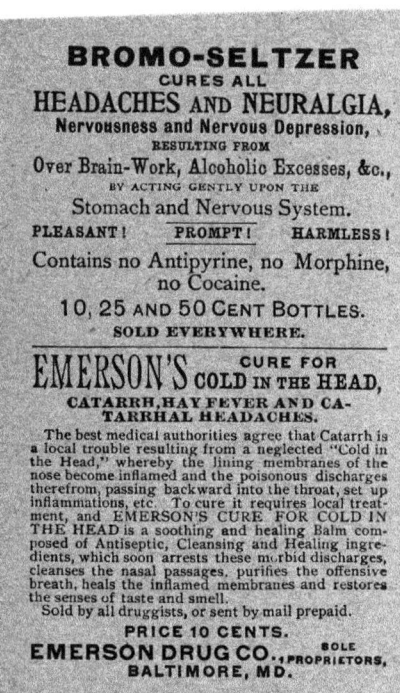

Page one of the Emerson Drug Company's booklet telling the story of barkeep Schneider parlaying its product into a successful run for Congress. Circa 1905. Note the disclaimers—"no antipyrine, no morphine, no cocaine"—designed to assure users that the product was safe but without divulging its ingredients. Also note the ad for another product, Emerson's Cure For Cold in the Head, a balm that did not catch on. Courtesy Warshaw Collection, Archives Center, National Museum of American History, Smithsonian Institution, Washington, D.C.

Bromo-Seltzer was there in full force in the form of exclusive contracts to sell and promote Bromo-Seltzer with the Columbia Soft Drink company and its 100 refreshment stands, the Moorish Palace, a casino, and the Terminal Building. Large Bromo-Seltzer signs adorned each facility. Attendees bought 20,000 doses a week. The effervescence arrived in railroad car lots of 56,000 cobalt blue bottles. In addition, Emerson's ornate Tally-Ho coach, pulled by four elaborately outfitted horses and sporting banners of the Emerson Drug Company, roamed the fairgrounds providing free rides to those in need, including ferrying poor children to Buffalo Bill's Wild West Show. Blue and white banners touting the Emerson Drug Company flew from the steamboats that carried people between the city and the fairgrounds. Emerson himself spent a week at the Fair in early September.²² He would continue to find innovative ways to keep his nostrum's name before the public.

* * *

Thanks to his bold advertising and the fact that his product actually worked, Emerson, by age 36, was becoming well-known beyond the confines of Baltimore. In 1894 *The American Druggist and Pharmaceutical Record* published a "sketch" of him shortly after the Fair ended. The article noted that he belonged to the Athenaeum and Pimlico Driving Clubs and owned a four-in-one hand Tally-Ho coach and the hunting yacht *Susquehanna* that he docked in Harve de Grace, Maryland, near Maryland's "ducking shores where he entertains friends." He was, the article continued, "known as a liberal minded, open-handed good fellow whose acquaintance is highly sought after and friendship highly valued."²³

The Bromo-Seltzer king expanded his professional network by joining the National Wholesale Druggists Association. He attended the group's convention in New York City in October 1894. There he mingled with other successful, "largely self-made" businessmen from all corners of America. Delmonico's Restaurant, famous for inventing the steak of the same name and one of the city's finest restaurants, prepared a banquet for the group in which over "400 covers were laid." The *New York Times* credited participants with possessing "the highest intelligence and most progressive methods." Those present, the *Times* continued, "represented more wealth than was ever gathered together before under one roof." Delegates sang patriotic songs and listened to speeches, some humorous and some serious. Halfway through the speeches, spouses and children, including Emerson's wife Emilie and ten-year-old daughter Margaret, were admitted to the musical gallery after a day of attending the Lyceum Theater and lunching on board the Cunard Line's ship *The Lucania*, known as "the Queen of the Ocean."²⁴ Five years later, as a member of the Proprietary Association of America, the Bromo-Seltzer king chaired the Banquet Committee at the Association's October 1899 semi-annual meeting in Niagara Falls, New York.²⁵

As the century was about to turn, the 41-year-old Emerson was well on his way.

3

Leading the Naval Reserves

At the same time that Emerson was building his Bromo-Seltzer empire, he was devoting considerable time, energy, and personal finances to the Maryland Naval Reserves.

Embracing the military heritage of his forefathers, the patriotic Bromo-Seltzer king joined the Reserves in December of 1893 as paymaster, a position of considerable trust, responsible for managing the finances, a subject in which he was well versed. Several months later, he became the unit's commander.[1]

Created by an act of Congress in 1892, the Reserves served as a backup force to the regular navy, much as the National Guard did for the army. Maryland Governor Frank Brown commissioned the state's oyster fishing boats that plied the Chesapeake Bay in search of crabs, clam and other shell food delicacies to serve as the Reserve's fleet. These were light-weight, small, relatively inexpensive to build and maintain, sail-powered craft commonly known as "skipjacks." Maryland's Adjutant-General, Henry Kyd Douglas, who was in charge of the Reserves, and Secretary of the Navy John D. Long thought Maryland law prohibited such an arrangement. Governor Brown then decommissioned the oyster fleet.[2]

In their place, the navy donated the United States sloop-of-war *The Dale* to the Reserves as a "practice ship." At 117 feet long and 32 feet wide, *The Dale* could accommodate the entire naval militia. She was the third-oldest naval ship still afloat, behind The Constitution and Old Ironsides, though smaller than both.[3] Built in 1839, she had once been a proud member of the navy's fleet, having sailed to "almost every civilized port of the world," and seen Civil War duty, capturing two Confederate ships trying to escape the Union blockade. Inactive since that time, she showed her age and needed work.[4]

Commander Emerson met his new ship at the U.S. Navy Shipyard in Washington, D.C., on January 3, 1895. He made arrangements for the tugboat *Britannia* to tow her to Baltimore. Upon arriving at the bottom of Charles Street, where she was to be docked, the navy's gift ran aground, becoming partly submerged. A bystander quipped, "Take her back and tell Grover [President Grover Cleveland] to give it to Ruth [his eldest child, who was four at the time] for her doll house." Another yelled out, "Say mister, when are you going to let the animals out of the ark?"[5] Undaunted, Emerson raised the sloop at his own expense. In a letter to Douglas, he explained his decision, saying, "No state funds for raising *The Dale*. Navy refused to fund repairing or towing *Dale* to Baltimore. I engaged the Baltimore Wrecking Company to raise her. I will carry the debt until funds are available from the State or the Navy." The project cost the new commander $450.[6]

That would not be the last debt he would assume for the Reserves. Emilie—she no longer went by Emma—testifying in court a decade later about a speeding ticket that two police officers had given to her chauffeur, which she contested and bitterly resented, claimed, in a plea to have the case dropped, "Mr. Emerson has spent nearly $10,000 on the Militia."[7]

By the end of June 1895, thanks again to the commander's generosity in funding repairs to the ship, *The Dale* was seaworthy enough to transport the Reserves, which now numbered 15 commissioned officers, 27 petty officers, and 147 enlisted men, and a U.S. Naval officer appointed by the Secretary of War to supervise the enterprise, across the Chesapeake Bay to Tolchester Beach for a week's training.[8] Pronouncing himself well-pleased with the week's activities, the Bromo-Seltzer entrepreneur complimented the men on their success in launching a boat in a storm, assisting a distressed vessel, and executing all on-board drills. In addition to developing skills, examinations in seamanship honed the men's knowledge. Those who excelled on the exams won "the Emerson gold medal."[9] The training would continue for several years.[10]

* * *

As Emerson was getting his charges acclimated to sea duty, the city of Atlanta was making plans to host the Cotton States International Celebration, referred to in the Baltimore press as the Atlanta Exposition, from September 18 to December 31, 1895. Designed to highlight the progress Southern states had made since the Civil War, the affair drew 800,000 people, including President Grover Cleveland, who gave the opening address, and a contingent of men representing Maryland's military and commercial organizations. Each state was assigned a day to tout its highlights. The men from Maryland took responsibility for Maryland Day. Emerson, for his part, led 100 officers and men from the Reserves and four pieces of artillery through Atlanta's city streets on December 7, 1895.[11]

As important as the Celebration was for Maryland and the other participating states, the affair in Atlanta is best remembered for Booker T.

Washington's controversial speech. It came to be known as the "Atlanta Compromise Speech." Washington, considered by many to be America's most influential African American leader from 1890–1915, spoke before a predominantly white audience, a rare occurrence in those days, especially in the South. Organizers of the event, while not unaware of many whites' hostile feelings toward blacks, thought Washington's presence would send a signal to Northerners that the South was making progress on the racial front.

Washington tried to calm whites' fears of the "uppity" black by proposing that blacks would work meekly and submit to white rule in exchange for a guarantee of basic education and due process under the law.[12] Many black intellectuals, including W. E. B. DuBois, thought Washington's proposal too subservient and advocated for a more assertive stance on the part of blacks. These efforts eventually led to the founding of the National Association for the Advancement of Colored People (NAACP) in 1909.[13] Washington's proposal found few takers among Southern whites as well. Most held fast to the culture of Jim Crow.

* * *

A year after Washington's speech, Cuban insurgents stepped up their resistance to Spanish occupation of their island and Spain's barbarous treatment of their people. Concerned that Spain, which controlled the Philippines as well as Cuba, might broaden its scope of occupation with attacks along the Eastern seaboard of the United States, American naval authorities encouraged other states to join Maryland in developing naval militias. States bordering the Atlantic Ocean formed the Association of Naval Militias of the United States. Sensing another leadership opportunity the always ambitious and public-spirited Commander Emerson invited representatives from each state to hold their first meeting in Baltimore in June 1896.[14] He welcomed the group on board his personal steam yacht, *The Nydia*, one of many yachts he would own. With an enclosed dining room on the deck and the interior finished in mahogany, the vessel was considered "up to modern yachting taste for brightness, convenience, and luxury."[15] Impressed by his leadership and hospitality, the representatives elected their host to become the Association's first president.[16]

Soon after the representatives returned home, Emerson, even though he had financed improvements to *The Dale*, became convinced that the Civil War survivor had outlived its usefulness as a "practice ship" for his men. The Commander and his second-in-command, Lieutenant Edward Geer, traveled to Washington, D.C., to ask the Secretary of the Navy, John Davis Long, to make the cruiser *Yantic*, which had also seen Civil War service, available for the Reserve's summer trainings. The cruiser was returning from duty off the shores of Argentina. The ship was better suited than *The Dale* for the shallow waters of the Chesapeake Bay and came better armed with four broadside guns. To Emerson's disappointment, Long sent the *Yantic* to the Great Lakes in June of 1897, still leaving Emerson and his men with *The Dale*.[17] The navy, however, did agree to make some improvements to the "practice ship." After removing her battery (a large gun at mid-ship), the navy installed four rapid-fire guns, two of 45-caliber and two of 50-caliber, giving, in the words of a *Sun* reporter, "the local battalion the latest improved equipment."[18]

As improvements were being made to *The Dale* in the fall and winter of 1896, Emerson kept the reservists busy by preparing them for two more upcoming ceremonies. The first was to join 2,000 Maryland troops, regular and reserves, in President William McKinley's March 4, 1897, inaugural parade in Washington, D.C. The men arrived in the nation's capitol by steamer the day before. Inauguration Day dawned under clear skies and a brilliant sun that highlighted the gaily adorned buildings along the parade route. Not since the end of the Civil War had decorations been so abundant for a presidential inauguration.[19] The reservists gave a splendid account of themselves as they marched the traditional inaugural route—down Pennsylvania Avenue from the U.S. Capital to the White House. A *New York Tribune* article complimented Emerson and his men, saying that "a battalion of Naval Reserve under the command of Commander Emerson ... made a fine picture in uniforms of grey-blue overcoats and white facings [the overcoats' linings]."[20]

The second parade was scheduled the following month for April 27, 1897. This one would celebrate the dedication of Grant's Tomb in New York City. Ulysses S. Grant had commanded the Union forces during the last 12 months of the Civil War and served as the nation's two-term, 18th President.

An arduous, 12-year process had been needed to build the General Grant National Memorial. The general's approaching death from throat cancer in 1885 sparked a spirited discussion over a location for his final resting place. Contending sites included cities where he had lived: St. Louis, Missouri, and his birthplace, Galena, Illinois; West Point, where he graduated in 1843; Arlington National Cemetery; and the Soldier's Home in Washington, D.C. New York's Irish-born mayor and the first Roman Catholic to hold the position, William Russell Grace, spiked the debate with a hurried telegram to the Grant family on the day the Civil War hero and former president died in the city on July 23, 1885. The mayor offered land in one of the city's parks for a memorial and burial site. Grant's son Frederick immediately accepted Grace's offer. Grace then appointed 85 wealthy New Yorkers, including John Jacob Astor, John P. Morgan, Joseph

Pulitzer, and William Steinway, to the newly-formed Grant Monument Association. Grace charged the group with creating a suitable structure.

In an unusual move for the times, Grace also appointed Richard Greener, the first African American graduate of Harvard University, a widely respected scholar and advocate for civil rights, and the Association's only African American, to be the group's secretary. Greener had met Grant both at Harvard and in the White House, where he proposed civil rights legislation to the president and his aides. To Greener fell the task of fundraising, which he vigorously and successfully pursued for seven years until the Association suddenly terminated his salary. After other tumultuous changes in the Association's membership, Grant's Tomb was finally completed in early 1897.[21]

Maryland Governor Lloyd Lowndes, Jr., accepted Emerson's request to include himself and five Reserve officers in the state's delegation. Emerson, ever on the lookout for opportunities to curry favor and make himself known, took to entertaining dignitaries as well as honoring Grant. Once ensconced in New York's Waldorf Hotel, two days before the parade, the Commander hosted Lowndes and his staff to breakfast at the New York Club, of which the commander was a member; held a reception for Captain Jacob W. Miller of the New York Naval Reserves; took his officers on a long afternoon drive on Riverside Parkway past Grant's Tomb in his Tally-Ho coach (a pleasure coach drawn by four horses and resembling a stagecoach, similar to those Emerson took for afternoon spins in Baltimore.[22]), and accepted a dinner invitation aboard the U.S.S. *New Hampshire*.[23]

On April 27, the 75th anniversary of the general's birth, the Maryland delegation, led by Emerson, stepped out smartly amongst the 60,000 marchers as over one million enthusiastic spectators looked on. Among the many notables present, including Grant's widow and two sons, was President William McKinley, who gave the dedication speech.[24]

Following McKinley's speech, the Association's president, former Civil War Brigadier General Horace Porter, a former aide-de-camp to Grant and now vice president of the Pullman Company, profusely thanked a long list of contributors. Greener's biographer, Katherine Reynolds Chaddock, points out, however, that in keeping with the racial culture of the times, "Porter ignored the African American population, many of whom had worked on the tomb's construction, in general and the splendid and enduring work of Greener in particular."[25]

* * *

In the midst of his militia responsibilities, the Commander found time to take to the seas for his personal pleasure. He favored high-profile sailing

3—Leading the Naval Reserves 31

events such as the annual cruise of boats from the New York Yacht Club in August 1897. He sent *The Nydia* ahead of himself and his Baltimore guests, who followed four days later by train to New York City. From the Yacht Club, *The Nydia* joined 300 other craft for a multi-day cruise to Huntington, Long Island; New London, Connecticut; Vineyard Haven, Massachusetts (the entry port for Martha's Vineyard); on to Bar Harbor, Maine, and back to the Yacht Club. The *Sun* reported that "Dr. Emerson usually entertains lavishly on his yacht."[26] This trip was no exception.

* * *

It would not be long, however, before his time at sea took on an official tone. By the winter of 1897–1898, with four years of training under their belt, the men of the Maryland Naval Militia, whose numbers had increased to over 400, were well prepared for their military responsibilities. They would soon be called on to exercise them.

On the evening of February 15, 1898, while resting silently at anchor in Havana Bay, the United States Battleship *Maine* exploded and sank, taking with her 260 American seamen. No cause for the explosion was ever found, but the Maine's demise added fuel to the arguments of those in the United States favoring intervention in Cuba to expel the Spaniards. Many American newspaper editors, most notably William R. Hearst and Joseph Pulitzer, fanned the flames of military intervention by exhorting their readers to "Remember the Maine" and criticized President McKinley for his inaction.[27]

Two days after the Maine's sinking, rumors circulated throughout Baltimore that the Naval Reserves would be called up. Commander Emerson assured the press that his men were well prepared and ready to move within 12 hours or less. He described the Reserves' rifles, side arms, and artillery as "excellent" and pointed out that "the men are thoroughly trained in the use for each gun." Emerson himself had taken courses on seamanship at the War College in Newport, Rhode Island, over the course of two years. Lieutenant Geer, Emerson's lieutenant commander, lent some specifics to Emerson's words in assuaging Baltimoreans' fears of an attack by the Spanish fleet on the city. With torpedo boats hiding in the many creeks and rivers emptying into Chesapeake Bay, the removal of all buoys from the Bay making it likely that invading ships would run aground, a cadre of scouts posted from the southern entrance to the Chesapeake Bay up to Baltimore to warn of approaching vessels, and the knowledge and experience gained by Emerson, himself, and other officers, Geer promised his fellow citizens, "We could make it warm for any Spaniard desiring to attack this city."[28]

Anticipation of war with Spain increased over the next six weeks.

On March 9, Emerson joined Naval Militia Commanders from New York City, Brooklyn, and Philadelphia in a conference in Washington, D.C., with the Assistant Secretary of the Navy to make plans for the Reserves in the event of war.[29] The Assistant Secretary was Theodore Roosevelt, soon to charge to glory up San Juan Hill with his Rough Riders. On March 12, Fitzhugh Lee, Jr., recently returned from Cuba and the son of the United States Counsel General in Havana, Fitzhugh Lee, Sr., a Confederate cavalry general in the Civil War and a nephew of Robert E. Lee, told a gathering in Tampa, Florida, "I am of the opinion that war between the two countries is imminent."[30]

On the same day Emerson offered his private steam yacht, *The Nydia*, which he purchased for $25,000 and refurbished to the tune of $5,000, to the navy. Emerson had used his yacht to cruise Chesapeake Bay, New York's Harbor, and the New England coast, and to travel to the American War College.[31] He engaged the services of Skinner's Shipyards, one of Baltimore's best, to convert the pleasure craft, which had been at the service of the Reserves' officers and men since its purchase a year earlier, into a torpedo boat. Among other modifications, engineers added two "rapid-firing guns" and a "torpedo tube."[32] The Bromo-Seltzer king paid for the conversion.

His many outlays had not gone unnoticed. A year earlier, the Rev. F. W. Clampett, pastor at St. Peter's Protestant Episcopal Church, which the Emersons attended, singled out the Commander for special praise. "Commander Emerson," Clampett told his Sunday faithful, "did not hesitate to prove his interest by the generous outlay of large sums so that the necessary steps might be taken to make a firm foundation."[33]

The anticipated war with Spain soon became a reality. Congress passed a resolution declaring Cuba an independent country. Spain refused to honor the resolution and declared war on the United States on April 22, 1898. President McKinley responded with a naval blockade of the island and a call for 125,000 volunteers. Three days later, on April 25, the U.S. Congress declared war on Spain.[34]

* * *

As the volunteers were being mobilized, Baltimore took time out to remember its first encounter in another war, the Civil War. A citizens committee invited the Sixth Massachusetts Regiment to parade through the city as they changed train stations on their way to Washington, D.C., and on to Cuba. Thirty-seven years earlier on May 19, 1861, a mob of Confederate sympathizers had greeted the Sixth with insults, rocks, stones, physical assaults, and pistols as the soldiers tried to reach the train station where they would catch a train to Washington, D.C. Several Union soldiers lost their lives, as did some rioters. This time Baltimoreans heartedly welcomed the Sixth on the afternoon of May 21, 1898. Like their predecessors, these soldiers had to march from one train to another to continue their journey. Officers and men marched four miles through streets lined six or eight deep with cheering onlookers. The soldiers were welcomed at the Town Hall by Mayor William T. Malster, given box lunches, and serenaded by bands before heading on their way. Emerson, always eager to participate in Baltimore's civic affairs, was a proud member of the citizens committee which organized the celebration.[35]

Two days before the celebration, the Commander, in compliance with orders from the Secretary of the Navy, sent eight officers and 167 men from *The Dale* to the warship *Dixie*, docked in Norfolk, Virginia, and soon to sail for Cuba. Emerson sent more officers and men, including Assistant Surgeon Ensign Smith Hollins McKim, to the *Dixie* the following week. The Commander, with wife Emilie, led a "group of society ladies and some official gentlemen from the state of Maryland," as Cabin Steward W. C. Payne described the group's visit to the Dixie shortly before she sailed. The assembled visitors joined the crew in a light lunch and offered a toast, "Success to the Dixie." This encounter, Payne reported, "inspired us with patriotism."[36] Massachusetts U.S. Senator Henry Cabot Lodge had paid an earlier visit to the Dixie to see his son, the Dixie's Acting Naval Cadet, George Cabot Lodge.[37] The younger Lodge became a poet in his later years.

The remaining Militia members and Emerson then spent three weeks on the *Dale*, "waiting patiently ... for the Navy Department to authorize our enlistment in the U.S. Naval Service," as Emerson put it in a report to Maryland's Adjutant General. After several more meetings in Washington with Teddy Roosevelt, the navy enlisted the Militia's remaining crew members into the regular navy. Emerson remained in command of *The Dale* in Baltimore, with orders to assist in defending the Atlantic Coast from Virginia to North Carolina.[38] He had to forgo his Commander title when the navy enlisted him. Lieutenant was the highest rank the navy could convey on a recruit. He took the demotion in title in good stride, saying "no petty pride should stand in the way."[39] The remaining reservists manned the *Dale*.[40]

* * *

The first battle of the Spanish-American War took place on May 1, 1898, in Manila Bay in the Philippines, where U.S. forces under the leadership of Navy Commander George Dewey defeated the woefully unprepared Spanish who were occupying the Philippines. The American forces, army and navy, in Cuba so overwhelmed the Spaniards that a cease fire there was negotiated by August 8. In the words of John Hay, formerly President Abraham Lincoln's private secretary, ambassador to Great Britain during the war, and soon to be Secretary of State, it was "a splendid little war."[41] Emerson saw no action but was applauded by *The Herald* (Los Angeles) as among the "society leaders who will fight Spain."[42]

While it may have been a little war as wars go, the people of Baltimore gave a rousing welcome to those Maryland sailors and soldiers who had fought in it. The *Dixie* entered Baltimore's harbor on September 12, 1898. Its crew welcomed the public aboard. Hundreds walked the decks, peered into the living quarters, and inspected the ship from stem to stern. Many in the crowd had relatives who had served aboard the *Dixie*. Accompanied by words of thanks for his support and leadership, *Dixie* crewmen presented a Spanish mortar captured at Guantanamo Bay to Lieutenant Emerson, who asked that it be kept on board the *Dale* while a decision on its final location was made.[43]

Starting at 10:00 a.m. on September 12, all of Maryland's veterans, army and navy, marched through the streets of Baltimore. Thousands lined the route, cheering and calling those they knew by name. Women handed large bouquets of flowers to the men. A man named "Charlie" received so many hugs and kisses from two women that police officers had to restrain them. The *Dixie's* band played a two-step. Lieutenant Emerson took it all in from the comfort of a carriage, as did the Dixie's officers.[44]

At a meeting in the Mayor's office the next day, the committee charged with planning "a peace celebration" in October called it off, deciding instead to distribute the funds already collected, $1,750, to the Naval Reserves and the Army Regiments. The committee published a resolution that said in part, "We tender to the members of the Fifth Regiment, the First Regiment and the Naval Reserves our heartfelt thanks for the courageous and manly manner in which they represented the State of Maryland."[45]

At the end of the war, Lieutenant Emerson was awarded an honorary discharge from the Navy. He earned a promotion in the Militia to the rank of Captain in May of 1900, a title he would use proudly for the rest of his life.[46]

* * *

With the war behind him and Bromo-Seltzer still selling briskly throughout the United States and Europe, Emerson returned his attention to two of his favorite leisure pursuits—hunting and sailing. In November 1898, Emerson indulged his hunting passion by arranging for exclusive hunting privileges for himself and friends on a Virginia game preserve known as Fauntleroys, famous for its partridges. The *Sun* speculated that he would buy the preserve and make it part of a larger preserve "that he is ambitious to own and stock."[47] Emerson did harbor such ambitions, but he would not act on them for eight years and not in Virginia.

Like many men of his station with a penchant for hunting, he went south for the winter. A typical trip entailed going by train from Baltimore to Georgetown, South Carolina, on the Waccamaw River. There he would meet the *Nydia*, now reconfigured for civilian travel. The yacht's engines and boilers had been overhauled; the armaments of war were removed, and ice machines and an evaporator added to produce cool drinking water. From Georgetown it was on to the Santee Gun Club, 12 miles to the south. The club, bordered by the Santee River and the Atlantic Ocean, provided its guests with 30,000 acres of lush hunting grounds.[48] Membership was capped at 40 but not just any 40. Members were drawn from the ranks of wealthy sportsmen from the East Coast—bankers, corporate attorneys, stockbrokers, and industrialists. President Grover Cleveland was an honorary member. The *Baltimore American* dubbed it "the most influential gunning club in the United States." Emerson received his membership certificate on June 3, 1899.[49] There he and other well-to-do gentlemen hunted primarily ducks, whose numbers blackened the skies on occasion, as well as turkeys and deer. Following the hunt, the Captain usually continued on to the Bahamas, Cuba, and three Florida ports—Key West, Miami, and Palm Beach.[50]

A frequent stop in Palm Beach was the Florida Gun Club, where the Captain displayed his skill with a shotgun in the Club's live bird shoots. Competitors came from Chicago, Baltimore, Philadelphia, and Wilkes-Barre, Pennsylvania. August Belmont, Jr., financier and builder of New York's Belmont Race Track, named for his father, joined the shoots, usually witnessed by several thousand onlookers. The Captain's best showing came in February 1904, when he outshot J. S. S. Remsen, a member of New York's Carteret Gun Club, by killing 25 consecutive pigeons.[51]

The Bromo-Seltzer king prevailed later in the month in a private match with John Jerome Kelly, a New York stockbroker and member of the New York Stock Exchange. Emerson downed 17 pigeons out of 20 to Kelly's 15 kills.[52] His most memorable match came two years later when he beat Dr. Daniel Karsner, a homeopathic physician from Philadelphia, in a shoot-off for second place money. The local paper termed the event "the most exciting shoot ever witnessed here." The winner, H. Yale Dolan, a multi-millionaire bachelor also from the City of Brotherly Love, downed 25 consecutive birds. The Captain and Karsner each missed their 25th bird.[53] A year later in February of 1907, daughter Margaret, 23 years old, married, and the only woman in a field of 12 shooters which included her father, won the event and was awarded the silver cup. She won in a tie-breaking shootout, five birds to four, with Walter Gibbs Murphy, president of the Importation Company in New York.[54]

One of Emerson's more memorable trips south started in January of 1899. He departed from Baltimore's damp and chilly winter weather for the warmer climes of Charleston, where he and his companions continued to hunt ducks and pheasants. Once the hunting was completed, the *Nydia* picked the hunting party up in Charleston for a cruise to the West Indies. The group proceeded to Miami without incident. The leg from Miami to Key West was a different story. They sailed in comfort at first. On February 12, Emerson reported to the *Sun* that

> Myself and my guests were enjoying our afternoon nap on the *Nydia's* comfortable divans, under the influence of Florida's balmy breezes, the seductiveness of our Havana perfectos, and just enough of old Madeira to vivify our dreams with pictures of Spain's sore disappointment in our demands for her relinquishment of sovereignty in the Western Hemisphere.[55]

The boaters' reveries came to an abrupt halt with the arrival of what the *Nydia's* owner described as "the heavens in an apparent state of intense madness ... roars of thunder adding to the grand spectacle illuminated by continual flashes of lightening [sic] ... and the sea like a boiling cauldron endeavoring to devour everything upon its surface." The storm roiled the boat for three days. One of the two smokestacks was almost carried away. The yacht's exact location was anyone's guess for two days. Crew and passengers went sleepless "with," as Emerson reported, "no desire for liquid refreshments or conversation." The seas finally calmed on the evening of February 15, allowing the crew to drop anchor. After all had a good night's sleep and a bit of sustenance, the *Nydia* arrived in Key West, Florida, with "but one bushel of coal in our tankers." Refurbished and refreshed, the crew and passengers continued their sojourn to Havana, where all were received by General Counsel Lee; then on to New Orleans, where Emerson visited his Bromo-Seltzer office; and finally back to Baltimore in April, ending an almost three-month absence from the city and his family.[56]

* * *

Shortly after his return, the inveterate sailor assumed yet another leadership position, this one as chairman of a committee to host the annual convention of the National Wholesale Druggists Association in October in Old Point Comfort, Virginia, near Hampton Roads, where he could arrive by boat.[57] Unfortunately, a Yellow Fever scare in Old Point forced the convention to meet instead in Niagara, New York, forcing Emerson to arrive by train.[58]

* * *

3—Leading the Naval Reserves

The Captain's time with the Reserves was nearing its end, but he and his reservists had one more presidential inauguration to march in. On March 4, 1901, he once again led the Maryland Naval Militia down Pennsylvania Avenue from the Capitol Building to the White House as part of Maryland's military contingent in President William McKinley's second inaugural parade. Evidently pleased with Lt. Smith Hollins McKim's performance on *The Dale*, Emerson included him as one of his four staff members for the parade. All the state's military bands played the state song, "Maryland My Maryland," as they passed the reviewing stand. The *Sun* reported the Militia "had many friends along the route of march who shouted and cheered them mightily."[59]

He returned to Washington several weeks later, where with 15 other men, including several U.S. Representatives and the Governor of Ohio, George K. Nash, the Captain hoped to establish the Military Club in Washington, D.C. The group filed incorporation papers in Delaware, and

The Captain's yacht *Margaret*, which he used extensively up and down the East Coast, in the Caribbean, and in Gulf of Mexico to entertain friends and associates with cruises and hunting expeditions. Some thought its relatively narrow width made it unsuitable for ocean voyages, though it did successfully crisscross the Atlantic once but without the Captain and his party on board. He preferred larger ships for ocean voyages. Author's collection.

PAY ROLL Steam Yacht "MARGARET," August

Copy to acct.

No.	NAME.	STATION.	Term of Service Mos. / Days.	Pay per Month.	Board	Due.
1	James H. Dungan	Master	1	150.00		150
2	Ernest Church	Mate	1	85.00		85
3	M. Doyle	2nd Mate	1	55.00		55
4	M. Schrader	Quarter-Master	1	35.00		35
5	A. Anderson	Quarter-Master	1	35.00		35
6	John O'Brien	Launch-man	1	40.00		40
7	O. Redbheim	Sailor	1	30.00		30
8	A. Madson	do	1	30.00		30
9	A. Hansen	do	1	30.00		30
10	A. Strange	do	1	30.00		30
11	John F. Oetel	Chief Eng	1	110.00		110
12	August Berite	asst "	1 / 23	75.00		57 50
13	Washington Smith	Oiler	1	45.00		45
14	R. Nelson	do	1	45.00		45
15	John Petterson	Fire-man	1	40.00		40
16	T. Aves	do	28	40.00		37 3
17	E. Sanchos	do	9	40.00		12
18	William Razzel	Steward	1	85.00		85
19	Ernest Temple	2nd Steward	1	60.00		60
20	Dick Brew	Pantry man	1	40.00		40
21	Ed Villez	Chef	1	85.00		85
22	Geo Neehim	Cook	1	60.00		60
23	John Kerst	Mess. man	1	30.00		30
						1226 8
	A H Devold	asst Eng	8	75.00		20
	Charles Jeelan	Fireman	2	40.00		2 6,
	David Huglind	do	21	40.00		28 0,
						1 7 5
						85 0
						1192 5

The *Margaret* required a crew of more than 20, as can be seen by the payroll list for August 1912. Courtesy of Andrew Murray.

members set out to raise $100,000 by selling 10,000 shares of stock at ten dollars each. The Club was conceived as an educational and entertainment membership organization for soldiers and sailors in state militias throughout the country. By 1906, however, the group had failed to raise the needed funds, and they abandoned the project.[60]

As the Bromo-Seltzer king was promoting the Military Club, the lure of the sea came calling. Captain Emerson resigned from the Naval Reserves on April 16, 1901, to travel around the world while leaving the management of the Emerson Drug Company to others.[61]

Preparations for the trip had been underway for some time. Emerson had sold the *Nydia* the previous November to a New York banker, Frederick J. Lisman. In her place, the Captain bought a larger yacht, the *Marjorie*, from Mrs. R. Van Winkle of Bristol, Rhode Island, for an estimated price of $110,000.[62] Emerson promptly renamed it *The Margaret*, in honor of his 17-year-old daughter. No record could be found of Emilie's reaction to the naming, but one could imagine she felt slighted and offended. The 185-foot, all-steel, coal-fired, extensively refurbished yacht boasted an interior finished in mahogany with its walls covered in silk fabric, seven staterooms, a library, dining room, extensive bar, music room with a piano, and several "handsome bathrooms, galley, and other necessary rooms."[63]

4

Breaking In

In addition to leading the Naval Reserves, finding new markets for Bromo-Seltzer, and indulging his passions for hunting and sailing, Emerson, often referred to in the press as "Dr. Emerson," though he held no degree, began establishing himself as one of Baltimore's leading citizens. In 1895 be built a mansion for his family, wife Emilie and three daughters, at 2500 Eutaw Place. The family had lived in several rental houses in the fashionable Druid Park neighborhood since moving to Baltimore. Ownership of a permanent home on Eutaw Place, home to many of the city's most prominent citizens including John Hopkins University's president Daniel Court Gilman and America's leading surgeon Dr. William Stewart Halsted, bestowed an appreciated aura of social status on the Emersons.[1]

Consisting of three stories built over a basement, sitting on one-third of an acre, with a prominent turret, a covered front porch, large bow windows (curved bay windows), dormers, and decorative window arches, the 15,600-square-foot structure joined the ranks of Baltimore's most prestigious homes.[2] Seven servants, including a maid, cook, waitress, valet, and chauffer, lived in the Emerson mansion. Five were African American.[3] His next-door neighbor was General Alfred E. Booth, a vice-president of A. Booth, Inc., the country's largest oyster-packing house, founded by his father in Chicago.[4] Booth was regarded "as one of the wealthiest men in Baltimore." His mansion was considered to be "one of the most elaborate homes of the old city."[5] Emerson took pride in both his new house and neighborhood.

The public's first access to the newly-built residence occurred on April 23, 1896. An evening reception following the wedding at St. Peter's Protestant-Episcopal Church of Emilie's daughter and Isaac's stepdaughter, Daisy, to T. Mitchell Horner provided the occasion. The groom came from a wealthy Baltimore family. His father, Joshua Horner, Jr., presided over the American National Bank. His grandfather, Joshua Horner, owned one of the city's largest fertilizer plants. Guests bestowed over 300 gifts on the couple, most of silver and cut glass. Following a honeymoon in Boston, they settled in New York before moving to Atlanta, where Emerson had given Horner charge of the Emerson Drug Company's office.[6]

* * *

Emilie demonstrated an interest in business as well as social affairs. Just before Christmas of the same year, Emilie took to the courts to file suit, or in legal terms, "to levy a distress," in City Court against J. Wesley White, a well-known druggist in the northwest part of the city, for non-payment of rent. White said he withheld the rent for his lease of Mrs. Emerson's house, which she had purchased from a former landlord, and which sat very near the Emerson's new mansion, because she had not reimbursed him $130.00 for his repairs to the property. In a first-of-its-kind ruling in Maryland, Judge Charles E. Phelps ruled in White's favor. Phelps' decision had nothing to do with the merits of who owed whom what. The judge cited an obscure Maryland law that reflected women's status before the court. A woman, the judge ruled, could not levy a distress on her own, but could only do so "with her husband or her next friend" (a person who acts on behalf of one who does not have the legal capacity to act on their own).[7]

Disappointment with the case's outcome did not deter Emilie or Isaac from continuing their climb up the city's social register. Five weeks later, on February 5, 1897, they again opened their home, this time for the first of many charitable and social events. Richard Burmeister headlined a musical performance to benefit the Hospital for Crippled Children. A German composer and pianist who had studied with Franz Liszt in Europe, Burmeister was a resident at Baltimore's Peabody Institute at the time.[8] Three hundred people were fortunate enough to obtain seats on chairs brought in. Others crowded onto the stairways and into the upstairs rooms. Many more had to be turned away.[9]

Several months after the musical performance, Emilie again found herself in court, this time for a case involving her diamonds, valued at the princely price of $25,000 (about $600,000 in 2018 dollars). At issue was whether her diamonds should be taxed. City Solicitor Thomas Elliott had ruled they should be. By a 2–1 vote, the Appellate Court overruled Elliott in February 1898, by deciding the gems were exempt from taxation. By wearing the greater part of her jewels constantly and all of them frequently, at least once a week, she met the legal definition of "habitually." Elliott had ruled that she only wore them "continually," which would subject them to taxation, whereas wearing them "habitually" avoided the tax.[10] While pleased she didn't have to pay tax on her jewels, Emilie would later rue the city-wide publicity about her diamond stash.

Two weeks before the Appellate Court's ruling, Emilie's second daughter, Lillie, married Walter Woodward White at St. Peter's Protestant-Episcopal Church in Baltimore, the same church where her sister had been married, on February 16, a day after the *U.S.S. Maine* had exploded in Havana Harbor. Many people, mostly women, had filled the church hours before the ceremony, seeking a glimpse of Emilie's jewels that the press had described in detail. Unfortunately for the early arrivees, Emile's clothing obscured most of the jewels. The couple left for a European honeymoon shortly after the ceremony. White, a junior member of the Roessler & Hasslacher Chemical Company in New York, was well acquainted with London, where his parents lived. The company's headquarters in Germany had exported products to the United States since 1894 and opened a manufacturing plant in Brooklyn in 1889.[11] The groom's experience with chemicals and his parents' connections sat well with Emerson, who soon appointed White to head Bromo-Seltzer's London office.

* * *

Two months after the wedding, Emilie joined a group of Baltimore women who, like herself, retained sympathies for the Confederacy. They held a Confederate Relief Bazar [sic], a two-week extravaganza in April at the Fifth Regiment Armory in Baltimore for the benefit of impoverished Confederate veterans and their families. The affair consisted of one table for each Confederate state and several in the name of generals such as Robert E. Lee and "Stonewall" Jackson. Donated memorabilia of all shapes and forms were available, including locks of hair from Lee and Jefferson Davis, and a sword worn by Jackson, to be auctioned. Raffle winners went home with prize livestock, including sheep, cattle, and pigeons. Entertainment in the form of races, games, contests, and fortune tellers, helped boost the attendance into the thousands. Emilie served as one of ten "Sub-Chairs" for the North Carolina table. More than 80 other women served as Assistants and Advisory Committee members for the tables. When the Bazar closed on April 22, 1898, $25,000 had been raised.[12]

In another volunteer effort, as the country was just a week away from the start of the Spanish-American War, Emilie joined the Ladies Auxiliary of the State Militia. She took charge of soliciting donations for a flag. "The naval militia," she told a reporter, "certainly deserve to have a stand of colors. The only flag they have ever owned is one I gave them three years ago, and this is a regular naval flag." In previous marches and parades, the men, wishing to fly the national colors, had to borrow an American flag. "The stand of colors we will present," she said, "will consist of the State as well as the national flag." Noting that all previous efforts for the militia have been done "at private expense," referring to her husband's outlays, she encouraged one and all to send donations to her Eutaw Place residence. Once enough donations arrived, the flag was made.[13]

While Isaac was taking his leisure on the water and attending meetings after the war, Emilie, who often did not join the Captain and their daughter Margaret on their sea-going adventures, continued to immerse herself in a variety of civic activities. As an elected honorary member of the Woman's Branch of the Society for the Prevention of Cruelty to Animals, she participated in the Society's early May 1899 efforts to expand beyond Baltimore to establish offices in Annapolis, Catonsville, and Towson, Maryland, and raise funds for the Society's work.[14]

She joined 124 other ladies who planned and put on a second benefit for destitute Confederate soldiers and their families in June. This one was held outside on the lawn of the Confederate Soldiers Home in Pikesville, Maryland. The weather cooperated with sunshine and clear skies. Emilie was among those responsible for the Ice Cream and Strawberry table.[15] Later that month, with her daughter Lillie, she planned and conducted a day-long cruise with lunch on board the *Nydia* for 26 June graduates, including daughter Margaret, of Baltimore's The Sisters of Notre Dame, a Catholic preparatory school on North Charles Avenue.[16] The outing, part of a week-long series of commencement activities, took the women south across the Chesapeake Bay just beyond Kent Island to Queenstown before returning to Baltimore.[17]

* * *

Three months later in September 1899, the Bromo-Seltzer king took another trip by himself, this one to London aboard a commercial steamer. He called the trip a mixture of business and pleasure. His time in London gave him a chance to review the Bromo-Seltzer operation in the British Isles and spend time with daughter Margaret. She had been enjoying a postgraduate tour of the Continent with an unnamed "instructress." The main topic of conversation on the steamer home was the conviction of Alfred Dreyfus, a young, Jewish French Army artillery officer, of passing secrets to the Germans. Tried and convicted once, his re-trial, with the same outcome, is still considered a judicial and political scandal of the first order. He was eventually pardoned. Emerson noted that the news of Dreyfus' second conviction, announced on board the steamer, "was received with great indignation by a large number of the Hebrew passengers."[18]

* * *

Though Emerson was by now a wealthy man and could afford trips to Europe and private yachts, he was thrifty with the dollar. A week after the Captain's return from England, the Emersons found themselves in court once more on September 27 and 28, 1899. A photographer, Daniel Brendan, had taken 11 photographs of the interior of their Eutaw Place mansion and one from the front porch with a view of Druid Hill Park. Emilie found them "unsatisfactory," but this time, as she had not done with the litigation about the tax status of her jewels, she let her husband go to court. She did not make an appearance. Magistrate Ayler ruled in the Emerson's favor, but on appeal, Magistrate John Dobler ruled for Bendann. The Emersons paid Bendann his $65 fee plus court costs.[19] Another example of Emerson's thrifty nature had occurred earlier in the spring. Needing a stable to be torn down and the bricks and wood removed from the rear of his office on West Fayette, Emerson sought estimates. The first one came in at $216.82. Subsequent estimates came in at $190.00, $235.00, and an offer from Timothy Bresnan, Dealer in Sand, Paving, and Grading, in the amount of $175.00. Bresnan got the job.[20]

While paying close attention to his day-to-day expenses, Emerson was, as we have seen, generous with his resources in the case of the Reserves. He also favored his alma mater and would make many gifts to UNC-CH. The first occurred in July 1895, when he gave $1,250 to UNC's Alumni Hall.[21]

* * *

In August 1900, Emerson took the *Nydia* on another trip to New England and this time docked at Narragansett, Rhode Island, a gathering place for the East Coast social elite of the day. Politicians, industrialists, financiers and other wealthy people spent all or a part of their summer in Narragansett and nearby Newport. Many in Newport built summer residences referred to as "cottages" even though they contained many rooms, had views of the Bay, and cost a pretty penny to build. The most famous "cottage" is The Breakers, a 70-room mansion built in 1895 in Newport by Commodore Cornelius Vanderbilt's grandson, Cornelius Vanderbilt II. A newspaper account of Emerson's visit cited 20 friends as accompanying him. No mention was made of Margaret or Emilie being among his guests, who came from Charleston, South Caroline, Paris, and New York City as well as Baltimore.[22] Emerson found Narragansett to his liking. He would return often.

* * *

The following year, the captain and his wife joined forces on the evening of February 15, 1901, to host the most lavish entertainment affair to date in their home. One-hundred and seventy-five invited guests heard world-renowned soprano Lillian Nordica sing selections from several operas. A native of Farmington, Maine, who had trained in Italy, she had a reputation as an "eminent prima donna" earned through her performances at New York's Metropolitan Opera House, in addition to appearances in Europe, Russia, and Australia. She made her entrance on her host's arm. Accompanied by French tenor Eustase Salignac, a French native who had trained at the Paris Conservatory and also sang at the Met, the duo received a standing ovation at the end of their program. The *Baltimore Sun* characterized the musicale as "one of the most artistic and beautiful ever seen in Baltimore." Emilie had arranged for programs to be engraved in gold and violet, American Beauty roses and "great masses of Southern Similax" to be placed throughout the house and its hallways, and an orchestra situated on the second floor to entertain with "popular airs" during dinner. The hosts and their 16-year-old daughter, Margaret, received their guests in the front drawing room. Guests included former Maryland Governor Frank Brown, a future four-term governor, Albert Ritchie, former Baltimore Mayor F. C. Latrobe, and assorted judges, attorneys, bankers, businessmen, and their wives. A physician, Dr. Smith Hollis McKim, who had served with Emerson on *The Dale*, also attended.[23] Emerson paid the performers a reported $1,800 for their evening's performance.[24]

The scale and magnificence of the event had a special significance for the couple. It marked their entrance and acceptance into Baltimore society. Mrs. "Bromo-Seltzer," as the press often referred to her, had attempted before to gain entrance, but none of the social elite in the city would accept her invites or invite the Emersons to their functions. The concert and dinner changed all that.[25] In March of 1903, the couple were guests of honor at a card party followed by supper and a musicale hosted by Mr. and Mrs. Edwin Faber. He was a prominent Baltimore attorney. She was frequently in the news for her charitable work with homeless dogs and aged horses. Thirty people attended.[26] The couple was later invited to a Christmas party given by Mrs. Andrew Melville Reid on December 24, 1904. Reid, a native of France, would become active in Maryland's Gold Star Mothers organization during and after World War I. She contributed to the work of the city's philanthropic organizations throughout her life. Mrs. Reid and Emilie stuck up a friendship and subsequently traveled together to Palm Beach, Florida, while the Captain was on one of his trips.[27]

By 1911, the Captain and Emilie were firmly established within the higher echelons of Baltimore society. In that year, they subscribed to an opera box at the Lyric Theater with such notables as Henry Walters, railroad executive and art aficionado whose collection would become the foundation for the Walters Museum; and brothers George and Michael Jenkins. George, a Confederate veteran, railroad and banking executive, founded the Bon Secours Hospital, while Michael was president of the Maryland Jockey Club and an executive of the Safe Deposit and Trust

Company. Other subscribers included B. H. Brewster, Jr., vice president of Baugh and Sons, Maurice Gregg, a director of the Baltimore and Ohio Railroad, and several who had estates in the Green Spring Valley, where the Bromo-Seltzer king would shortly take up residence himself.[28]

* * *

Life at the Eutaw Place mansion would be remembered for other reasons as well. In January 1901, a burglar, perhaps learning of Mrs. Emerson's stash of diamonds from the publicity generated by the tax litigation, set off an alarm at 2:00 a.m. on a Sunday morning. Awakened by the noise, Mrs. Emerson raised her bedroom window and fired two shots into the air from the pistol she kept by her bed, to attract attention. "I keep a revolver in my bedroom all the time," she told police, adding, "I can handle it or a rifle and am not afraid to fire either." The Captain was in New York at the time of the break-in, but two of her daughters, Margaret and Daisy, were in the house along with four servants. The intruder escaped capture.[29]

This had not been Emilie's first encounter with those of criminal intent. Several unsuccessful robbery attempts had been made previously. Each time, Emilie managed to scare them off. Only on one occasion was the robber caught. In this instance, on the night of December 9, 1897, the intruder, who had reportedly followed Emilie home from the Bromo-Seltzer office on West Fayette Street, where she had stopped to pick up some cash, quietly ransacked her bedroom while others in the house were at dinner. He tried to escape with $10,000 worth of jewelry. Spotted on the roof by a police officer, the thief, a John Davis, fired three shots from his revolver at the officer, who returned the fire. All shots missed their marks. Davis was pulled to the ground and subdued by the officer's partner.[30] Davis, whom police knew as a pickpocket artist at the World's Fair, denied following Emilie. He claimed that his inebriated state induced him to attempt the robbery and fire his gun at the officer. Be all that as it may, his faulty derring-do and arrests for three other robberies in the Emerson's neighborhood netted him seven years in the penitentiary.[31]

Emilie was no shrinking violent. She was pursuing activities and developing friends on her own as the Captain was spending more time away from Druid Park.

5

Separation Strains

By the end of May 1901, Emerson was ready for his "globe girdling" adventure that would cover 44,000 miles across 18 countries over the course of a year and two weeks. Joining him from Baltimore were daughter Margaret, Mrs. Edmund P. Jenkins, and Martha Lee, the wife and the daughter of the late Edmund Jenkins, paymaster for the B&O Railroad,[1] and Dr. Smith Hollins McKim, whom the Captain thought very highly of by now. McKim, who had served in the Reserves with Emerson, worked as a physician at the Hospital for Crippled Children at Charles and Twentieth Street, serving as the party's physician and surgeon.[2] Described by a *Sun* reporter as "one of Baltimore's prominent young physicians and a general favorite as a club man," McKim belonged to the Maryland Club, the Baltimore Club, and the Elkridge Fox Hunting and Catonsville Country Clubs.[3]

New York City friends Gerard and Minnie Stuyvesant and B. B. Kirkland completed the party. Gerard was a seventh-generation descendent of Petrus Stuyvesant, who played a major role in the development of Manhattan in the late 1600s. Minnie's hometown newspaper, the *Courier-Journal* in Louisville, Kentucky, described her as "one of the most charming women in New York and is one of the best dressed women in the East."[4] Kirkland owned a prominent Manhattan investment firm.[5] Noticeable by her absence was Emilie, who elected to remain in Baltimore to pursue her own interests and enjoy her ever-widening circle of friends and acquaintances.

The group assembled in New York and boarded the German ocean line *Kaiser Wilhelm der Grosse*, the fastest and largest ship of its kind when built in 1897. The ship carried the party to Southampton, England, where the *Margaret* was waiting.[6] After a visit to London and Scotland, the group traversed the North Sea to Germany's Elbe River and passed through the Kiel Canal to St. Petersburg. From there, the *Margaret* took the party to Gibraltar, Italy, and continued on to Alexandria, Egypt. Passage through the Suez Canal and crossings of the Red Sea and the Indian

Ocean took the group to its next point of land, the city of Bombay (now Mumbai), India. The cruise ended in China after stops in Colombo, Ceylon (now Sri Lanka), and Singapore. The *Margaret* returned to Baltimore via the Atlantic Ocean, while Emerson and party continued on to Japan, China, and the American West.

The sun had yet to set on the British Empire. The proliferation of ships flying the British flag that the party encountered throughout their voyage impressed the skipper. He noted, "in almost every port we visited there was found some vessel flying the English flag, while our own in many ports was a curiosity, and people looked as if they had never seen it before."

The "hail fellow, well met" Captain made a favorable impression on England's royalty, as he did with most people. They invited him to a dinner at the Royal Yacht Club, whose members were all of royal blood. He characterized the invitation as an "unusual honor." Lord Landsdowne, formally known as Henry Charles Keith Petty-Fitzmaurice, 5th marquis of Lansdowne, an English statesman and Foreign Secretary at the time,[7] invited the party to a week-long hunt for grouse on his estate in the north of England.

Known for his intelligence and shrewdness, the Captain was a keen observer of people wherever he met them. He recorded his impressions of those he met on the voyage and shared them with a *Sun* reporter who relayed his adventures and included his social commentary in an article entitled "Globe Girdler Home." In Germany, the Bromo-Seltzer king saw the people "as most progressive ... and ruled by a progressive monarch [Wilhelm II]." The Italians he thought to be "a dirty class of people, but still I think there is a great future for Italy."

While on Italian soil Margaret, Dr. McKim, Isaac, a crew member from the *Margaret*, and a local guide embarked one day on a hunting trip in the mountains. It proved to be more adventurous than anticipated. The guide's dog attacked a goat. An angry and vocal crowd of some 500 people, one armed with a pistol, surrounded the group and demanded payment for the goat. Emerson, who did not take well to being ordered about, refused on the grounds that the goat recovered and suffered no lasting harm. Seeing that his words had only added to the crowd's anger, Isaac gave one of his pistols to the crew member, while he and the others loaded their shotguns. A military officer arrived just in time to defuse the situation. "It was a wonder we were not all killed," Emerson reported on his return to the *Margaret*.

On the group's visit to Egypt, Emerson commented on the contentment of its people and that of all those "in the English colonies." Emerson suffered a heat stroke in India which kept him from accepting the Governor of Ceylon's invitation to hunt tigers which, he said, "I was very anxious to do." The people, he noted, "are remarkable and the country throughout is most interesting."

In Japan, the group attended the Mikado's (Emperor's) garden party, a formal affair at which men wore high hats and long coats. Women in mourning were not permitted to attend. The Captain described the assembled crowd as a "sprinkling of pig-tailed Chinamen, mustached Germans, Hebrews and Englishmen." He observed that "the Japanese ladies are not particularly beautiful and the men are all small." During his time in Japan, he said "the influence of American and British commercial interests can be seen throughout the land." He made the acquaintance of Baron Eiichi Shibusawa, then the richest man in Japan and credited with introducing capitalism to Japan. Shortly after his arrival home, Emerson reciprocated Shibusawa's generous hospitality by giving the industrialist and his entourage of wealthy Japanese businessmen a tour of a large steel plant in Steelton, Pennsylvania, while the Baroness dined with Mrs. Emerson.

An outbreak of the plague in Hong Kong cut short the party's visit to China, but while there, the Captain, an inveterate collector during all of his trips abroad, "surreptitiously bought a gown formerly worn by the Emperor and stolen from the palace." Clearly pleased with his purchase, he said, "It is of the finest silk ... with the colors that only royalty is allowed to wear in China."[8] The Captain's gown was not the only purchase made in China. Margaret bought a monkey, the size of a small kitten, named Jingo, who became the party's mascot.[9]

Emerson's party crossed the Pacific by ocean liner and toured the American West in a private rail car—*The Rosalind*. Eighteen-year-old Margaret clearly missed being away from her mother for more than a year. Thrilled to be finally home, she was first off *The Rosalind* when it pulled into the Baltimore station and "threw herself into her mother's arms."[10]

* * *

The *Margaret* survived her return journey to Baltimore via the Atlantic Ocean in fine shape, dousing doubts expressed by some that she wasn't seaworthy enough for such a round-trip voyage. "She has passed through storms fierce enough to tax the endurance of an ocean liner and has borne herself with a staunchness that has won the admiration of her officers and crew," enthused a reporter for the *Sun*.[11] The Captain himself may have been among the doubters, for he obviously preferred commercial liners to the *Margaret* for ocean crossings. The Captain continued to use the *Margaret* as his yacht for trips up and down the East Coast until she was pressed into service by the navy during World War I. When he wasn't using it, the astute businessman rented his yacht out on at least five occasions, for a noticeable sum each time. New York stockbroker and racing enthusiastic Ross Proctor leased the *Margaret* in June 1904 for three and-a-half months for $2,500 a month. The lease came with an option to buy for $85,000. Proctor didn't exercise the option. Four other rentals between 1908 and 1912 brought in $30,000 in another demonstration of the Bromo-Seltzer king's business acumen.[12]

* * *

Three months after circling the globe, the Captain indulged another of his passions—automobile racing. Driving what a reporter referred to "as his famous red automobile," Emerson and three friends, Col. John M. Carter, former aide to Maryland Democratic ex-Governor Lloyd Lowndes and president of the International League of Press Clubs,[13] among them, regaled diners at Washington, D.C.'s elegant hotel, The Willard, located just two blocks from the White House, with the events of their trip from the Monument City to the Nation's Capitol earlier in the afternoon. The Captain boasted that the trip had been made in an hour and three-quarters, which would have required the then-heady speed of a little more than 20 miles an hour. The return trip was another story. At 8:00 p.m., Emerson and friends entered the machine, which had been "thumping and grunting" curbside as steam-powered cars did while warming up, and "shot eastward along Pennsylvania Avenue." They had not been heard from by 10:00 p.m. A caller to his home at midnight was told that the Captain had retired, but no one would say when he arrived.[14]

A month later on October 19, 1902, the Captain, with daughter Margaret and step-daughter Lillie onboard, again entered a race pitting his French red machine, the largest car in the field, against the roadsters of five other members of the Automotive Club of Maryland, for a race between Baltimore and Frederick, Maryland. Everyone, chauffeurs included, wore Russian calf automobile coats and goggles to ward off the dust from the dirt roads. Emerson's car finished fourth, 28 minutes behind M. Gillet Gill's American steam machine's winning time of two hours and 11 minutes. Gill, a prominent Baltimore businessman and one of the first in Baltimore to purchase a "horseless carriage" in 1898,[15] claimed that the results proved the superiority of American automobiles. Emerson disagreed, saying Gill's reckless driving and good luck made the difference. Gill retorted, "The public will know who did reckless running when they find you ran over two chickens and I killed only one on the road."[16]

Another example of the Captain's passion to test his racing skill behind the wheel of the fastest, most expensive car he could buy, involved a new "big red French automobile," the *Bollee*. January of 1905 found both on Ormond Beach, Florida, 20 miles north of Daytona Beach. Also present was Ernest S. Partridge, Vice President of the Decauville Automobile

5—Separation Strains

Co., a French firm that also produced a 40 horsepower car. Partridge often sought opportunities to race his car as a way to advertise it. Emerson, ever up for a challenge, took him on in a ten-mile race along the sands of Ormond Beach, with a stake of $500 agreed upon by the two men in the twilight hours of January 27.

The Bollee, with Emerson at the wheel, got away first and led for the first five miles. Professional driver Guy Vaughn, who would go on to set many race track records, drove Partridge's car. Vaughn overtook the Bollee by the six-mile mark and won the race by five lengths. More than $5,000 had been bet on the race among spectators. Several thousand had come to watch a 50-mile race between seven cars earlier in the day. Among the drivers in that race was Barney Oldfield, a popular race car driver who began his career driving for Henry Ford and was the first man to achieve 60 miles an hour in an automobile.[17]

* * *

Another of the Captain's automobiles, his touring car, had made news in January of 1903 when two Baltimore police officers pulled it over for speeding. Roger Magondux, who came from France to drive for the Captain, was at the wheel. Emilie and Lillie were in the back seat. The officers took all three to the Northern Police station. Emilie threatened to file charges against the officers for arresting her without cause. She insisted the car had not been speeding but later changed her mind. The officers, however, resented Emilie calling them "liars," "thieves," and "puppies." Each filed a $10,000 suit against her in Superior Court. The officers' superior, Captain Bernard J. Ward, filed a similar suit against Emilie. The court dismissed the officers' suits, but Ward's went to trial.

Hundreds of spectators, mostly women, attended the four-day jury trial in late January 1905. *The New York Times* reported that "hats were torn off, satchels were lost, faces scratched, and gowns torn in the scrambles [for seats]." The court found for Ward in the amount of $4,000. Emilie threatened that she and the Captain would sell their mansion and move to New York. "I consider the verdict a most unjust one," she fumed to a *New York Times* reporter. She added, "I expected a verdict against me, because in a jury there is always prejudice against people who have money." Upset though she was, Emilie decided not to appeal the verdict. Within two months, attorneys for both sides arranged a settlement in which Mrs. Emerson paid Captain Ward $1,000.[18] The couple stayed in Baltimore.

* * *

A month before Emilie's first court appearance in the speeding case, the romance between Margaret and Smith Hollins McKim, that flourished during their around-the-world adventure, culminated in their December wedding, an event that captured the attention of Baltimore's elite. At the time of the couple's engagement in October 1902, the *Sun* described the bride as "tall and fair, possessing much individuality as well as a charming grace of manner. She is a fine linguist, a finished musician upon the harp, and endowed with a rarely beautiful voice." On the evening of the engagement announcement, Isaac and Emilie hosted a theater party to see "The Little Duchess" at Ford's Opera House, followed by dinner at the Hotel Stafford.[19]

Wanting to give their daughter every advantage as she entered adulthood and marriage, her parents had made sure she received the benefits of a fine education coupled with an extensive introduction to Europe. She had attended Baltimore's Notre Dame of Maryland Collegiate Institute for Young Ladies (a preparatory school where she converted to Catholicism), and, at age 17, studied at Misses Ely's School on Riverside Drive in New York City for a year. She spent three summers in Europe, traveling with a governess.[20] McKim, a physician, came from a long line of socially prominent Baltimoreans, many of whom had made fortunes in banking. He resumed his work at the Hospital for Crippled Children after returning to Baltimore. He was 29 and Margaret 18.[21]

The Emersons spared no expense for the December 30, 1902, wedding. The *New York Times* described the ceremony as "the most splendidly appointed event ever seen in Baltimore."[22] Fifteen hundred invited guests, some from Philadelphia, New York City, Washington, and other cities, filled the Christ Protestant-Episcopal Church at Chase and St. Paul Streets for the 8:00 p.m. nuptials. Most arrived by carriage. Flowers and twinkling lights lent a festive atmosphere to the church. A *Sun* reporter noted that the women were "brilliantly gowned," and the gentlemen "stalwart."

The catered reception that followed at the Emerson mansion was no less spectacular. Seventy tables filled a 100-foot-long dining room built especially for the occasion. The Hungarian Band of New York, in native costume, performed throughout the evening and into the early morning. Five hundred light bulbs of various tints colorfully lit the room and the floral decorations that appeared on every wall and table. Following an elaborate dinner of French cuisine for the 400 people invited to the reception, the newlyweds received a bounty of gifts that included chests of silver, jewels of various types, crystal glassware, and works of art. They departed Baltimore for a honeymoon in Europe.[23]

The Captain, again without Emilie, joined them in April 1903 for a two-month motor tour through Europe. Stops included Monte Carlo in the principality of Monaco, known for its casinos and, in the early 1900s, master chess tournaments; Genoa, Italy; and Madrid, Spain, where the group attended a bullfight; Switzerland and Germany. The Baltimore tourists rode in style. The Bromo-Seltzer king added a "touring machine" bought in Paris to his French automobile collection. The car featured "seats for several guests and servants and ample space for luggage."[24]

* * *

Throughout the trip, Emerson sought out gardens to inspire him as he worked on designing a garden for his Baltimore estate. "Whenever we heard of a specifically beautiful garden," he told a *Sun* reporter, "it at once became our objective point, no matter how far out of our selected route it carried us." He made sketches of the gardens they visited and said his garden "will be a plaything for me." Soon after arriving home, he had built a sunken garden consisting of three terraces rising toward the piece de resistance, a marble fountain about which the captain allowed, "I believe I have selected a peculiarly unique and beautiful design." A ten-foot-high marble wall, with replicas of Bromo-Seltzer bottles arrayed along the top, that intentionally resembled the wall surrounding the Garden of the Tuileries in Paris, blocked the view of passersby. Marble statuary, urns, trees and shrubbery with "some of the curious, yet tiny, yet ancient Japanese trees among them," completed the garden. He planned to extend the north side of his residence later so it would extend into and overlook the garden that one would enter from ground level through an iron gate.[25]

Among the many people involved in executing the Captain's flight of floral ecstasy was the then-little-known sculptress, Sally James Farnham. Emerson hired her to design and cast a bronze statue for his garden. Born Sarah Welles James into a wealthy family in Ogdensburg, N.Y., in 1869, despite constraints typically endured by young girls at the time she was encouraged by her father, Col. Edward C. James, Civil War veteran and one of the state's best-known trial lawyers, to pursue her love for hunting and horseback riding. At age 27 she married George Paulding Farnham, an internationally famed designer of jewelry and silver for Tiffany & Co.

During a serious illness which kept her bedridden throughout most of 1901, George gave her some modeling clay in an attempt to raise her spirits. His gift launched her into a celebrated career in sculpture. Largely self-taught, though she did benefit from some tutoring by Frederick Remington, she became one of the pre-eminent sculptors of her time. Her prominence was all the more remarkable given her responsibilities to her three children following a divorce from Farnham, and the preponderance of male sculptors. Her most famous work is the statue of Simon Bolivar, the South American liberator, on horseback, originally placed in New York City's Central Park and subsequently moved to Central Park South and the Avenue of the Americas.[26]

Her bronze sculpture for the Captain was her first important private commission.[27] Always anxious to move quickly on projects, her impatient patron was ready to accept her design sight unseen. She cautioned him in a letter "to [not] accept it until you have seen the design completed," which he agreed to.[28] What emerged was a bronze fountain of three life-size nude maidens dancing around a center sprout topped by a fanciful figure of Pan, the Greek god of the wild, a hunter and companion of the nymphs. Art historian Michael P. Reed assessed the work "as typical of Farnham's early output in being ambitious in scope and a bit daring in content."[29]

While the final product pleased them both in the end, their relationship had gotten off to a rocky start. An exchange of letters between the two in early January 1904 shows her assertiveness and his response to his feathers being ruffled. Commenting on a letter received from him, she expressed "surprise, to put it mildly," at its contents. Apparently thinking he had reneged on an oral agreement, she cast aspersion "on the word of a Southern gentleman which," she wrote, "I had an idea—mistaken, it seems—was binding." In response to what she construed to be his expectation that the fountain would be a gift, she wrote, "[That] is concerning. I am as yet not an object of charity, my dear Captain, artistically or otherwise. Only have known you as a sportsman [they first met at a 'shooting event'], I expected you to play fair."

The price was also an issue. She had quoted him a price of "in the neighborhood of $3,000" but added in her letter, "the actual expenses of setting up etc. would amount to about $4,000, and my price completed is $5,000 which does not seem exorbitant considering my time, etc." She closed with, "Waiting your reply and with my kindest regards to your good wife. Believe me. Sincerely yours."

Captain Emerson wrote back, saying he received her letter "with sadness and sorrow," and stated his belief that unnamed "others outside of your home" had influenced her "to abuse me as you have seen fit to." He stated in his defense, "Never in my life have I repudiated an obligation ... Neither have I sought 'bargains' in works of art.... I have never in my life questioned, or halted at the price of a work of art if I desired it and felt that I could afford it."

He went on to say that he thought the cost of "casting, etc. is too high (though I may be mistaken)," and asked for a meeting at New York's Waldorf-Astoria Hotel where, he said, "I feel confident I can arrange the matter to our entire, mutual satisfaction ... and I will explain to you what I mean by 'outside' influence which will probably interest you." After assuring her that he cherished their "comradeship" and invoking "the name of fairness," he closed by assuring her they need not meet if "you still feel you have been mistaken in your idea of a 'Southern Gentleman.'" He signed his letter "Very Respectfully."[30] They did meet. She got her price. The unnamed others remained unnamed, at least in the public record.[31]

Farnham inscribed a poem on the base of her sculpture which read,

> Graces in alluring shapes
> Played and danced among the grapes.
> None to question or to hamper,
> Naught on fun to cast a damper.
> Joyous spontaneity,
> Knowing not propriety,
> Why should maiden, stiffly bodiced,
> Stand the type of all that's modest,
> Or the consciousness of virtue
> Be expressed by shoes that hurt you?
> Would the All Wise Power saw fit
> To unlace our lives a bit
> Give us room to breathe, and be
> Like the gods in Arcady![32]

The garden, first envisioned by Emilie two years earlier, but taken over by the Captain with such gusto that it became his primary diversion at the time, was unveiled to the public on May 28, 1904. The *Sun* called the Italian garden, covering 3,000 square feet and partially enclosed by a 27-foot-long wall of Texas marble, "magnificent" and filled with "splendid statuary." Two prominent examples of the statuary, in addition to Farnham's contribution, were a marble sun dial brought back from Naples by the Captain and a marble fountain carved from a sketch the Captain made of a fountain in Monte Carlo. More than a hundred varieties of flowers covered the three terraces in a lush panorama of spring blooms. Adding to the aura of the garden were the "charming vistas of Druid Hill Park and the blue lake in the distance."

At the same time the garden was being constructed, Isaac adorned his mansion's main entrance with two life-size lions carved of stone, one on either side of the front steps.[33] The lion, the garden planner explained, "is the Emerson crest, of English origin."[34]

Emilie, recently returned to Baltimore from a trip to the baths at Hot Springs, Virginia, left immediately the day after the garden opened to visit Margaret and her husband at their country home at Irvington-on-the-Hudson, N.Y., 30 miles north of New York City, an estate Emerson had purchased for the couple as a wedding gift.[35]

* * *

Construction of the garden had proceeded unhindered by the fiercest fire ever to strike the city. Starting in a downtown dry goods store on February 7, 1904, the flames barreled eastward, propelled by heavy winds.

Fifteen hundred buildings were destroyed. More than a thousand firemen tried unsuccessfully to extinguish the blaze as it burned out of control throughout the next day and evening. H. L. Mencken, then a reporter for the *Evening Herald*, recalled seeing a six-story office building burn "as if it had been made of matchwood and drenched with gasoline." A shift in the wind to the south finally blew the intruder into Baltimore's harbor. Miraculously, no one died, though property damage ran into the millions.[36]

The blaze was a topic of conversation at the Emerson Drug Company stockholders December 1904 meeting. Emerson's mansion was far enough north of the downtown that the fire never threatened it. Nor did the flames touch his Bromo-Seltzer warehouse. "We were most fortunate," he said "in escaping the ravages of the disastrous conflagration." Others, particularly his competitors, had not been so fortunate. "Nearly all the wholesale drug houses," he continued, "and many proprietary medicine manufactures, were destroyed ... yet we sustained no losses in accounts as a result of the fire, and we feel that we should offer our thanks to Providence for so sparing us." He made no comments about his less fortunate competitors.[37]

At the same meeting, Emerson told his shareholders that "we have to contend with imitations and substitutions on the part of unscrupulous dealers." He assured his audience, "We are constantly on the alert and whenever a trademark pirate appears, we endeavor to bring him to justice."[38] An example of bringing a trademark pirate to justice had occurred that same year in New York City. T. Mitchell Horner, during a visit to New York from his new location in Atlanta, came upon the pharmacy of one Charles Herzenberg, proprietor of the People's Pharmacy. Large Bromo-Seltzer signs appeared inside the store and in the store's windows. Herzenberg made the mistake of handing Horner a bottle of Bromide Seltzer when Horner had asked for Bromo-Seltzer. When challenged, Herzenberg said, "It's the same thing. Some call it Bromo-Seltzer and some Bromide Seltzer." Horner contacted Emerson, who hired an attorney to hand-deliver a letter from him to Herzenberg. If Herzenberg refused to sign the accompanying bond (a written promise not to misrepresent Bromo Seltzer in the future)Emerson promised his stockholders, "we will at once take steps to prosecute him." Herzenberg signed.[39]

An earlier misrepresentation of Bromo-Seltzer had brought Emerson an unexpected publicity bonanza. A box marked Tiffany & Co., containing two candlestick-shaped bottle holders and a blue bottle of what appeared to be Bromo-Seltzer, arrived at the New York office of Mr. Harry Cornish, physical director of the Knickerbocker Athletic Club, the day before Christmas 1898. After showing the contents to his aunt, Mrs. Kate Adams, he put them in a bureau drawer in his bedroom. Several nights later, Ms.

Adams, after a night on the town, retrieved the bottle, poured herself a teaspoon of the "Bromo-Seltzer," mixed it with water, drank it, and died almost immediately. The bottle contained cyanide of mercury, a highly toxic substance.

Cornish identified Roland B. Molineux, a chemist and a club member who strenuously disagreed with Cornish's management of the establishment, as the most likely perpetrator.[40] Molineux's trial drew sensational press coverage that reported every salacious detail throughout the nation. The term Bromo-Seltzer became familiar to millions of readers who followed the trial. Molineux was convicted and sentenced to the electric chair in 1900. While awaiting execution, Molineux received an authentic bottle of Bromo-Seltzer while in Sing Sing Prison from an anonymous person with the message, "Brace up, Roland." In a second trial in 1902, however, he was acquitted and released from prison. Molineux maintained his innocence throughout both trials, but the stress proved to be too much for him. Following 15 years of freedom, he was committed to the Kings Park Asylum on Long Island, where he died in 1917.[41]

Similar cases came to light. One gentleman, unfortunately mistook a bottle of mercuric chloride for Bromo-Seltzer.[42] Called to testify at his 1900 trial, Emerson said the bottle in question was not from his company.[43] Bromo-Seltzer came in distinctive, cobalt blue bottles of various sizes, yet another component of Emerson's advertising genius.

* * *

In the time between the 1904 fire and the stockholders' meeting, Margaret and the Captain, who enjoyed traveling the Continent together, embarked on yet another European foray in the fall of 1904. It was on this trip that Emerson bought his powerful French car, the red Bollee with a 40 horsepower motor that, as we have seen, he would soon race in Florida. The car, he said, "is regarded as the latest and best on the French market and enthusiasm for automobiles is like the craze for horses—one can't resist buying." He and Margaret toured France and Germany in his new purchase, including a week's stay at Trouville, France, on the Normandy coast. A picturesque fishing town and resort 120 miles north of Paris, Trouville offered horse racing, historic architecture, and luxury hotels and restaurants to the well-heeled tourist.[44] There, father and daughter indulged their craze for horse racing. "We enjoyed it greatly," he told a reporter, "hearing the crowd 'hurrah' for Vanderbilt [William K.] when his horse won the grand prize."

Their road trip ended in England. Upon arriving there, the Captain told a local reporter, "It was good to hear the Anglo-Saxon speech after weeks of French and German." The twosome later met up with Smith Hollins in Plymouth, England. The trio enjoyed a hunting trip outside of London before returning to New York in mid–September, where they were met by Emilie.[45]

* * *

Barely two months after father, daughter, and son-in-law arrived home from Europe, a family tragedy struck. On November 25, 1904, his sister Cornelia's husband, Josiah Stockton Murray, was shot and killed by his nephew, W. R. Murray, at 10:00 a.m. on Durham, North Carolina's Main Street, in front of his music store and in full view of many pedestrians. W. R. had gone to the store with his brother, Earle, to confront his uncle over a business matter. Josiah pulled out a revolver and fired several shots that struck Earle. W. R. wrestled the gun away from Josiah. The tussle resulted in W. R. fatally, albeit accidentally, shooting his uncle in the chest. Earle survived. A jury convicted W. R. of manslaughter and sentenced him to two years "on the county roads."[46]

Josiah left a wife and seven children, six girls and a boy. Hearing of the shooting, Isaac went immediately to Durham. He set up financial trusts to provide for his sister and nieces.[47] Emerson paid for his nephew's (J. Edward) studies at UNC-CH and the University of Virginia. After completing his coursework, J. Edward moved to Baltimore, joined the Emerson Drug Company, first as assistant treasurer and later as treasurer. Years later, in 1936, he became president of the company, a position he held until his death two years later.[48]

* * *

The Captain's diversions during the first few years of the twentieth century, extensive travel and his garden foremost among them, did not detract from Bromo-Seltzer's sales, over which, as was evident during the December 1904 stockholders meeting, Emerson kept a close watch. Employees continued to work day and night, manufacturing the fizzy white effervescence to meet the demand. Newspaper ads appeared in an ever-increasing number of dailies throughout the country and the world.

By 1902, Bromo-Seltzer was doing so well financially that shareholders received a dividend of 145 percent on their investment that year. The *New York Times* pointed out in 1903 that "Emerson, who not many years ago was the proprietor of a little drug store is now a millionaire, ... owns one fine yacht and has given the contract for another ... to cost a fortune ... and has plans for the construction of a beautiful and costly Italian garden adjoining his mansion on Eutaw Place."[49] Emerson had made his mark.

Emerson limited his newspaper advertising largely to white-owned papers. A few ads appeared in Baltimore's African American paper, the

Afro-American. One banner ad for Bromo-Seltzer appeared in the paper on April 25, 1903. Seven months later, a block ad did appear in the *Afro*. It carried the familiar ditty in large print, "With nerves unstrung and heads that ache, Wise Women Bromo-Seltzer Take. Trial Bottle 10 cents."[50]

The *Afro* also took ads from other purveyors of patent medicines. Directly above the Bromo ad was one for Cascaret Tablets. That ad serves as an excellent example of the outrageous curative claims made by many of Emerson's competitors. The company touted the pills as a "guaranteed cure for all bowel troubles, appendicitis, bad breath, bad blood, wind on the stomach, headache, indigestion, pimples, pains after eating, liver trouble, and sallow skin and dizziness." Scientists at New York's Memorial Sloan-Kettering Hospital, while not endorsing the product, noted that the tablets produced "propulsive contractions." A laxative by any other name. But a lucrative one that had sold 5 million boxes in 1899 and was still going strong in 1903. The tablets appealed to the belief at the time that constipation was the cause of the aforementioned ailments.[51] Emerson made no such extravagant claims for Bromo-Seltzer, limiting the powder's curative powers to headaches, upset stomachs, and nerves. His restraint helped sales, which continued to boom.

6

Problems with the Nostrum

By age 45, Emerson and Bromo-Seltzer had achieved such visibility that Abram P. T. Elder, a purveyor of books with a shady past most likely unknown to Emerson, invited him in 1903 to "subscribe," with a payment of $500 a page, to a book of biographies of famous men. Emerson opted for two pages. Elder had been fined several times and jailed once in Chicago for a variety of publishing acts that fell under the charge of "using the mails for fraudulent purposes." Elder maintained his innocence in every instance, claiming that the publicity did him more harm than good.[1]

The book, a heavy tome measuring 16 × 12 inches, with the text encased in green leather boards and a ribbed spine, all liberally embossed with gilt decorations, was published, but not by Elder. The job fell to Col. William D. Mann, publisher of *Town Topics*, a magazine carrying gossip and items of interest about New York City. To write the Introduction, Mann recruited Constance Cary Harrison, a prolific writer of magazine articles and short stories, and who, with her two cousins in 1861, had sewn the first example of the Confederate Battle Flag. She gave as a rational for the book, "It is well worthwhile to record in permanent form instances of some of the men who by their personality, influence, and surroundings give character and form to American society of this period."[2]

The Captain's entry and those of 85 others, including the likes of Alfred Gwynne Vanderbilt, Theodore Roosevelt, Grover Cleveland, J. Pierpont Morgan, appeared in the spring of 1905. Mann gave the missile the flowery title: *Fads and Fancies: Representative Americans at the Beginning of the Twentieth Century, A Portrait of Their Tastes, Diversions, and Achievement.*

Before Mann took the helm, Elder, after soliciting the Captain's participation, drafted a statement for him. Elder wrote for Emerson's review:

"Captain Emerson has a keen eye for the artistic and beautiful, has pronounced musical and literary tastes and is an artist of some ability. He is physically a picture of vigorous manhood and in business affairs, possesses unusual executive ability. His decisions are deliberate and thoughtful but when once made are final, and he is noted for a serenity and temperament which few things have power to disturb."

Flattered, Emerson returned a lightly edited version, including crossing out the date of his birth. He added the modest notation, "I am likely not totally deserving of all your good words."[3]

Following publication, charges and counter-charges, none involving Emerson, of blackmail, broken promises, financial transgressions, and arm twisting were leveled against Mann's employees.[4] *Colliers Magazine's* editor Norman Hapgood, for instance, charged Mann's agents with "compelling" some of New York's most prominent men to subscribe to the book. Mann sued Hapgood for criminal libel in New York's West Side Court. After many days of spicy and salacious testimony, Hapgood prevailed. The District Attorney then charged Mann with perjury regarding his testimony in the case but failed to win a conviction.[5]

The book did not enjoy a wide distribution. Each subscriber received a copy, as did four libraries. The printing plates were destroyed.[6]

* * *

In spite of the Captain's growing fame and the financial success enjoyed by Bromo-Seltzer and other patent medicines, they were not without detractors. Bromo-Seltzer's formula at the turn of the century included acetanilide as the analgesic (pain killer). While effective, it was known to be poisonous in large amounts and had caused some people's skin to turn blue. The formula also included a bicarbonate to calm the stomach by reducing acidity, and sodium bromide (from which came the term Bromo) to settle one's nerves. Sodium bromide was found to be the cause of some users' dizziness, confusion, slurred speech, and acne-like outbreaks on the skin.[7]

As these conditions gained greater notoriety around the turn of the century, the federal government began to take a greater interest in the welfare of its citizens in general and patent medicines in particular. A well-known example is the Meat Inspection Act of 1906. Congress enacted the legislation after Upton Sinclair published his famous expose, *The Jungle*. His novel spotlighted the harsh and cruel conditions faced by low-wage workers in Chicago and other large industrial American cities. U.S. President Theodore Roosevelt, in office from 1901 to 1909, proposed a "Square Deal" to improve conditions in the country's working class and immigrant communities. He also doubled the number of national parks by putting privately held lands under government control.

Bromo-Seltzer had come under government scrutiny as early as 1899. The U.S. Senate's Pure Food Committee, chaired by William E. Mason (R-IL), held a series of hearings to, among other objectives, stop the sale of "adulterated foods dangerous to health" and to have the labels of such foods clearly marked with their ingredients.[8] On May 11, the committee took testimony from three university professors and a New York City physician, Henry G. Piffard. Piffard singled out Bromo-Seltzer, technically not a food but of interest to the committee nevertheless, telling the panel it should properly consist of bromide of potassium but "it appears," he testified, "acetanilide is being used extensively instead." The doctor considered the drug "deleterious."[9]

Piffard was not the first to sound an alarm about acetanilide. German and French scientists had reported similar conclusions in Europe as early as 1886.[10] In 1904, a U.S. Department of Agriculture publication noted an increase in the number of poisonings and death caused by the drug. The increase, the authors concluded, "could be explained only by the fact that control of acetanilide during recent years has passed from physicians to those people extensively advertising so called patent medicines."[11] That finding certainly must have gotten Emerson's attention.

More journalists and academics joined the fight to instigate government control over patent medicines, including Emerson's invention. S. H. Adams, a muckraking journalist known for exposing public health problems, stated in the introduction to six articles he wrote in 1905–1906 for *Collier's Weekly*, "The series will contain a full explanation and exposure of patent-medicine methods, and the harm done to the public by this industry, founded mainly on fraud and poisoning."[12] He included Bromo-Seltzer in "the following well-known 'remedies,' both 'ethical' and 'patent,' [that] depend for their results upon the heart-depressing action of acetanilide."[13]

Adams was among the first to point out that the mere existence of acetanilide in Bromo-Seltzer and other headache remedies was not so much the concern as was its overuse. The drug, Adams said, "will undoubtedly relieve a headache of certain kinds ... but when taken steadily produces constitutional disturbances of insidious development which results fatally if the drug be not discontinued."[14] Charles Spencer Williamson, Chair of Clinical Medicine at the College of Physicians and Surgeons in Chicago, pointed out in 1906 that acetanilide "produces chronic poisoning in some cases" and that a prescribed dose of Bromo-Seltzer contained 10 grains of the substance, while "five have been known to prove fatal.... Most people," he added without citing any documentation, "who take Bromo-Seltzer have nothing serious the matter with them, anyway, so they get along all right."[15]

Harvard-trained Dr. Harvey W. Wiley, chair of the USDA's Department of Chemistry, who had joined Senator Mason in the 1899 Senate hearings, campaigned against impure foods such as "soothing syrups laced with cocaine and glucose syrup diluted with honey." Many pure-food bills, based on Wiley's work, had been introduced in Congress during the 1880s and 1890s, only to die under the assaults of armies of lobbyists.[16]

Such works were, however, credited with finally convincing Congress to pass and President Theodore Roosevelt to sign the Pure Food and Drug Act on June 30, 1906. The Act required only that patent medicine producers accurately describe their ingredients on a label attached to the product, just as Mason's committee had proposed seven years earlier. The Act, while a step forward, fell far short of the reformers' aspirations. The U.S. Supreme Court, in Plaintiff in Error v. O. A. Johnson on May 29, 1911, did not require, to the dismay of President William Howard Taft and the American Medical Association (AMA), that curative claims made by producers be truthful. Taft, a month after the Court's ruling, asked Congress for an amendment to the Act that would require truthful curative claims to accompany the list of ingredients. Congress demurred. The AMA chastised the Court's ruling, saying that a patent medicine label could now boldly and legally proclaim "Canceroid: A Positive and Never Failing Cure for Cancer, Tuberculosis, and All Other Diseases."[17]

More physicians voiced concerns about the harmful effects of Bromo-Seltzer. William J. Mayo, one of the seven founders of the Mayo Clinic, wondered in 1906, "Will the American people continue to use Bromo-Seltzer which causes them to experience blueness of the skin surfaces from poisonous coal tar products?"[18] William J. Robinson, MD, of New York City, said that if a patient of his, whom he described as "a Bromo fiend," did not stop his two-bottle-a-day use of Bromo-Seltzer, he would die. The patient stopped. He lived. His headaches lessened, and his impotence problem improved. "Self-administration ... contributes significantly to the mortality rate though it does not appear as one of the causes on death certificates," the doctor said.[19]

Another physician, Henry Bixby Hemenway in Evanston, Illinois, offered a starker warning. Bromo-Seltzer, he claimed, caused the death of a patient after she took a dose for headache and indigestion. He gave "acetanilide poisoning from Bromo-Seltzer" as the cause of death. The autopsy findings agreed with Hemenway's statement. The mortician noted "much damage to internal organs and lungs completely engorged; a condition typical of acetanilide poisoning."[20] Hemenway said nothing about the size of the dose or how often the patient had used it. A year after the passage of the Pure Food and Drug Act, an article in the *Chicago Daily Tribune* warned readers to avoid Bromo-Seltzer. A small dose of acetanilide may cure a headache, but careless clerks, the article said, might measure out a dangerous dose.[21]

Journalists cautioned against the use of the remedy. Dr. W. A. Evans, who wrote a daily "How to Keep Well" column for the *Chicago Daily Trib-*

une in the 1920s, warned readers to avoid excessive doses and habitual use. To a reader inquiring about a friend's practice of taking Bromo-Seltzer "in ever increasing quantities for years and now consumes two, two pound bottles in eight to ten days," Dr. Ware replied, "When used habitually, changes in blood and nerve cells could occur and "bring on headaches." To a reader asking if Bromo-Seltzer harmed the heart, Dr. Ware advised, "repeatedly taking this begets headaches. It is unwholesome."[22]

Wiley, whom President Theodore Roosevelt named to administer the Federal Drug Administration, which was responsible for enforcing the new law, continued to lobby Congress to pass legislation that would force patent medicine producers to "stick to the truth in advertising their wares,"[23] to no avail. "Why," Wiley lamented in 1911, five years after the Act became law, "can an unknown layman, with neither knowledge of physiology, therapeutics, medicine or pharmacy, sans degree or license, manufacture and sell, unchecked, harmful or dangerous cure alls?"[24] A frustrated Wiley left the FDA in 1912 to continue his crusade under the auspices of the Good Housekeeping Institute, a subsidiary of the magazine of the same name.[25]

Dr. H. W. Wiley, on the left, and W. G. Campbell, on the right, in a discussion at the U.S. Department of Agriculture's Bureau of Chemistry in 1910. Both were pioneers in the struggle to protect the public from the harmful effects of Bromo-Seltzer and other drugs. LC-USZ61-768, Prints and Photographs Division, Library of Congress, Washington, D.C.

6—Problems with the Nostrum

In the case of Bromo-Seltzer, the answer to Wiley's lament lay in the fact that the nostrum was becoming firmly entrenched in America's popular culture. The findings and warnings were overshadowed by an avalanche of advertisements and testimonials. The remedy was the only one in Tim Daly's 1903 *Daly's Bartenders' Encyclopedia*. In the middle of over 100 cocktail recipes appeared one for Bromo-Seltzer, the only such potion in the book. Daly recommended it to his customers, saying, "This is one of the best known and most speedy cures for a headache known to the profession, and it is perfectly harmless in its results."[26] Daly's directions specified taking "two spoonfuls," size of spoon not specified. What constituted a safe dose would soon become an important issue.

Five years after the World's Fair, Chicago held its first cat show. A tame wildcat named Bromo-Seltzer came in second place in the most popular cat category.[27] In 1904, Brooklyn Magistrate Judge Edward J. Dooley, appalled at the number of people brought before him who were drunk, ordered officers to sober people up before bringing them to his court. Officers laid in large supplies of aromatic spirits, malted milk, bitters, and a healthy supply of Bromo-Seltzer.[28] Bromo-Seltzer even attained a measure of scientific legitimacy when, in 1915, the *Scientific American*, without commenting on its usefulness or safety, dubbed it "noteworthy" along with such contemporary developments as the mercury arc light, centrifugal snow plow, the Kodak, Edison's telegraph improvements, and Livingston radiators.[29]

Bromo-Seltzer even found its way onto the Western Pacific Railway's 1915 wine list. Under listings for "Ales, Beers, Waters, Etc." could be found "Bromo-Seltzer." A glass of the mixture cost riders ten cents. No other remedy appeared on the menu. Amory Blaine, the main character in F. Scott Fitzgerald's first novel, published in 1920, *This Side of Paradise*, and his friend Carling were enjoying themselves in New York's Knickerbockers Bar, Blaine more so than Carling, who asked the bartender to "give him a Bromo-Seltzer."[30] The same year, during a meeting of National League baseball executives and players, including Casey Stengel, then an outfielder with the Philadelphia Phillies, a lone patron at the hotel bar "was having a bromo seltzer" which, the reporter noted, had not been seen at bars during previous league meetings.[31] Ten thousand bowlers took part in the American Bowling Congress' international tournament held in Chicago. On opening night, February 23, 1924, the Bromo-Seltzer five-man team finished in third place.[32]

The headache remedy featured prominently in sad tales of romances gone awry. In 1918, after two hours of marriage in Chicago, one Anthony Lucas told his bride he was going "out for a bromo seltzer" to cure his headache. He never returned. A woman in 1922 waiting patiently for her date at a New York drug store asked the clerk, "in a weak, tired voice," for a Bromo-Seltzer after realizing she'd been stood up.[33]

Two men approached a druggist in Bath Beach, Brooklyn in 1923, saying the woman in car parked at the curb needed a Bromo-Seltzer. As he turned to get a bottle of the nostrum, the men pulled their pistols, emptied the cash register, and sped away in the woman's car.[34] H. L. Mencken, the dean of Baltimore letters, in a 1926 critique of what encyclopedias chose to include and exclude, bemoaned the fact that "aspirin is mentioned but not bromo seltzer."[35] Will Rogers, American humorist, previewing a 1927 debate scheduled between silver-tongued lawyer Clarence Darrow and his overmatched opponent, corporate lawyer Wayne Wheeler, predicted that Darrow would soon have Wheeler "under the table and hollering for Bromo Seltzer."[36] Afro-American writer A. William Dunn, III, in 1929, advised readers who partook of all-night merriment in New York City to pause at 3:00 a.m. for a Bromo-Seltzer. "More than likely" he wrote, "you won't know what it is, but drink it nevertheless."[37] Four years later in 1933, etiquette writer Alice-Leone Moats described the proper way for a servant or employee to address their employer or boss by using the example, "Please tell Mr. Lamb that Bromo-Seltzer is what he needs."[38]

As time went by, Emerson's invention attained ever greater popularity.

* * *

Emerson was not unaware of the negative publicity and took what steps he could to counteract the cautions being spread about his invention. While he was an unequaled advertising genius, there is no public record of Emerson or the Emerson Drug Company championing the safe use of the product. In an effort to counter the claim that acetanilide was harmful, the Captain queried Dr. Harry S. Houghton, a New York physician who had graduated from The Johns Hopkins University School of Medicine in Baltimore.[39] Houghton referred the query to Dr. George N. Slattery at New York University and Bellevue Medical College. Slattery sent Emerson a list of 1,000 patients admitted to Bellevue and added in his letter, "acetanilide poisoning, acute or chronic, is very rare."[40]

Emerson took dead aim at efforts to require truthful description of ingredients on bottles and packages in his December 1905 annual report to shareholders. The passage of such a bill in North Dakota, the first state legislature to do so, he warned his audience, "will encourage our enemies in other states and there never was a time when they were so numerous, influential, and active." Such efforts, he felt, were not in the public's interest, "for in no instance," he argued somewhat ingenuously, "is it demanded by the public." Such laws, he feared, "would force manufacturers of popular remedies to expose their secret formulas." He went on to decry the efforts of the Women's Christian Temperance Union, the American Medical Association, and the First National Co-operative Society, as well as physicians and legislators in Bromo-Seltzer's home state of Maryland, who wanted to limit the sale of all medicines, patent or otherwise, to doctors. He asked all present at the meeting to urge their state legislators "to defeat these unjust bills." The first draft of his remarks read, "most vicious and unjust bills," but he deleted the words "most vicious" for the final draft.[41]

Asked by the editor of the *Journal of the American Medical Association* (JAMA) for a reaction to the North Dakota law, Emerson replied, "we have decided to withdraw our goods from the market ... so if Bromo-Seltzer is sold there it is through some other source and we are not responsible." The editor asked himself, "When the law goes national, will they not ship to any state or comply with the law?"[42]

In the end, Emerson had no choice but to put the required descriptive labels of ingredients on his bottles. Prior to the Food and Drug Act's passage, the only reference to ingredients on the bottles' labels was "a granular effervescent." The rest of the label read, "Cures nervous headache, neuralgia, brain fatigue, sleeplessness, mental exhaustion, alcohol excesses." No instructions appeared on the labels concerning how often to take a dose or exactly what a dose amounted to.[43] In spite of the publicity about the fatal effects of his product and perhaps buoyed by Slattery's letter, he did not alter the ingredients.

Negative publicity and Emerson's fear that the exposure of "secret formulas" would harm business failed to derail Bromo-Seltzer's rising popularity. The modest manufacturing facility above a restaurant in 1889[44] had become a factory, now housed in a 17-by-30-foot extension of the building at 311 W. Fayette Street, which Emerson had built for a cost of $43,540.[45] From that factory came the world's supply. Emerson initially packaged his invention in aqua-colored bottles, but by 1907 he had incorporated his own glass plant—the Maryland Glass Corporation—which by the late 1970s had produced more than 20 variations in at least seven sizes of his trademark cobalt blue bottles.[46] By 1912, 30 tons of the powder packaged into two-, four-, eight-, 12-, and 16-ounce bottles emerged from the warehouse daily.[47] Specially designed dehumidifying equipment kept the air as dry as possible. Excess moisture in a bottle could cause the glass containers to burst, "causing," according to drug historian Henry C. Fuller, "inconvenience to the purchaser and embarrassment to the company."[48] Fuller anointed Bromo-Seltzer "the most popular effervescent [sic] on the market today."[49]

The appeal to the public of patent medicines in general and Bromo-Seltzer in particular was evident by the fact that such nostrums had survived the Panic of 1907, a national financial meltdown second in intensity only to the Great Depression. Gilbert Percival, MD, noted in 1907 that "statistics show that commercial hard times have less influence on successful 'cure alls' than on any other commodity." In the case of Bromo-Seltzer, he pointed out that one share of stock issued at a par value of $100 was now worth $2,000.[50] Bad times made for good times for Emerson, but he could not escape the controversy forever.

By 1917, the Emerson Drug Company had made several concessions to the growing demand for more transparency on its labels. The new labels now disclosed the amount of acetanilide in each ounce (20 grains) and specified taking a dose of "a heaping teaspoon in half-glass of water." The directions continued, advising users to "repeat in half-an-hour if not relieved or until three doses have been taken. It is not often," the directions continued, "that the second and third dose is required." The label also disclosed that each teaspoon represented about 3.7 grains of acetanilide. If taken three times, a user could consume about 11 grains, a level many authorities considered dangerous. The company also now added a more detailed description of the mixture's curative power as "a speedy and reliable remedy for nervous headache, neuralgia, brain fatigue, sleeplessness, over-drain work, depression, following alcoholic and other overuses, mental exhaustion, etc."[51]

These would not be the last changes the company would make.

* * *

Having built a company and amassed a fortune that allowed him to enjoy a rich man's pursuits, Emerson promoted Hindes to president to take over day-to-day responsibility for the company in 1906.[52] The Captain took the title of Chairman of the Board and would go on to spend the bulk of his time on world travel, racing, philanthropy, family, and real estate.

7

Arcadia

One of the Captain's most significant real estate ventures involved land on the Waccamaw Neck, a narrow peninsula of land across the Waccamaw River from Georgetown, South Carolina. The Neck is bounded by the eastern side of the river and the Atlantic Ocean. Often called "the lowcountry," the area had supported numerous rice plantations since the 1750s. Slaves, many from the West African countries of Senegal, Gambia, and Sierra Leone, and selected by planters for their knowledge of growing rice, performed their back-breaking work in the alligator and water moccasin-infested tidal swamps. Using only axes, hoes, and spades, they cleared the area of trees hundreds of years old and cultivated the land. They built a system of wooden gates and ditches to drain the land at planting time, allow water in from the Waccamaw during the growing season, and drain the land in the fall so the rice could be harvested. A series of high banks along the river kept flood waters out.

Rice growing on the Neck, which accounted for 30 percent of the country's total in 1860,[1] fell off sharply after the Civil War. Prices plummeted due to competition from other states, the absence of free labor once the slaves were freed, floods, and storms that ruined the rice crops, destroyed the gates, and filled the ditches with sediment. Cotton plantations fared no better thanks to the arrival of the boll weevil. What did not change was the hundreds of thousands of ducks—mallards, black ducks, teal, scaup, and wood ducks that "over flew" the Neck each year.[2]

The battered economy forced many residents to resort to sharecropping to scratch out a livelihood in the face of poverty, poor public health, and little education. The economy picked up in the early 1900s once wealthy Northern sportsmen, like Emerson, started buying the decaying rice plantations and improving them. Locals greeted the new arrivals with mixed feelings. Charleston resident Jonathon Daniels noted the financial benefits to the low country while at the same time pointing out the changes to the culture, of which he was not so fond. "Rice" he said, "has vanished and the boll weevil has slain the cotton. Today ... millionaires are the successors of rice. They are the cash crop."[3]

Realtors in the area struck a similar financial tone by aiming their ads directed at potential sellers with the slogan, "GET YANKEE MONEY."[4] The *Georgetown Times* welcomed the influx of Northern money, if not the Northerners themselves. "Good!" its editorial read. "Those rich people only stay for a few weeks or months during the ducking season, but they spend lots of money. The more the merrier, we say."[5] The editor of the *Georgetown Times* opined that a better use of the plantations would be "to sell the land to actual settlers from the Midwest who would make two blades of grass grow where one grew before. We want a community of small farms adjoining one to the other."[6] Such farms never materialized.

On December 29, 1906, the Bromo-Seltzer King joined the influx of "rich people" when he bought two adjoining rice plantations on the Neck, Prospect Hill and Oak Hill. The *Georgetown Times* applauded his purchase, saying "a valueless old plantation was being turned into good, hard Yankee cash."[7] There, in the words of historians Julia Brock and Daniel Vivian, he created an estate "that is highly cultivated, not by striving for authenticity, but making it a setting for upper-middle class activity once again."[8] The land, heavily timbered with pine and cypress trees and a stand of 175-year-old magnolia trees, comprised 5,500 acres. The property stretched from the river to the Atlantic Ocean. Three elevations to the front lawn spanned the space between the "Big House" on the Prospect Hill plantation and the canal that fed into the Waccamaw, where one at the Big House could see boats cruising up and down on its waters.[9]

To reflect his feelings about the property, he named his estate Arcadia after a region of Greece recognized by the Roman poet Virgil as an isolated and bucolic area. The term designates a place of rustic innocence for simple, quiet pleasure.[10] Emerson may have been introduced to the term by Farnham. The last lines of the poem she added to her bronze sculpture for him read:

> Would the All Wise Power saw fit
> To unlace our lives a bit
> Give us room to live and be
> Like the gods in Arcady!
> —*Funk and Wagnall's* lists Arcadia as a synonym for Arcady.

The only way to reach Prospect Hill from the mainland until 1935, when a bridge was built, was by boat. Soon after buying Arcadia, the new land baron purchased the *Gardenia*, a power yacht, which he and guests used for "gunning" (shooting ducks) when not transporting people, mail, telegrams (there were no phones), food, and supplies from Georgetown.[11]

"The Big House" at Arcadia, circa 1900, six years before Emerson made his first purchase of land at Arcadia. HABS SC 22-GEOTO.V, 5-12, Prints and Photographs Division, Library of Congress, Washington, D.C.

His nearest neighbor, Bernard Baruch, born in Camden, South Carolina, a leading financier with a seat on the New York Stock Exchange and future advisor to President Franklin Delano Roosevelt, purchased similar plantations to form neighboring Hobcaw Barony. The two often sponsored holiday galas including New Years Day's barbeques.[12] At Christmas 1921, a reporter for the *Gaffney Ledger*, a local newspaper, wrote, "one could hear the sounds of horns and hounds and many a fine buck and doe did fall." The same reporter called attention to the "generous hospitality" both showed to their guests.[13] Other notables who owned property near Emerson's included members of the DuPont, E. F. Hutton, Guggenheim, and Huntington families.[14]

Finally in possession of land where he could hunt and shape the property to his liking, the Captain spent so much time there that some thought the Emersons would make Arcadia their permanent home. The *Sun* reported that the couple, while maintaining their Eutaw Place mansion, "were abandoning" Baltimore for the new property, which "would claim the family for its own."[15] The *Georgetown Times* stated that Arcadia would be their "permanent home."[16] As it turned out, Emerson kept Baltimore, where his business was headquartered, as his primary residence, though his extensive travels kept him away from the city and Emilie for long periods of time.

The Captain invited guests to Arcadia every winter to join him but at times neglected to follow local laws, to the displeasure of local residents. In the winter of 1913, his guests included daughter Margaret, business associate George Ewing, his wife Bettie, wealthy long-term residents of Brooklandville, Maryland, where the Captain had by then purchased an estate, and several others, "all wealthy and well-known tourists." State law required everyone to buy an out-of-state hunting license. The state's chief game warden, J. A. Richardson, suspected that fewer such licenses had been issued in Georgetown than he expected. The warden spotted a private rail car on a siding in Georgetown and thought he'd catch himself an unsuspecting Northerner. It soon came to light that only Emerson had a license.

Richardson's deputy, a Mr. Funderburk, encountered Ewing on Arcadia's grounds and arrested him on a Sunday afternoon, imposed a bail bond on him, and telegraphed Richardson to come at once from Columbia to decide the fate of the other hunters. Richardson arrived in Georgetown on Monday morning to find only Ewing present. The others had skipped town on Sunday evening on Emerson's private car. Ewing's case was dismissed that Tuesday on a technicality.[17]

The chain of events brought about disdain for both Richardson and Emerson, though for different reasons. The *Georgetown Times*, mindful of Emerson's financial value to the area, thought Funderburk had overreacted. "Just such cases," read the editorial, "as this is what gives Georgetown a black eye. These gentlemen buy property and spend their money lavishly to have a few days sport when some little sorehead runs before a magistrate and swears out a warrant."[18] An anonymous letter writer to the *Times* took issue with Emerson, saying, "It is the lawless conduct of men of the Emerson stripe, who imagine that their dollar elevates them above the law ... that creates whatever feeling of prejudice against the inordinately rich that exists in this country."[19] No other encounters with the local constabulary occurred, and life on the plantation continued on its busy yet peaceful pace.

By March of 1907, a crew of men, mostly African Americans, had refurbished the "Big House." They repaired and painted the deteriorating, two-story wooden house, added two wings, each containing several rooms, and electrified the house with an electric-light plant putting it "ablaze."[20] During the work, Emerson lived aboard his new purchase, a

A view of the approach to the "Big House" in 2017. Notice the pond, brick lining of the walkway, shrubs, and tress, all examples of the landscaping improvements Emerson made to the grounds of Arcadia. They are maintained today under the care of Matt Balding (author's photograph).

houseboat that he also named *Margaret*. A large bottle of Bromo-Seltzer was always within arm's reach on the boat.[21] Once the property was suitable for guests, he invited daughter Margaret, Mr. and Mrs. F. C. McCormack, and their daughter Ethel to join him for an extended stay. Mrs. McCormack was a childhood friend of Margaret's.[22]

He made continuous improvements to Arcadia. In later years he designed a 38 × 40-foot, two-story "gymnasium." The ground floor consisted of a large sitting room, gun room, kitchen, butler's pantry, library, two servant's rooms on the back, and a steam-heated swimming pool that connected to a marble-lined sauna and exercise room. Four bedrooms and baths and an open-air deck made up the second floor, where guests stayed. He stocked his property with pheasants and quail to add to the existing game stock of ducks, deer, wild turkeys, and quail. As the years went by, he designed projects large and small—fences, gates, terrace steps, stables, a laundry building, and the occasional house or cottage. Construction crews dug up old English bricks from abandoned sites about Arcadia and used them, where possible, to complete the projects.[23]

* * *

Prospect Hill came to Emerson with two historical anecdotes, one true, one in need of correction. On April 21, 1819, President James Monroe, accompanied by Secretary of War John C. Calhoun, a South Carolina native and staunch defender of slavery, and other dignitaries, spent the night at the home of Benjamin Huger, Jr., a rice planter, major in the South Carolina militia, and Congressman. Huger laid a red carpet for the party to walk on from the canal, which brought boats from the river to Huger's house that sat on land that would eventually become Arcadia.[24] On departing the next morning, they boarded "one of the plantation's barges, profusely decorated and adorned for the occasion with the United States colors proudly floating at its head. Eight negro oarsmen dressed in livery propelled the barge."[25] Monroe's visit to Huger's house on his way to Charleston, was the first by a sitting American president to South Carolina since George Washington's Southern Tour in 1791.[26] Locals will tell you Huger's red carpet was the first of its kind in the United States.[27]

Another more controversial historical anecdote involves the Marquis de Lafayette, a French aristocrat who fought for the United States in the American Revolution. In dispute is the frequently repeated tale that Lafayette spent his first night in the United States at Huger's Prospect Hill home. A counter narrative is that he and four officers, rowed by seven sailors in a "jolly boat," plied the coast of South Carolina the evening of June 15, 1777, looking for someone who could pilot the *Victoire* safely through the British blockade to Charleston. After many lonely hours they came upon a group of slaves dredging for oysters. The fishermen led Lafayette to their master's house, Huger's summer home. Huger's main house sat on North Island near Georgetown and the land that would become Arcadia. Arriving at midnight they were initially greeted by barking dogs and a wary Huger suspicious the group might be marauders from a British ship. Lafayette reported he received "a cordial welcome and generous hospitality."[28] Lafayette's entourage, after being assured by Huger that he could find a capable pilot, departed overland the next day for Charleston.

Bernard Baruch confirmed the story. In response to a September 1936 letter from Miss Gladys Newman, secretary to Admiral Cary T. Grayson, long-time personal physician to President Woodrow Wilson and then Chairman of the American Red Cross, Baruch wrote, "Lafayette was supposed to have landed at North Island and slept the first night at Mr. Huger's place, which lies to the north of me. . . . The house in which Lafayette is supposed to have spent his first night is still standing."[29] Newman's query may have been prompted by an article in Charleston's evening paper, *The News and Courier*, a month before her letter to Baruch. The article does not dispute Lafayette's presence on North Island but does challenge a local myth that Lafayette spent the night in Huger's Prospect Hill house, eventually to become "The Big House" at Arcadia, calling the story "a persistent myth." The Prospect Hill house, the article pointed out, was built 17 years after Lafayette's arrival. Lafayette's party, *The News and Courier* reported, "was sheltered in the beach house of the Huger family."[30]

* * *

Emerson bought adjoining plantations and smaller plots of land until 1929, eventually building an estate of over 10,000[31] acres at a cost of about $98,000.[32] In addition to designing gardens and overseeing the landscaping of the grounds around the Big House, he tried his hand at poetry. One of his verses can be seen today as the welcoming refrain etched on a bronze plaque that he mounted on a brick arch at the entrance to one of the gardens.

> Here art and nature
> On equal grounds did meet
> And wrought a picture beautiful
> Which your presence makes complete.[33]

He repaired enough gates and ditches to allow some rice to be grown at Arcadia. A 50-acre plot, known as the Barnyard Field, in front of the Big House, produced rice to be used as bait for ducks and turkeys. Most of the laborers and tenants were elderly "Negro" women and older children. They plowed and hoed the land with ox and mule teams, then planted, cultivated, and harvested the rice by hand, hard work in the hot and humid South Carolina climate. Each family of workers, who lived year-round at Arcadia, received a plot of land where they cultivated rice to eat.[34] Emerson also provided them with a church, St. Anne's, which had served as a hospital for slaves until after "The War Between the States," a small school, and an infirmary.[35] By the eve of World War I, historian Daniel J. Vivian credited Arcadia's owner with "creating one of the most elaborate estates in the lowcountry and … the most stylish."[36]

Arcadia took on the appearance of a small community when the Emersons were in residence. It took many people to maintain the facilities as well as to buy, prepare, and serve the food and beverages. Guests always had ample access to fine imported whiskey and wines, liberally available even during Prohibition. Some staff lived at Arcadia year-round, including a dozen or so African American families who worked on the property in Emerson's absence and served as guides for hunting parties. Other staff, from the Bromo-Seltzer operation in Baltimore, arrived by train via the Atlantic Coast Line during his stay at Arcadia, which usually lasted from Thanksgiving to Easter. Neal Cox, whom Emerson hired as a 21-year-old gardener in 1930 and who stayed at Arcadia, with his wife Mary Alice and their son Edward, assuming ever-increasing responsibilities until his death in 1999, recounted the Captain's retinue in 1930 and, in so doing, painted a picture of life at Arcadia during the social season.

> This special crew included Mr. Weatherly, personal secretary, and Mrs. Gerhart, housekeeper. Mr. Gerhart and John Lasley were in charge of the huge central steam-heating systems and a series of generating units for furnishing electricity and steam heat for the big house the gym, the stable building, the Dingles' house (the resident superintendent, his wife, and three children), the laundry building and two other cottages. A Mr. Rickets acted as chauffeur and mail boat captain.... There was Ernest, the English head butler, with two assistant butlers. Also in the crew from Baltimore were Mrs. Emerson's personal maid, two upstairs maids, two Irish women who did the laundry. Several Negro men and women from the plantation helped out whenever needed. Also there was Michael Healy, head groomsman, with a young man to help take care of the 10–12 horses.... There was Harry Shearer, head carpenter; Nick, the head brick mason; and two young men to milk the cows.... There was a head chef with an assistant.[37]

In their spare time, the Captain encouraged his staff to protect the plantation's wild turkeys, ducks, and deer, by hunting what he considered to be vermin. Encouragement took the form of bounties—eagles, $5; $3 for foxes, wild hogs, bobcats, and alligators, and $2 for coons, hawks, and possums.[38]

The owner's departures were emotional times for those who lived and worked at Arcadia. Everyone accompanied the Emersons to the dock where his yacht was anchored and usually stocked for a cruise in southern waters. The staff from Baltimore made plans to return there by train. Youngsters waved flags or palm leaves. Everyone sang Negro ballads and spirituals they knew the Emersons liked to hear. Older women danced and shouted "Thank the Lord, Thank the Lord," in gratitude for the life the Emersons provided for them.[39] Had it not been for the Captain and others like him who purchased and maintained plantations throughout the Waccamaw Neck, life would have been much harder for the year-round residents.

Not all departures, however, were so harmonious. Arcadia's superintendent, A. W. Baker, confronted the Captain who, with a party of friends, arrived at Georgetown's train station at 5:00 p.m. on December 2, 1911, to return home after a week of hunting. Emerson had fired Baker, who lived at Arcadia and managed the truck farming, for sloppy work that morning. Emerson asked Baker to leave the premises within the week. Baker's wages, he promised, would continue to be paid through the end of the month. J. W. Ford, Emerson's Georgetown financial agent, would issue Baker a check, as he normally did at the end of the month. Baker, who had spent the afternoon in Georgetown's taverns, demanded his remaining salary there and then. Emerson said he'd have to wait. Baker called Emerson a "liar." The Captain promptly landed a swift right hook to the bottom of Baker's chin, which only staggered the tall, muscular Baker. He swung back but missed. Blows continued to be exchanged. As Baker reached into his right pants pocket, a guest, Mr. George P. Mordecai, well-known Baltimore sportsman and Brooklandville resident, grabbed his arm and subdued him with a half-nelson. The police found a loaded pistol in Baker's pocket. The Captain declined to press assault charges. The police took Baker into custody. The Captain and his party boarded the train.[40]

8

Coping with Marital Strife

Barely a year after Emerson bought the first section of Arcadia, he confronted the first of several family divorces. The relationship between Emerson and T. Mitchell Horner, who had married his step-daughter Daisy and had been the Captain's first representative in New York, soured in September of 1907. The couple, married in 1896, seemed to be living a compatible life until Daisy left her husband behind in Atlanta in May 1906 to join her father, Margaret, and Anne McCormack on a three-month tour of Europe. Previously, she had often visited her parents in Baltimore, occasionally accompanied by T. Mitchell, but never for three months.[1] Daisy cabled Horner to meet her in New York on her return. He did.

They went back to Atlanta, where they lived together until Daisy walked out on him again the following May, this time for good. She told Emilie over the phone that she could no longer live with Horner. She moved in with Margaret and Smith Hollins McKim at their mansion in Irvington-on-the Hudson. Emerson informed Horner that the Atlanta office would be closed and that his services were no longer needed. Horner's letters to Daisy, addressed to her parents at their Baltimore home, went unanswered. The Horners' divorce was granted on November 5, 1907. Horner stayed on in Atlanta and opened a broker's office but did not take the divorce easily.

After consulting his brother, Joshua P. Horner, Jr., T. Mitchell filed a $100,000 suit against the Emersons, charging them with alienation of affection. "They did," the charging document read, "cause, and procure, and wickedly procure the estrangement of the affections of Mrs. Horner from her husband." Emilie Emerson responded that the suit was merely "an attempt to extort money from Dr. Emerson and me."[2] The suit was settled in December 1908 for a mere $500 paid by Isaac to Horner, who stayed in Atlanta.[3]

Daisy, who had again gone to live with step-sister Margaret, later married James McVickar, a wealthy New York stockbroker, in January of 1909. The newlyweds met when McVickar, recently returned from a trip

8—Coping with Marital Strife 79

to Africa, was a guest of Margaret's at Irvington-on-the-Hudson. One afternoon, Daisy leaned a bit far over the gunwale of a small boat and fell into the Hudson River. McVickar gallantly dove in after her and pulled her safely to shore. They married in front of a small group of family and friends in the Red Room of New York's Plaza Hotel. After a brief honeymoon, the newlyweds took up residence in an apartment on Park Avenue. McVickar became the Emerson Drug Company's agent in the city.[4] The couple divorced in 1915.[5]

Her marriage to McVickar did not put Daisy's Atlanta experience entirely behind her. Eight months after the marriage, she faced charges of having carried on an "inappropriate relationship" in Atlanta with the president of the Central Georgia Railway, Major J. F. Hanson, a Confederate veteran of the Civil War and a Republican who had declined President McKinley's offer of a cabinet position. His wife, Cora L. Hanson, sued for divorce from J. F. in August of 1910, charging that he earlier had "become infatuated" with Daisy to the extent that he was willing, in his words, to "give up everything I have and leave the state."

Major Hanson's disdain for his wife's attraction to Theosophy, a movement seeking to understand the mysteries of life and the universe, so embittered her that she took her son and daughter to live with her in Point Loma, California, where the Theosophy movement was headquartered. The major was often seen with Daisy afterwards. Daisy denied all of Cora's charges to a *New York Times* reporter, claiming that her relationship with both Hansons had been purely social. "It is an outrageous affair.... There is nothing to substantiate the charges ... or to justify her dragging me into her domestic affairs," she said. In a telegram to Cora, Daisy exploded, "You are guilty of the most infamous falsehoods, and you know it. I defy you to produce a single shred of proof in support of such cruel and malicious statements." Her parents, who had socialized with the Hansons, backed her up. Cora raised the same charges on the occasion of the major's death in December 1910, while contesting his will, but nothing came of them.[6]

* * *

In the midst of this family conflict, and more was in the offing, the Captain and his daughter had been granted a peaceful interlude the previous summer in Newport, Rhode Island. The *Margaret* docked at Newport, in July 1908, with the Captain, Margaret, and two other women, a Mrs. Howard and, once again, Mrs. Fred McCormack, on board. Margaret rented a "cottage" for the group while her father, continuing his lavish approach to entertaining, hosted lunches at the Narragansett Pier Casino, one of the nation's most prestigious resorts, located on Narragansett Pier across Narragansett Bay from Newport. The casino offered its guests boating, billiards, bowling, cards, shooting, and tennis as well as restaurants, stores, reading rooms, a bandstand, and a ballroom.[7]

Newport attracted many of the nation's wealthiest families, including Vanderbilts and Astors, for the socially prestigious summer season. Margaret, now 24 years old, fit right in, described as "a brilliant new social light on the Newport horizon" by the *New York American Magazine*. The article suggested that Margaret, part of "the New York-Newport Colony," was well-positioned to become the next "Queen" of New York City's Four Hundred, a group of the city's most prominent families.

The article listed her qualifying qualities, most of which she owed to her father, which might help her become a "society leader." They included a country home at Irvington-on-the Hudson, a Newport villa, an ocean-going vessel, a South Carolina estate, one of the finest apartments in the Plaza Hotel, a handsome arm with which to play the harp, and friends in the younger set of the Four Hundred.[8] The *Oakland* (Rhode Island) *Tribune* called her rise to such social prominence "a triumph," given that she was not New York-born, and young to be considered as "a possible ruler of New York society."[9] Young though she may have been, Margaret was not new to Newport society. Six years earlier, the *New York Times* noted that she had been the hostess on her father's yacht in the absence of her mother, who had remained in Baltimore.[10]

Another of Margaret's assets was the high regard in which members of the Vanderbilt family held her, especially Mrs. "Reggie" Vanderbilt, wife of Reginald Vanderbilt, an older brother of Alfred Gwynne Vanderbilt. The two women "were inseparable" and regular patrons of the Narragansett Horse Show. At the end of the season, Margaret and Smith Hollins McKim joined the Reginald Vanderbilts for a stay at Alfred Vanderbilt's, Camp Sagamore in the Adirondacks, followed by a tour of horse shows in Louisville, Kentucky, Syracuse, and White Plains, New York.[11]

By this time, Margaret had become known to the press as a lavish party-giver, gracious hostess, and socializer with the glitterati. Less well known was her developing interest in horses and the outdoor life, both encouraged by her father. Life in the wild extended beyond Camp Sagamore to include big game hunting in the Rocky Mountains and Africa. She killed a grizzly bear on one of her trips west with her father. On trips to the "Dark Continent," she hunted rhinoceroses, hippopotami, lions, and tigers.[12]

* * *

While Margaret's social status was being elevated, rumors circulated that not all was well at home. A formal announcement confirmed the rumors in May 1909. After almost seven years of marriage with Margaret in Paris and Smith Hollins McKim in New York, the couple announced their separation, that it was amicable, and that no plans had been made for a divorce. Her parents denied rumors that Margaret wanted a divorce in order to marry a wealthy and recently divorced but unnamed man in New York City.[13]

The separation may have been amicable, but life for Margaret with McKim the three previous three years had been anything but. McKim's devotion to the bottle led her to leave him five times, but each time she went back, "filled," she said, "with pity and thinking he was not responsible." The final straw came in their sixth-floor Plaza Hotel apartment in New York City, where she fainted after seeing that "he was so drunk he forgot we were going out." He set her on the ledge of an open window in a successful attempt to revive her. "I fell inside the window instead of out. I could have just as well gone inside as out in which case we would not be having this conversation," she told a *Sun* reporter. During previous drunken rages, he had attacked her, thrown her across a room in their apartment, and hit her once with his fist. She finally walked out for good taking refuge with her father at Arcadia. In February of 1910, following another successful social season in Newport, she departed the Big Apple for Reno, Nevada, and a divorce.[14]

At the time, a six-month residency was required to obtain a divorce in Reno, later raised to one year. By 1931, the required length of stay was down to six weeks. Changes in divorce laws in many states since then now make getting a divorce even simpler, and Reno is no longer singled out as the "quickie divorce" city. In its day, however, Mary Pickford, Cornelius Vanderbilt, Jr., Jack Dempsey, Rita Hayworth, Gloria Vanderbilt and many others who could afford the travel, hotel bills, legal fees, and living expenses sought Reno's divorces.[15] Thanks to her generous father, cost was no problem for Margaret. Upon arriving in Reno, she purchased a bungalow and adjoining lot on Plumas Street which she claimed as her principal residence.[16]

Determined to prevent a divorce, McKim arrived in Reno in June 1910 to contest the proceedings, claiming that she had falsely claimed Reno as her residence and was there simply to acquire a divorce. He also claimed she had not lived in Reno continuously for six months, which she had not. Accompanied by Isaac and Anne McCormack, both of whom had escorted her to Reno, she made a week-long trip to San Francisco to entertain friends. McKim, nevertheless, lost on both counts in Reno's district court.[17]

She did not stay idle during her time in waiting. The historic James J. Jeffries and Jack Johnson heavyweight boxing match on July 4, 1910, gave her an outlet for her considerable energies. Known as "The Great White Hope," Jeffries came out of retirement to fight Johnson, the reigning heavyweight champion of the world and an African American. On that sweltering hot Independence Day, 20,000 spectators surrounded a specially built ring in downtown Reno. Whites across the country rooted for Jeffries, blacks for Johnson. Jeffries' handlers stopped the fight in the 15th round after Johnson floored their man three times. Race riots ensued in several cities. A search was launched for a new Great White Hope.[18]

Aware of the fight's importance, Margaret approached the editor of the *Nevada State Journal*, asking for an assignment. He assigned her the job of "copy boy." As the telegraph operator transcribed results of the fight round by round, she raced through the paper's building, shouting the information out to the linotype operator. Once the presses published the extra edition, she grabbed a copy and collapsed from exhaustion.[19]

She also attempted to establish a Nevada branch of the Junior Republic Association for Boys. Initially founded in New York City, the Association established a living situation for wayward boys where they could take on the responsibilities necessary for governing themselves in a shared living arrangement. With the help of her father, she promised Association officials that they would endow the institution. Their plans fell through when they were unable to buy the Carson City, Nevada, mansion of Lemuel Sanford "Sandy" Bowers, whose fortune had come from the state's Comstock Silver Mines.[20]

Margaret as she looked during her marriage to Smith Hollins McKim. LC-B2-1185-13. 10. Prints and Photographs Division, Library of Congress, Washington, D.C.

* * *

With her divorce, granted in August, on charges of non-support and cruelty, in hand, the newly-freed Margaret departed Reno for San Francisco, where she caught a ship for Honolulu and Japan, accompanied by Baroness de Chaboulon, a frequent companion and chaperone. On board just before the steamer sailed was Margaret's attorney during her divorce proceedings, 33-year-old Raymond T. Baker. An Oakland, California, native, Baker moved to Reno, where he made a fortune in mining and established a law office in the silver capital of the West. A reporter described him as "a handsome young man." He was the last to shake her hand good-bye on deck and blew kisses to her from the wharf as the ship was leaving port. Rumors that the two would marry on her return to the States soon permeated the press. Margaret debunked the speculations, but it would not be their last encounter. After a stay in Yokohama, Japan, which she had visited in 1902 during her trip around the world, she returned to the States in September to hunt wild game in the Rocky Mountains with her father.[21]

* * *

Toward the end of Margaret's stay in Reno, the Captain continued the family's summer presence at Narragansett, this time with Emilie. After arriving on the *Margaret* in late July and again giving a lunch at the Casino, they went, not to a cottage, but to the Mathewson Hotel "for an indefinite stay."[22] Known for its capacity to accommodate 500 guests, fine dining, hot and cold running water, fresh and sea water baths in some rooms, and an expansive piazza overlooking the Atlantic Ocean, the establishment suited the Emersons well.[23]

The couple frequented the ever-popular Narragansett Club, known for its fine dining and as a gathering spot for the well-heeled. Not so well publicized but certainly known to its patrons and others in the town was the Club's gambling facility. Although illegal, the practice had flourished for years under the inattentive gaze of the local constabulary. At the urging of three women who claimed that "the epidemic of gambling in this town" had caused property values to fall and the town's character to change for the worse, Constable John G. Cross and his deputies staged a midnight raid on August 8. The 30 society matrons present, fearing they would be charged with a misdemeanor and their names made public, tried to give false names and swore they were only watching, not playing. One got down on her knees and begged Cross not to divulge their names. He took the names of all present anyway. A melee ensued when the police arrived, with male patrons and officers exchanging blows, resulting in arrests and subsequent court dates. To the relief of Emilie and the other women, none were charged with gambling. Several men later faced assault and battery charges.

While avoiding arrest, Emilie fared less well in the notoriety realm. One of the women present, Mrs. J. H. Hanan, considered the raid a joke and said that no one should take Cross seriously "because he's just a country bumpkin." Hanan forced Emilie to take her seriously when she reported that no New York women were present but some from Baltimore were. Among those she named was "Mrs. I. E. Emerson."[24] Emilie would have none of it. "I was not in the club and am not in the habit of attending it at any time," she indignantly told a *Sun* reporter who asked her about the incident when she returned home. "I wish my name would be kept out of the papers," she said. "What I do is of no interest and I hate to see my name in print."[25]

* * *

The remainder of the summer went smoothly for the Emersons. Rumors of Margaret's impending marriage to the man in New York who now had a name, Alfred Gwynne Vanderbilt, blossomed again in the fall, fueled in part by Emilie herself. Asked by a reporter if her daughter would marry Alfred, she said, "Well, I won't deny it: but I just don't bother about the matter." Margaret, however, did bother about the matter, saying to a reporter at the end of October—"with her eyes flashing fire"—"I have no expectations of becoming engaged to anybody.... These constant rumors are causing me the greatest annoyance." Standing by her side and nodding in agreement, the Captain supported her, saying, "It is time these foolish reports stopped. There is no foundation for them."[26]

The reports continued, nevertheless, with their foundation becoming ever more firm. Alfred, divorced a year ago by his first wife, socialite Elsie French, said he would not leave his Rhode Island farm to live in New York unless he intended to marry again. It was, therefore, of some interest to the society pages when on November 10, 1910, he invited the directors and exhibitors of the upcoming horse show in New York City's Madison Square Garden to lunch at his new home at 11 East 62nd Street. He did not invite Margaret. She was having lunch at the time with her parents and several friends at the Waldorf-Astoria.

The two had, however, spent time together at the Belmont Park Aviation Meet two weeks earlier.[27] The Meet, international in scope and occurring only seven years after the Wright Brothers' first flight at Kitty Hawk, North Carolina, awarded prizes to pilots for speed, distance, duration, and altitude attained.[28] Both had been registered at the Plaza after her return from the Orient, and she had attended a play a week earlier as a guest in his box.[29] Rumors of upcoming nuptials grew louder when Margaret, who still went by the name Mrs. Smith Hollins McKim, was spotted at the Madison

8—Coping with Marital Strife 85

Square Garden horse show ensconced in Alfred's box, sitting next to Walter Webb-Ware, a close friend and confidant of Mr. Vanderbilt.[30]

* * *

As rumors and gossip continued to swirl about Margaret and Alfred, the Captain laid plans to build a hotel in Baltimore. Not just any hotel but, in Emilie's response to a *Sun* reporter's question in November 1909, while the Bromo-Seltzer king was at Arcadia, "one of the most attractive hotels in the country."[31] Emerson hired architect Joseph Evans Sperry to design the structure.[32] Born in Georgetown, South Carolina, just across the Waccamaw River from Arcadia, Sperry designed many prominent buildings in Baltimore including hospitals, churches, and several Johns Hopkins University buildings.[33]

Proprietors of existing hotels in the city had mixed opinions about the project. Harry D. Busick, manager of the Caswell and New Howard Hotels, welcomed the project, believing it would attract more business to the city. James L. Kernan, manager of the Kernan Hotel, disagreed. He thought a new hostelry would harm the business of existing hotels. George Blakistone, president of the fashionable Belvedere Hotel, agreed with Kernan. "Downtown and uptown," he argued, "there are hotels well fitted and fully capable of supplying all demands.... Any new hotel would have to draw its clientele from the established hotels."[34]

Blakistone may have had another reason for opposing Emerson's hotel. The story is often told, by among others Baltimore native and long-time *Sun* reporter Gil Sanders, of a run-in Emerson had with the Belvedere's maître d' on the hot and muggy evening of August 10, 1908. The Captain, the story goes, removed his jacket and hung it on the back of his chair. The maître d' forcibly reminded him that gentlemen do not take their coats off during dinner at the Belvedere. "Fine," Emerson reportedly snapped as he grabbed his coat and stormed out, "I'll build my own hotel and take my coat off as I please."[35]

In an undated, double-spaced, typed statement titled "A few incidents of my travels at home and abroad that possibly had some effect in influencing me to build a hotel," written shortly before the hotel opened in October 1911, Emerson explained why he built the Emerson. While the Belvedere incident may have happened, he made no mention of it. He did, however, describe his travels at length: "I have circled the Globe once, crossed the American Continent a number of times, and wandered from 'The Land of the Midnight Sun,' and the borders of Siberia to the wilds of African and Asia, to say nothing of my numerous tours over the Continent of Europe." He commented on the variety of food he ate, "oysters of Ostend, English Sole, duck of Rouen, curried Chicken and rice in India." And on places stayed: "homes of English Royalty, palaces of French Princes and Venetian Doges," and "roughed it in the bungalows of India and the ranches of our Western frontier."

From these travels, he continued, "I have returned to dear old Maryland tired and hungry and have endeavored to build for the way worn traveler and for the citizens of our beloved city a home embodying all the comforts of the best." The one "nuisance" he encountered frequently had been tipping. As an example, he recalled 18 "servants of different vintages" lined up with their palms outstretched as he approached the doorway to leave a Moscow hotel. He wondered, facetiously, if the "same formidable crowd" may have caused Napoleon's retreat and not "the Russian Army." He vowed to keep the "nuisance" at a minimum at his new hotel. He thanked the "Knights Of the Quill" for "proclaiming the hotel's virtues to the World in their morning issues, 'A new house is born and soon its banner will unfurl!'" He invited them "to call the house any name that appeals to you. Call it, if you wish, 'The House That Would Stop a Clock.'" He ended with this verse:

> It is so wondrously fair,
> So full of comfort, so free from care,
> That even time would stop,
> And linger there.[36]

The 18-story Emerson Hotel—what else would he have named it—located at Baltimore and Calvert Street, the former site of the B&O Railway station destroyed by the fire of 1904, soon became **the** place in Baltimore for luxurious lingering. As he did in constructing his Italian garden, the Captain sought inspiration for the Emerson from his travels abroad. The dining room, for instance, 62 by 32 feet in size, was furnished in the style of Louis XIV. The floor was marble, the ceiling beamed and decorated in shades of gold. Ten massive chandeliers provided light. The floor-to-ceiling windows were draped in Du Barry damask—a soft rose color—chosen to harmonize with the French grey wood used in the walls and window frames. A marble balcony provided space for an orchestra. Pictures from the era of the French king hung on the walls.[37]

The Chesapeake Room, one floor below the dining room, served that estuary's famed morsels to diners surrounded by 20 oil paintings with titles like "Chesapeake Bay Dog Retrieving Geese" and "Tonging Oysters and Treading Clams" that adorned the room's walls.[38] These succulents and the traditional Maryland fried chicken were prepared "by a Southern darky" whose previous employer had been the Czar of Russia.[39] Food for the restaurants came from the city markets. William H. Barse, whom Emerson hired away from New York's Waldorf-Astoria to manage his hotel,

8—Coping with Marital Strife

was especially pleased with the vegetables, fruit, and seafood on sale at Lexington Market, which he praised as "being by far the best I've ever seen, not excepting the big markets of New York City." Meats, fowls, and fish came from a variety of Baltimore city markets as well.[40]

New York had introduced Barse to major league baseball, where he had his choice of the Brooklyn Dodgers, New York Yankees, or New York Giants. A major league club in Baltimore, he thought, "would advertize the name of Baltimore all over the country and do it better than any other scheme that could be availed of.... That will do much to carry the name of our city abroad and, along with the advertising, will go increased commercial and industrial activity."[41] Emerson, always attuned to advertising opportunities, Barse said, also favored the idea. The political and financial resources needed to introduce Baltimoreans to "The Show" failed to materialize, perhaps because, among other reasons, Baltimore had a respectable minor league club at the time, the Baltimore Orioles, who finished the 1911 season with a 95–58 record, good for second place in the eight-team Eastern League. Between 1913 and 1915 a third league, the Federal League, would attempt to compete with the American and National leagues but failed to do so as the result of numerous player contract conflicts and insufficient financing. Baltimore's entry, the Baltimore Terrapins, played for two seasons, 1914 and 1915, before folding. The city's major league aspirations would have to wait until 1954 when the St. Louis Browns would move to Baltimore.

The lack of major league baseball did not detract from the Hotel Emerson's style and elegance. Eight large bronze chandeliers suspended from the ceiling with figures of huntsmen and fishermen in relief on each, supplemented by seven smaller chandeliers on the walls, lit the Chesapeake Room. In the "well" between the first floor and the mezzanine hung a one-ton chandelier, the only one of its kind in the country and an exact replica of the one in the Cathedral of Pisa, of which Emerson had no doubt made a sketch during one of his trips through Italy.[42]

Not only did each of the guest rooms have a private bathroom, a luxury at the time, but each featured several other tradition-breaking touches. Running ice water replaced the bellboy delivering a pitcher. Emerson insisted on this convenience to spare the guest a tip. Sanitized paper cups replaced heavy-bottomed, cut glass tumblers. Paper of a "pretty hue" replaced pictures on the wall which, as Barse noted, collect dust. Instead of placing the telephone box with its two bells on the wall, Emerson sealed the box in the wall. Only a cord coming out of the wall and attached to the phone on the desk could be seen.[43]

To prevent the possibility of a tuxedoed male guest being mistaken for a waiter, Barse decreed mustaches verboten for employees. Anyone

An outside view of the Emerson Hotel. Its décor and menu changed as Emerson constantly brought back ideas from his travels in Europe. It was a favored watering hole for Democrats of all stripes and tourists from around the world. Courtesy of Andrew Murray.

who insisted on facial hair could look elsewhere for employment.[44] Male guests who needed a haircut or a trim in the early years availed themselves of the eight-chair emporium in the basement, where Emerson required the barbers to wear white uniforms of pure silk. One observer described the barbershop as "glistening white like an arctic snow scene, giving at once an effect and a reality of absolute sanitation." The same observer likened the shop's marble wainscoting "to the walls of a hospital operating room."[45]

* * *

Knowing the crucial role advertising played in the success of Bromo-Seltzer, the Captain spared no effort or expense in touting his hotel. Barse opened a booking agency in Washington, D.C., which arranged package deals for groups of tourists from throughout the country. He established partnerships with premier East Coast Hotels such as the Waldorf-Astoria and Philadelphia's Bellevue-Stratford. The new manager hired a "special traveling agent" to visit every city and town of more than 500 people to extol the hotel's virtues. A group of Baltimore businessmen commissioned renowned city artist James Doyle, Jr., to etch the invitations and menus for the hotel's gala opening.[46] Barse sent invitations for the hotel's opening to members of the city's trade associations, civic organizations, and city and state officials, including all police and firemen.

Barse chose September 12, 1911, Defenders Day (commemorating Baltimore's successful defense of the city from a British invasion during the War of 1812) to open the hotel. He arranged for special trains to bring newspaper correspondents from New York and Washington at his expense. Barse and Emerson would host them to lunch on opening day. Baltimore Mayor James H. Preston, Democratic Maryland Senator and former governor John Walter Smith, and General Murray Vandiver (Maryland's Treasurer) headlined Maryland politicians in attendance. Emerson invited representatives from many hotels up and down the East Coast, including Walter Harper Marshall, secretary to Alfred G. Vanderbilt, owner of New York City's Hotel Vanderbilt, considered one of the finest in the world.[47] The *Sun* credited Emerson and Barse with "blazing the way in hotel advertising."[48]

The Captain chose his friend of twenty years, Col. Benjamin L. (Lyons) Farinholt, a Confederate veteran of the Civil War, to be the hotel's first official guest. Farinholt had been captured by Union forces at the Battle of Gettysburg, but escaped from a Union prison camp in Ohio in time to, on February 22, 1864, lead 938 men, mostly reservists and local citizens, in the successful defense of the Stanton River, Virginia, railroad bridge against 5,000 Union troops. His performance, in what has become known as "the battle of boys and old men," earned him a promotion to Colonel. By 1900, he was a glass merchant in Baltimore.[49]

Another indication that the Captain retained fond feelings toward the Confederate cause and those who, like his father and uncles, had served, was evident in his $500 donation in January of 1912 toward the $2,000 cost of restoring the house that Robert E. Lee and his wife, Mary Anna Randolph Custis, had occupied from 1848 to 1851. The West Point graduate had been assigned to assist in the design and building of Fort Carroll as a defense against an invasion of the city like that launched by the British in the War of 1812, located on an artificial island in the Patapsco River just south of Baltimore.[50]

All went as planned save for the opening date, which, due to construction delays, got pushed back to October 30. The staff served dinner to 1,000 people in the main dining room. Another thousand were reluctantly turned away for lack of space. A singer and orchestra performed in the background.[51] Ten days later, over 200 men with businesses surrounding

A resolute-looking Emerson as he appeared at age 53 in 1911, on the occasion of the banquet in his honor given by 200 friends and businessmen at the Emerson Hotel. This memorable year saw the completion of the Emerson Hotel, the Bromo-Seltzer Tower, his divorce from Emilie, and his marriage to Margaret's friend, Anne Preston McCormack. Courtesy Andrew Murray.

8—Coping with Marital Strife

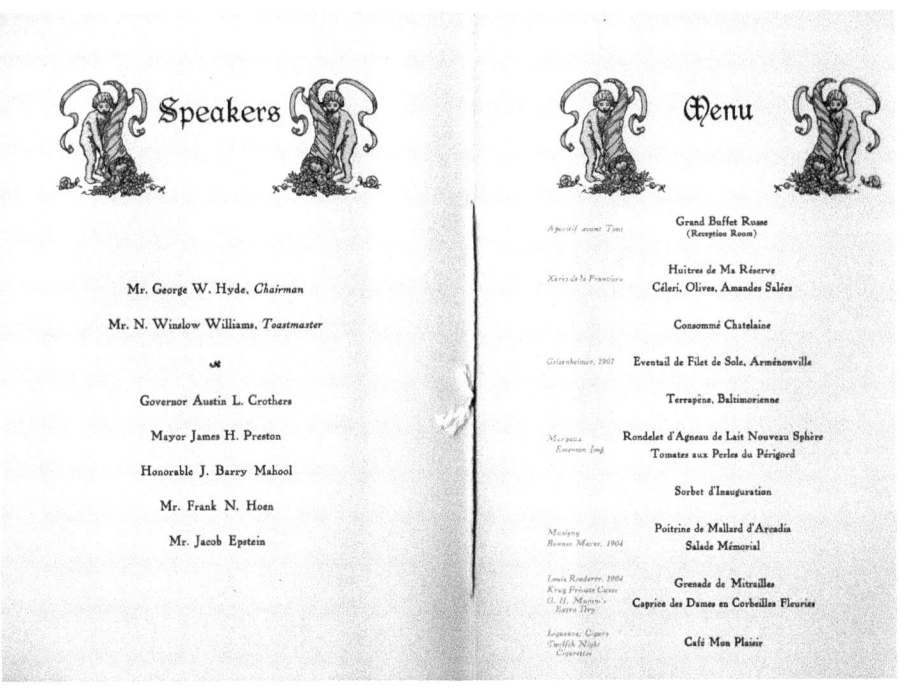

The speakers and menu for the banquet. Notice that the Margaux wine accompanying the Rondelet d'Agneau, lamb from a male sheep aged less than a year, has Emerson's name on it. Courtesy Andrew Murray.

the Emerson, Mayor James H. Preston, former Mayor J. Barry Mahool, and a representative from a bedridden Governor Austin Lane Crothers hosted a French cuisine-inspired banquet for its owner.

Directly behind the dais in the banquet stood the evening's decorative masterpieces, four-foot-high replicas of the hotel and of the Bromo-Seltzer Tower, both made of sugar and gum. Emerson had built the tower while his hotel was under construction. Duck from Arcadia, listed on the menu as "Poitrine de Mallard d'Arcadia," was the featured entrée. Speakers showered Emerson with praise for his hotel, which, they thought, would speed Baltimore businesses' recoveries from the devastation caused by the 1904 fire. Maryland's Secretary of State, N. Winston Williams, lauded Emerson as "the pioneer of Baltimore greatness." Emerson, after explaining his objectives for building the hotel, thanked the speakers for their praise and promised that "no effort has been spared or will be spared to make you feel at home within our walls and trust that our exertions will be satisfying."[52]

During the years that his hotel was being conceived and built, blacks in Baltimore faced a sudden increase in discrimination. In 1905 blacks and whites eating together at cafes and restaurants was a common sight in

Baltimore. Two years later most food establishments in the city had been segregated. Over the next three years racial tolerance came to an end in, among other facilities, department stores, theaters, cemeteries, and symphony concerts. The Supreme Court ruled in 1917 that laws or ordinances supporting segregated housing were unconstitutional. White homeowners and real estate agents in Baltimore and elsewhere then turned to covenants to exclude anyone of the seller's choosing, most notably blacks and Jews, from buying the seller's house. In the words of Baltimore historian Antero Pietila, "Baltimore became segregated from cradle to grave."[53]

It was in this racial environment that Emerson operated his hotel and drug company to the adulation of city and state leaders who themselves actively supported segregation. Civil rights activities challenging segregation in the form of court suits, protests, and marches would not gain city-wide or national traction until the 1950s.

9

Politics, Buildings and Jim Crow

As is often the case in successful ventures such as The Emerson Hotel, timing plays an important role. Just hours after the Democratic National Committee announced in early January 1912, that Baltimore would once again host their party's presidential nominating convention from June 25 to July 2, calls for reservations flooded the hotel's switchboard. Baltimore had been the site of seven previous conventions, dating back to 1832. This time the city beat out St. Louis, New York, and Denver for the 1912 event, thanks in large part to a $100,000 donation which had been raised by Emerson and other local leaders and the renovation of the Fifth Regiment Armory, where the delegates would meet.[1]

The Captain, still keeping his hand in the Bromo-Seltzer business while promoting his new hotel, invited the Proprietary Association to forgo its usual annual meeting site, New York City, and convene their 1912 meeting at the Emerson. The three-day meeting in late April attracted 200 manufacturers of patent medicines in the United States and Canada, men whose combined wealth the *Sun* estimated at $150 million to $2 million. Speakers announced the Association's support of "all fair investigations of all attacks made on patent medicines," and laid plans to reduce taxes levied on alcohol used in their products and to continue the growth in exports of patent medicines to foreign countries.[2]

While Emerson was hosting the Proprietary Association, reservations for the convention continued to flow in. Woodrow Wilson's supporters booked a large number of rooms at the Emerson. Wilson, the eventual standard bearer, reserved the large banquet hall on the mezzanine and two adjoining rooms, though he would reside at the Belvedere during his stay in the Monument City. No stranger to Baltimore, Wilson had boarded with the sisters Jane and Hannah Ashton on McCulloh Street while he pursued his PhD studies at The Johns Hopkins University. Publisher William Randolph Hearst took the Emerson's entire roof garden plus a large suite of rooms for his personal use. The Democratic National Committee chose The Emerson as its headquarters, as did the national committeemen and their state delegations from seven states, including Texas, Minnesota, and Washington. Large parties from Brooklyn and New York City also booked rooms there. Scores of reporters from newspapers around the country and a large contingent of *Associated Press* scribes would call the Emerson home.[3]

They and the candidates' staffs burst on the Baltimore scene in early June and stayed until July 12 when, after much wheeling and dealing and pro–Wilson oratorical flourishes by William Jennings Bryan, the party's unsuccessful nominee at its three prior conventions, Wilson, the governor of New Jersey and former president of Princeton University, won the nomination on the 46th ballot, the most ever cast at a national political convention up to that time. The convention was also noted for including the first African American delegate, J. D. Harkless (an alternate), and a sole woman delegate, Anna Pitzer, both from Colorado. She had a special entrée. Champ Clark, speaker of the U.S. House of Representatives and a major contender for the nomination, was her brother-in-law.[4] Regardless of who won the nomination, the name of The Emerson Hotel was carried far and wide throughout the land.

* * *

Having helped bring the convention to Baltimore and garnering his share of the associated hotel business, the owner turned his attention to other matters of business, sport and politics. On January 26, 1912, the hotel hosted the 35th annual banquet of the city's Merchants and Manufactures Association, which represented small businesses. Maryland Governor Philips Lee Goldsborough and Baltimore Mayor James H. Preston headlined the more than 300 invited local businessmen. Four United States senators, from Maryland, Alabama, Utah, and Indiana, made the trip up from Washington, D.C., to lend their support to the Association's call for direct election of U.S. Senators. Congress would pass such a measure, the 17th Amendment, in 1913 to replace the practice of state legislatures electing senators.[5]

As the Emerson Hotel was flourishing, Commodore Emerson, a title bestowed on Emerson by the Baltimore Yacht Club, was re-elected to head the organization. Emerson had supervised construction of the modern yacht club near Fort McHenry, from which an imprisoned Francis Scott Key had seen "that our flag was still there," on the Patapsco River, at an estimated cost of $15,000.[6] The new club was completed in September 1912.

Captain Emerson again found himself the guest of honor at a banquet to thank him for his efforts. Seated at a table placed in the center of the club's dining room overlooking the river, the Commodore listened to a flood of accolades directed his way from members seated at surrounding

9—Politics, Buildings and Jim Crow 95

tables. Emerson, in turn, thanked the members for their contributions, saying, "Well, we got together. We hustled…. This attractive building … is not the result of the efforts of the commodore, but of the combined efforts of the members." Clearly pleased with and proud of the new club, Emerson told the group that during his trip around the world, he'd seen "all the important yacht clubs" in Europe and Asia. Only two, he said, surpassed the Maryland Yacht club: The Royal Yacht Squadron of Cowes, located on the Isle of Wight in the English Channel, and the Bombay (now Mumbai), India Yacht Club. Appreciative of his leadership and modesty, the members ended the evening with a rousing chorus of "For He's a Jolly Good Fellow."[7]

* * *

The hotel's personnel policies at its opening reflected the city's Jim Crow culture. The city council had carried the city's tradition of segregation into the 20th century by unanimously voting on December 19, 1910, to prohibit "any black" from living in a house on a block where more than half of the residents were white. The ordinance similarly prohibited any white person from living on a predominantly black block. Violators faced a maximum fine of $100 and a prison term of 30 days to a year. The *Baltimore Sun* cited "colored people invading Northwest Baltimore" in 1909 as the cause of the ordinance.[8]

Democratic Mayor J. Barry Mahool earnestly told a *New York Times* reporter that the measure "was not passed in a spirit of race antagonism but passed to meet a critical condition." The condition included several parts, among them the decline, according to Mahool by more than half, of property values in white neighborhoods after a black family moved in, and a loss of social status.[9]

The ordinance sat well with many whites. "Experience and time," said Edgar Allan Poe, city attorney and grand nephew of the poet, "have conclusively proved that the co-mingling of white and colored races invariably leads to grave public disaster." Poe did not elaborate. A white woman, whose ancestry traced back to the days of the Calverts, the family that founded Maryland in the 1630s, recalled her fond feelings for "my old Negro mammy and my little nurse girl playmate." Yet, she added, "It is a most deplorable thing that even the best of the well-to-do colored people should invade our residential districts. The idea of Negroes living next door to me is abhorrent."[10]

Contrary to whites' popular beliefs at the time, African Americans did not always aspire to live next to them. Anna McMechen, wife of black lawyer George W. McMechen, whose lease of a house at 1834 McCulloh Street Mayor Mahoor cited as an example of the need for the ordinance, rebuffed Mahoor's assertion that the first thing blacks did after acquiring money and property "is to leave his less fortunate brethren behind and nose into the neighborhood of white people." "I have," said Mrs. McMechen, "no desire to associate with white women one whit more than they have to associate with me. My husband and I moved into the house because we wanted to be more comfortable."[11]

The Maryland Court of Appeals unanimously invalidated the ordinance on August 5, 1913, for technical reasons but upheld the Council's right to pass such an ordinance. Milton Dashiell, a prominent attorney who had authored the original ordinance, promptly redrafted a second to address the court's concerns.[12] The Council passed Dashiell's second ordinance a month later. Hours after its passage, a race riot broke out over, as the *Washington Post* put it, "the invasion earlier in the day at the 1300 block of North Mosher street by a negro family." White and blacks threw bricks and stones and fired marbles from slingshots at each other and nearby homes, injuring three people, smashing windows, and splintering plate-glass store windows.[13] The ordinance stood until 1917, when the U.S. Supreme Court declared it, and others like it, unconstitutional.

African Americans worked at the hotel as waiters and busmen, though denied supervisory positions, such as the headwaiter in the Chesapeake Room, and as bellboys, who would come into close contact with guests, all of whom were white, as African Americans were not allowed beyond the second floor.[14] Emerson first hired only French cooks in the belief that they would attract diners with the flavors and subtleties associated with the haute cuisine of France, which the Captain no doubt enjoyed on his European jaunts. But by 1913, the hotel's manager, John J. Kincaid, decided, "we simply had to get negro cooks to keep our patronage.... When they [patrons] ask for 'chicken, Maryland style' or for terrapins or oysters, they want them prepared by cooks who know how. French cooks might do pretty well for New York—but for Baltimore, never."

Kincaid made the change at midnight on a June evening in 1913. The French cooks sullenly gave their aprons to the nervous African American cooks, who had been stationed just outside the kitchen. A squad of Baltimore policemen stood by to keep the peace, but their services weren't needed. Pleased with the changeover, Kincaid reported on June 29, 1913, "Our guests are ordering double portions of those good things which only a negro chef of Maryland birth knows how to prepare."[15]

The 21 African American cooks lasted until May of 1922, when the Captain suddenly replaced them with white cooks "for the good of the service," he explained. An efficiency expert, he said, had studied the kitchen operation and concluded, "some of the cooks were good and some of them were bad." He gave no further details to support the wholesale change of black cooks to white cooks. African American waiters were not affected. Emerson told them, "so long as you and your subordinates look after the interests of the Emerson Hotel Company … there will be no change in your Department." A separate locker room was built for the white cooks, thus "separating the two departments, in which each department will have ample room to keep themselves neat."[16]

African American visitors experienced discrimination at the hotel. Members of the Committee on Christian Education of the Presbyterian General Assembly, during their June 1926 convention, refused to eat a lunch they had paid for and left the hotel en masse when the hotel staff refused to serve the lone African American delegate.[17] Earlier in the year, the hotel's management had canceled New York poet and Harvard student Countee Porter Cullen's engagement, citing its policy that African Americans were not allowed above the first floor. The poet later gave a well-attended reading at Baltimore's Ames Memorial M. E. church.[18]

Two years later a hotel employee, William H. Walker, intercepted two Howard University professors, Daniel H. Smith and Antoine Green, in the lobby on their way to attend a session sponsored by the Colleges of Pharmacy and the National Association of Boards of Pharmacy, held in the hotel's Club Room on the second floor. Walker told the two that African Americans were not permitted in the hotel. Other delegates rescued the duo and led them to the meeting. The following day, the two were asked to remove their hats in the lobby. They refused and were again rescued by fellow delegates. Both said they had not been so insulted in any other city.[19]

As late as February 1941, an orchestra playing dance music for the Maryland state convention of the American Legion laid down their instruments when they spotted "two colored couples" on The Emerson's dance floor. They would not continue playing until the couples left the dance floor. A hotel spokesman said the hotel's policy "wouldn't allow dancing by colored couples."[20] A year later, labor leader George Meyers, seeking to book a convention at the hotel, was told "The colored will have to use the freight elevator. We don't want them sitting around here like they own the place." Meyers found a more hospitable hotel in Washington, D.C.[21]

Many of the city's leading white citizens, including judges, supported Baltimore's culture of discrimination and segregation. Judge Charles W. Heuisler's 1924 speech was a case in point. He stated to 200 members of the city's Real Estate Board at a luncheon at the Hotel Emerson that "segregation is practical and satisfactory as applied in schools here and on railroad trains in some parts of the State only because the negro is afforded facilities in those cases equal to those given whites." That statement would be invalidated 30 years later with the Supreme Court ruling in Brown v. Board of Education. The judge told the realtors that the same conditions must apply to "living quarters" before zoning segregation could be practical. He also proposed improving hygienic condition in "negro" neighborhoods and holding conferences of whites and "negroes" to devise "ordinances that would be satisfactory to each race and possible under the constitution." The judge's proposals were prompted by his anticipation of a great increase in the city's "negro" population, predicting it would rise to 250,000 by 1944.[22]

* * *

The hotel had not been Emerson's only venture into the world of magnificent city edifices. Speakers at the testimonial dinner feting the city's newest hotel also applauded the Captain for building the Emerson Tower, also known as the Bromo-Seltzer Tower, during the same time his hotel was being built. Emerson hired the two men most responsible for constructing the hotel to do the same for his tower. Sperry designed it, and William H. Parker saw to the construction.

The tower, located at West Lombard and South Eutaw Streets, rose to the then-unprecedented height for a building in Baltimore of 357 feet. The Renaissance tower in Florence's Palazzo Vecchio had captured the Captain's imagination and served as a model for his Baltimore tower. Parker used 750,000 bricks with a yellowish hue and blue and brown tints. A 17-ton, 51-foot-high, 20-foot-wide, steel facsimile of a ten cent, blue Bromo Seltzer bottle that rotated 107 feet a minute sat atop the tower. It weighed 20 tons. Electric lights, 506 by count, lit up the bottle at night, ensuring that the Bromo-Seltzer label would be visible across the city 24 hours a day.

On a clear night, people on Tolchester Beach, 20 miles away on the opposite shore of the Chesapeake Bay, could see the glow. Four clock faces, one on each side of the tower at its top, marked the time. Twelve large letters spelling out Bromo-Seltzer surrounded the Roman numerals, marking the clock faces' hour locations. At the time, it was the world's largest four-dial gravity clock, larger even than London's Big Ben. The tower, which became known as the Emerson Bromo-Seltzer Tower, in addition to its obvious advertising purpose, provided additional manufacturing and office space for the prospering Emerson Drug Company. The structure was another example of Emerson's ability to combine the practical with the innovative.[23] An article in the *American Druggist and Pharmaceutical Record* referred to the massive structure as "undoubtedly

9—Politics, Buildings and Jim Crow

A night view of Emerson's Bromo-Seltzer Tower, circa 1920, with the twinkling lights at the very top. Notice how it dwarfs the surrounding buildings and the letters B-R-O-M-O-S-E-L-T-Z-E-R surrounding the Roman numerals on the clock face. Author's collection.

one of the most effective advertising schemes ever devised by any manufacturer of medicine."[24]

* * *

The tower, the hotel, and the yacht club were examples of Emerson's voracious work appetite. Soon after he embarked on building the Emerson Hotel, he described his Type A personality to a *Sun* reporter. "Do you know that I am fifty-one years old," he told the scribe in June of 1910.

> But I'm capable of doing as much work as ever. I tried to give it all up about three years ago, but soon found that I couldn't. I went around the world and kept on traveling, but work is what I want and plenty of it. Even though I am not any longer the president of my company, I like to hang around and see how things are going.

The same reporter observed that the Captain "grasps one by the hand like a man who is thoroughly enjoying life, and wants everybody to know it. He smiles and talks affably…. He sees the city on the crest of a prosperous wave and that a big, fine, up-to-date hotel like the Emerson will be just the thing to keep up interest."[25]

Things were going quite well for the Captain, at least in the realms of business and finance.

10

Vanderbilts

The Captain's domestic affairs were not going as smoothly. As he was directing the building of a luxurious hotel, a dominating clock tower, and a modern yacht club, and fending off charges about Bromo-Seltzer from journalists, reformers, and the American Medical Association, the Bromo-Seltzer King became embroiled in a number of marital clashes.

Splashed across page two of the *Chicago Daily Tribune* on January 20, 1911, ran a story citing a loud argument between Isaac and Emilie in the lobby of the Waldorf-Astoria, where both had been staying in separate apartments. An embarrassed and angry Isaac immediately moved to a room in the New York Club, where he began preparing divorce papers. He spent Thanksgiving at Arcadia with daughter Margaret and a group of friends. Emilie returned alone to the Baltimore mansion.[1]

Another marital conflict erupted soon after Margaret returned to Baltimore following her divorce and trip to Japan. Ex-husband Smith Hollins McKim filed alienation of affection suits against the Captain, Alfred Vanderbilt, whom Margaret was still widely rumored to soon marry, and Mrs. Frederick McCormack, a friend of Margaret's since childhood who, along with her father, had accompanied her to Reno. McKim said he filed the suits "to test the validity of the divorce." The parties reached an out-of-court settlement in late February of 1911, in which McKim was reportedly guaranteed a one-time payment of $50,000 for his attorney fees and an income of $7,500 a year for life from a $150,000 trust fund. In return, Margaret's ex dropped all three suits.[2]

While maintaining a public display of marital accord, the Emersons had become estranged a number of years earlier. Isaac's divorce suit brought the conflict into open view. He named as a co-defendant C. Hazeltine Basshor, Vice President and General Manager of the Thomas C. Basshor Co., which identified its business in the 1912 city directory as "engineers, contractors and machine supplies." The company had been incorporated in 1900 by his father, Thomas, and four partners.[3] It was well known among Isaac's and Emilie's friends that each had their own set of friends and spent large amounts of time apart from each other. Emerson had earlier offered Emilie Bromo-Seltzer stock that would pay her $15,000 to $20,000 a year in return for a quiet divorce. She refused. When Isaac filed the papers, Judge Charles W. Heuisler ordered them sealed so as to be unavailable to the public. "I was asked to do this," he told a *Sun* reporter, "and in my opinion good reasons were given."[4]

The *Sun* roundly criticized Heuisler's decision. In separate editorials, the newspaper made two points. In spite of Emerson's public spirit, money, and many contributions to the city, "none," one editorial argued, "should secure for him any advantage before the law … which would tend to encourage the distrust of the fairness and impartiality of the courts."[5] A second editorial said that no newspaper should go beyond "the line set by good taste and decency in reporting on scandals and divorces, but the suppression of any information in such cases would, the editorial argued, "lead to a tremendous multiplication of divorce suits and of the practices that make divorce suits possible."[6]

The *Sun* need not have worried, for the particulars did not stay private for long. In March 1911, the *Sun* reported that Isaac had charged Basshor with "inappropriately visiting Mrs. Emerson during his absences without his knowledge or consent." She counter-sued, adamantly denying any inappropriate behavior. "I have never been untrue to my marriage vows," she testified when the case was heard by Judge Heuisler in Circuit Court. She said their relationship had been congenial in the early years of the marriage. She added that Isaac "was poor" at the time, and that she worked long hours, seven days a week, in his drug stores. They both agreed they had lived apart since the hotel lobby argument.

During that time, an auditor appointed by Judge Heuisler concluded after listening to all the evidence given by witnesses, "Captain Emerson never shared his apartments with Mrs. Emerson; that his attitude toward her was not that of a member of the household … and their matrimonial relations entirely ceased." Emerson in fact had spent little time in Baltimore for the past seven years. For the sake of public appearances, he stayed at his mansion when in town. On those occasions, a maid locked Emilie's bedroom door and kept the key. Isaac, when not at Arcadia, New York, Newport, or Europe with Margaret and Anne Preston McCormack, lived with the McKims prior to their divorce in their Irvington-on-the-Hudson estate.[7]

Judge Heuisler granted Emilie an "absolute" divorce on May 29 on the grounds of abandonment. The decree allowed Emerson to keep one-third of the bound volumes in his library, an oil painting of Margaret, and a few items from his trips overseas. Heuisler awarded Emilie $28,800 a year in alimony, ownership of the Eutaw Place house, and most of its contents.

The Italian garden was to be kept undisturbed as long as Emilie occupied the house. Emerson lived on the *Margaret* until a suite was available for him at the Hotel Emerson.[8]

* * *

Days after the divorce, rumors circulated that the Captain and Anne Preston McCormack would marry and honeymoon on the *Margaret*. Asked about the gossip by a *Times* reporter on June 27, 1911, Emerson dodged the question of marriage by replying,

> That's just what they know about it. The *Margaret* had been chartered to Edward P. Smith, [a Philadelphia banker] until September 1 and the houseboat, a recent purchase also named the *Margaret*, to J. Pierpont Morgan, Jr., until the same date. Tomorrow you will find me here at my office.... I have work to do.... In the summer I will go abroad and expect to meet in Europe my daughter, Mrs. McKim.[9]

Part of what he told the reporter was true. He did go to Europe and he did meet up with Margaret. But before departing for Europe, Isaac, age 52, married McCormack, 13 years his junior,[10] in a private ceremony on July 6 at the Marble Collegiate Church (now the Collegiate Church of New York) on New York's Fifth Avenue, just a week after he said he was not going to marry her.[11]

* * *

Emerson met his future wife while he was staying with Margaret and her then-husband McKim. She introduced her father to her best friend, Anne McCormack. Anne and her husband, Frederick C. McCormack, an insurance salesman, lived in Dobbs Ferry, New York, just ten miles from the McKims' Irvington-on-Hudson residence.[12] Anne, who had known Margaret since childhood, was known as a handsome brunette with a charming personality. At the time of their marriage, she had two children, a boy 15, Frederick, and a girl 17, Ethel.[13]

Emerson took an immediate liking to Anne. The relationship between the two blossomed and was well known to their families. Anne had frequently joined Margaret and her father on trips to Arcadia, Newport, Europe, and Florida.[14] On Isaac's and Margaret's first extended trip to Newport in July of 1908, for instance, the Captain invited Anne and a Mrs. Howard to accompany him on the *Margaret*. Emilie stayed in Baltimore. Margaret rented a villa, The Orchard, owned by New York businessman Col. George R. Fearing, for the group's summer stay.[15]

Shortly after meeting the McCormacks, Anne's husband was struck with a life-threatening disease. Emerson, thinking South Carolina's warm climate and the nearby Georgetown hospital would benefit him, brought him to Arcadia on a special train shortly after he purchased the plantation. Despite everyone's best efforts, Frederick died after several weeks at the Captain's property. Anne turned to Emerson to act as executor for her husband's estate. Their relationship had been one of close friends, and some suspected more. Two photographs spawned the speculation. One, taken in St. Augustine, Florida, in the winter of 1905, showing a distinguished, portly Emerson seated on a chair with Anne McCormack standing beside him, appeared in the *Sun*.[16] In a photograph of the three taken in Florida onboard the *Margaret* in January 1906, the caption stated that Emerson was in his pajamas and the two ladies in "filmy lingerie."[17] "It is the merest nonsense," the Captain replied when asked by a reporter about the photograph. "The women members of my party wore morning gowns and I was decked out in a library gown," he added.

To bolster his claim of innocence, even though he and Emilie were by now estranged, he told a reporter for the *San Francisco Chronicle*, "Mrs. Emerson was in Palm Beach at the time, and I gave her one of the pictures." Both appeared in the *Sun* on June 22, 1911, just days before the wedding between the Captain and Anne. "How," a reporter wondered, "had the *Sun* received the photo like the one that Isaac had given to Mrs. Emerson?" The question was never answered publically. The suspicion, of course, was that Emilie had supplied the photo. Shortly before the wedding, she had been quoted as saying, "On the day that Captain Emerson re-weds, I shall have something to say." She made no further public pronouncements on the matter.[18] Publication of the photographs did not bother the groom. Reiterating his claim that all three were fully dressed in the on-board picture he said, "It was a beautiful morning, and Ernest, the steward of the yacht, took the picture, one of which was given to Mrs. Emerson."[19]

The new Mrs. Emerson did not dwell on the controversy. She told the reporter, "I have been cruelly maligned by those who have their own interests to serve. My future happiness will not suffer, however.... I am going away on a long European tour with my husband. Just what my plans are I cannot say now. But I know I am going to be happy."[20]

After a honeymoon in France and Germany, during which Margaret joined them for a time, the newlyweds arrived back in Baltimore in mid–September. The stayed on the *Margaret* until a suite was ready for them at the Emerson Hotel. He once again denied rumors of an engagement between Margaret and Alfred Vanderbilt. "It does not exist so far as I know … and I think I would know if the engagement did exist," he told a reporter for the *Sun*.[21]

As was often the case, Emerson was inspired by what he saw in Europe. On this trip it was food. German hams and bacon would now be served at the Emerson Hotel in place of Virginia-based Smithfield pork products purchased at Lexington Markets. "Crinkles [a cookie] of all kinds

The oil painting of "Magnolia Blossom" as it appears over the Maryland Club's bar. In a letter conveying the painting to the Club in 1996, Edward Emerson Murray said, "Art experts have advised that the Madeleine is excellent quality art ... all curves and nothing offensive to the senses. She radiates quality and pleasure!!" The Captain, Murray added, would "be pleased with such an allegation." Courtesy Andrew Murray.

as found in European hotels," the Captain promised, would be added to the menu.[22] He ordered a French oven for the Emerson that could cook 15 chickens at a time after reveling in the flavor of chickens so cooked at a restaurant in Vichy, France.[23]

In addition to ideas for his hotel's menu offerings, the newlywed husband also returned from France with a life-size oil painting of a nude woman titled *Madeleine Repentante*, by Jules Armand Hanriot (1853–1930). Emerson installed the painting high over the dark, mahogany-paneled men's bar in the hotel. A spotlight highlighted the painting, nicknamed "Magnolia Blossom" by J. Edward Murray. He received the painting from Emerson's estate in 1935, at which time he was president of the Emerson Drug Company. Murray family lore has it that "Magnolia Blossom" was Emerson's mistress in Paris.[24] The painting has remained in the Murray family and currently graces the wall behind the Maryland Club's bar in Baltimore.

* * *

A little more than a year after the Captain's wedding on August 22, 1912, Emilie married Charles Basshor, who at age 45 was 11 years younger than his bride. A few close friends attended the ceremony at the St. John's German Evangelical Lutheran Church in Jersey City, New Jersey. Margaret, "due to a temporary indisposition," could not leave England to attend her mother's wedding. The couple took a European honeymoon before taking up residence at the Eutaw Place mansion.[25]

Their union did not sit well with Isaac. Immediately after hearing the news, he asked Baltimore's Circuit Court to relieve him of paying alimony to his ex. He did not think he should have to support another man's wife, particularly one whom he thought "was abundantly able to provide for her." The Court turned him down. Undaunted, he took his case to the Court of Appeals, where he met a similar fate. Emilie continued to receive her alimony.[26]

In November, the newlywed couple moved from Eutaw Place in Baltimore to Algonquin Manor, an estate on the Choptank River two miles from Cambridge, Maryland. Named for the Indian tribe, the estate had been the former summer home of the late U.S. Democratic Senator from Maryland, Isidor Rayner. Described by the *Baltimore Sun* "as one of the show places on the Eastern Shore," the three-story, 17-room house sat on 135 acres that sloped gently down to the Choptank River, affording the occupants a water view that stretched for 12 miles. Original growth shade trees dotted the lawn.[27] Life in the country and the dairy farm they created there agreed with the former Baltimore residents so much that Emilie sold her Eutaw Place house in May of 1913. The buyer, Henry J. Matthews, reportedly paid $65,000 in cash and conveyed his residence at 231 Laurens Street to Emilie to complete the sale.[28]

The couple's seemingly tranquil lifestyle came to an abrupt end just two years after their marriage, when on August 19, 1914, servants at the Manor found Basshor lying on the floor unconscious and bleeding profusely from a charge of mustard-seed shot fired into his neck from a rifle lying beside him. He had returned from an early evening hunting outing while Emilie was visiting friends.[29] He lingered for a week, with only brief moments of consciousness. During one of those, he reportedly told his physician, Dr. W. Brice Goldsborough, "I came in holding the rifle by the barrel. I went to get a chair to use the telephone. I remember nothing more."[30] Some, citing rumors of discord between the two and business problems for Basshor, thought the wound had been self-inflicted. Emilie vehemently denied the suggestion, saying the gun discharged unexpectedly as he was putting it away after returning home from hunting, shooting guinea fowl. Dr. Goldsborough ruled the death accidental, as did the State's Attorney, Calvin W. Price and Chief of Police W. G. Pritchell.[31] There the matter rested.

Emilie, after recovering from a mild heart attack, turned to Margaret, with whom she'd maintained a close relationship notwithstanding the Captain's obvious preference for Margaret over herself, for comfort. After returning from a trip to Newport with Margaret, the widow sold the manor in May of the following year and took up temporary residence at the luxury Severn Apartments in Baltimore, before relocating to an apartment in New York City to be near Margaret. Located in the heart of Baltimore at Mt. Vernon Square, the Severn, built in 1894, was the first high-rise apartment building in the city.[32]

* * *

Eight months before her mother remarried, Margaret, 27, quashed the ongoing rumors linking her to Alfred Vanderbilt, 34, by marrying him in a private ceremony on Sunday, December 17, 1911, in the Registry Office at Reigate, Surrey, England, 25 miles south of London. The ceremony was a far cry from the grand scale and sumptuousness of most Vanderbilt weddings and that of Margaret and McKim. Only four witnesses attended: Anne McCormack, Walter Webb-Ware, one of Alfred's attorneys, and two Registry officials. The marriage was the second for both.[33]

Margaret cabled the good news to her parents, "Married to Alfred Vanderbilt today." The event did not surprise friends. The two were frequently seen together at horse shows on the Continent and in England, where Margaret had gone after receiving a cablegram from Alfred asking her to join him. She said goodbye to her father at Arcadia, where she had gone right after her mother's divorce was settled. Anne Preston McCormack joined her there. Both sailed to Paris under assumed names to keep the press at bay. Alfred met them at a hotel in the City of Lights.[34]

* * *

Being no strangers to divorce, their own and those of friends and relatives, Margaret and Alfred, having in Alfred's words, "suffered too much publically and newspaper notoriety," inked a pre-nuptial agreement designed to minimize any divorce-spawned spats that, he complained, "attract the press like moths to a light" should they divorce. They spelled out financial arrangements. Margaret would receive $3 million, each son $3 million, and each daughter $1 million if Alfred was at fault. Margaret's settlement would fall to $100,000 a year if she was at fault. Amounts to children remained the same. Alfred would pay all child expenses in any case. The children would spend six months with each parent regardless of who was at fault. They would not begrudge the other their passions. Alfred did not like Margaret's penchant to sail the seas, which had been a bitter bone of contention between her and Smith Hollins McKim, but, he said, "If you want to live at sea, I'll buy you a beautiful house boat." Likewise, she would not file for divorce based on time he spent with horses. They agreed to like each other's friends and agreed that flirting with them was okay.[35] The need to implement the agreement never arose, but it did give Alfred license to continue his passion with horses and a well-funded, flamboyant life style.

* * *

The Vanderbilts were the closest thing America had to a royal family in the late 19th century. Commodore Cornelius Vanderbilt, starting with a $100 loan from his mother, built a shipping and railroad empire worth $100 million when he died in 1877. Son William Henry doubled that figure. William's son, Cornelius II, continued to enhance the family's fortune and built the Breakers in Newport. He had seven children, three girls and four boys, Alfred, Cornelius III, Reginald, and William, who died in 1892 at age 22.[36]

Following his graduation from Yale University in 1899, where his classmates voted him the "Playboy of Yale Society," the "tall, handsome, athletic" graduate, noted for his "striking countenance and light blue eyes," embarked upon a life full of pleasure and excesses.[37] Helped by an inheritance from his father, Cornelius Vanderbilt II, thought to be between $70 million and $100 million, making him, in the estimation of the *New York Times*, "the richest young man in America," Alfred eschewed any interest in the family's corporations. Instead, he bought property in Portsmouth, Rhode Island, which he named Oakland Farms and claimed as his primary residence.

A partial view of Oakland Farm, a working farm that Alfred cherished as his main residence. His son, by his first wife Elsie French, William Henry, inherited the property from Alfred, made it his principal residence, and sold it after World War II. Subsequently sub-divided, little evidence of the original property remains today. Author's collection.

Alfred maintained a nine-room suite at New York City's elegant Plaza Hotel from 1907 to 1912, when he built the stately Vanderbilt Hotel in the heart of New York City at 34th and Park Avenue. He maintained townhouses and apartments in London and Paris. In 1909, he commissioned the world's largest houseboat, outshining that of England's Royal Family, from which he and friends watched Regattas on the Thames. He traveled to Europe as often as ten times a year, once with 100 horses that he stabled in England. Horses were his passion. He exhibited them at international horse shows, where he became known as a "fine whip" for his skills with the reins.[38]

In England in 1908, he took up the English upper class sport of coaching. He drove his custom-made coach, the *Venture*, between London and Brighton, a town on England's south coast, Tuesdays through Friday, over a period of six weeks in May and June. The manes of horses in the first team were braided with red and white ribbons. Red and white carnations adorned their heads. The *Venture* was painted maroon with red and white stripes.

The seven-hour trip, with nine stops along the way and eight changes of the four-horse teams, brought out enthusiastic spectators along the route. His passengers were in no hurry. The first class train, the *Brighton Belle*, made the same trip in an hour, at a fraction of the coach fare, but lacked the social status of being seen in Alfred's coach. The paying passen-

When not driving a coach, riding a horse, cruising in his yacht, or riding the rails in his private railcar, Alfred took to the road in open-air machines. Seen here behind the wheel of one of his machines, no doubt an English vehicle as the steering wheel is on the right, his outfit, with the exception of his hat, is not unlike that he would wear when boarding the *Lusitania*. LC-USZ62-118341. Prints and Photographs Division, Library of Congress, Washington, D.C.

A coach similar to ones that Alfred drove. This one is stored at Arcadia. Courtesy of Matt Balding.

gers could take an inside seat or an outside seat. The most desirous seat was that beside the driver. His coaching activity ceased with the outbreak of World War I. The British army commandeered all of his horses in England, an event which saddened Vanderbilt, who treasured every one of them and knew the temperament of each. The war did not, however, affect coaching in the States, where Alfred operated his coaches between New York and Philadelphia and between Manhattan and various destinations in Rhode Island.[39]

* * *

Alfred's life before marrying Margaret consisted of more than coaching and managing his considerable number of horses. Alfred enjoyed relationships with several women. His father, Cornelius II, had disinherited Alfred's brother, Cornelius III, for marrying a woman of whom he disapproved. Alfred avoided his father's displeasure by marrying a woman his father welcomed into the family, socialite Elsie French, described by a *New York Times* reporter as "a pretty girl of rather slight frame."[40] Her father, president of the Manhattan Trust Company, left a fortune estimated to be worth $15 million. Elsie's mother owned properties in Newport and New York City. She took Elsie on trips to Europe, where they frequently spent time with Alfred. The two had been friends since childhood. He was known as a modest man who excelled in all outdoor sports, particularly those involving horses. They married in January 1901 in Newport, Rhode Island. He was 24, Elsie 22. Alfred's father, in his will, rewarded his son's marital choice by naming Alfred head of the family and heir to the bulk of his estate.[41]

While his parents approved of Elsie, playboy Alfred wasn't ready to be tied down to one woman. In 1906 he had started an affair with St. Louis-born Mary Agnes Ruiz, daughter of a boilermaker and renowned for her beauty and daring. She twice ran away to New Orleans as a teenager and returned home each time by hopping freight trains. Both Alfred and Agnes loved horses. She was an excellent horsewoman, having been raised on a farm. Alfred was the most famous horseman at the time and operated a successful breeding operation. They met in New York's Central Park, where Alfred rescued her from a runaway horse when its saddle girth broke.[42]

Among many indulgences, Alfred bought her an $11,000 automobile. Elsie, in residence at Newport, had heard rumors of her husband's fondness for Agnes, but was infuriated by news of the car purchase, disclosed to friends in his private rail car, the *Wayfarer*, on a trip from Richmond, Virginia to Norfolk, Virginia; the fact that it occurred on his 30th birthday, October 30, 1907; and that Agnes herself had peeled off 11, $1,000 bills to the car dealer. She filed suit for divorce, charging him with "misconducting himself with an unknown woman." Alfred made only a "general denial" of her charges. New York State Supreme Court Justice James A. O'Gorman, later to serve as a Democratic Senator from New York (1911–1917), found for Elsie by signing an "interlocutory decree of divorce. The decree allowed her to marry after three months and forbade Alfred ever to marry again."[43] The Vanderbilt family made it clear they also sided with Elsie, making Agnes persona non gratis in New York.[44]

After Alfred's divorce was finalized, Agnes left for London, where Alfred had a residence. There she bought a large house in fashionable Grosvenor Square, servants included. She rode regularly on a path known as Rotten Row. Alfred, while still in a relationship with Margaret, visited her daily during his visits to London. His visits stopped suddenly in April of 1909.[45] Agnes was crushed. Firmly believing she and Alfred would marry, she lost weight and sleep, suffered from depression, and was seen by servants weeping and beating her chest. Reports of Alfred riding daily in the London parks with another woman of equal equestrian skills, no doubt Margaret, deepened her depression. She fired a single shot into her chest on May 16, 1909, from a pistol she kept by her bed.

The news of her death and the verdict of the coroner's jury, which ruled the death a "suicide while of unsound mind," were successfully withheld from the press for three weeks. When the facts finally became known, several members of the House of Commons demanded an investigation into why the news had been suppressed. The chief clerk ruled the demands out of order.[46] Not until later did it become known that Alfred's attorney in London and cousin, Walter Webb-Ware, had paid each reporter who had been present at the inquest $50 to keep the story quiet.[47] City newspapers at the time relied entirely on "news agency" reporters for such stories. Often underpaid, most were amenable to trade silence for cash. In this case, so much money was spread about that suspicions were quickly aroused and the truth revealed in a relatively short time.[48]

Adding to the mystery of Ruiz's death was speculation that Alfred had purchased many of her jewels sold at auction in December 1909. His attorney, W. G. Webb-Ware, served as the attorney for the administrators of Ruiz's estate. Public information about the auction resulted in less interest than might have been expected. Ruiz's maiden name, Miss Mary O'Brien, appeared in the catalogue, and her address was wrongly listed as "10 Grosvenor Street" instead of 19 Grosvenor Street. A physician, Sir Henry Weber, lived at #10 and expressed indignation at his address appearing in the papers.

When asked by a reporter if the jewels belonged to Ruiz, Ware refused to answer. He explained away the wrong address as a "typo" even though it appeared that way in all the city papers. Ware had visited the auction site days beforehand but did not attend the auction, which was limited to dealers only. The names of successful bidders were not made public, but the amount of money, $35,000, realized by their sale was.[49] *The New York Times*, however, reported that Alfred had been represented at the auction "by an agent," most likely someone hired by Walter Webb-Ware, who bought Ruiz's jewels.[50] A reporter for the *St. Louis Post-Dispatch* found among the jewels a dressing bag with silver-gilt, tortoise-shell fittings to be "most interesting." It bore the monogram: A.R. (Agnes Ruiz no doubt), a fact not reported in the sales catalogue.[51]

Alfred, though reported to be stunned by Ruiz's suicide, continued partying, racing his coaches, and attending horse races. He had been presented to King Edward VII at the International Olympia Horse Show a few days before the scandal broke. After the news became public, Alfred and Edward again found themselves at the same horse race. This time His Majesty snubbed Alfred by inviting many prominent Americans in attendance but not him to the royal box. "His gay, bohemian life style without atonement" was given as the reason for the royal snub by the *St. Louis-Post Dispatch*.[52]

Some in America had the same opinion of Alfred. Ill-timed rumors of a pending marriage between Alfred and Margaret sparked a *Los Angeles Times* editorial saying, "Mrs. McKim may marry Alfred Vanderbilt if she wishes, but if she were the sister of some men we know, she would have a fine horsewhipping coming to her."[53] Adding to Alfred's reputation problem was a rumor circulating that not only had he deceived Agnes, to say nothing of Margaret, but that he was using his affair with her to mask an affair he was having with Washington, D.C., socialite Caroline Lorillard, who had committed suicide in March 1909 amid rumors of an affair with the rich playboy.[54]

* * *

His marriage to Margaret improved his mood, as did the prospect of installing his family on the top floor of the recently opened Vanderbilt Hotel in New York City. Their "flat" consisted of the entire top floor and part of the one below. A two-story dining room could accommodate banquets and more intimate affairs. Views of Long Island and the amusement park, Coney Island, could be had on clear days. Other amenities included "rooms three times larger than most, lavishly decorated, bedrooms with bath and dressing room attached, a library, reception hall, smoking room, private library and office for Alfred, madame's boudoir, breakfast room, and tea room."[55]

* * *

The newlyweds arrived in New York in November 1912, six weeks after the birth of Alfred Jr., but without their son. His doctor deemed him too young to travel. His parents left him in the care of servants at Alfred's London estate.[56] The couple spent most of their time during their month-long visit to the States at the Vanderbilt Hotel and Camp Sagamore in the Adirondacks, where Margaret's father joined them for several days. Sagamore offered guests a rustic retreat from city life. Alfred bought the property from William West Durant, a noted designer of camps throughout the Adirondacks which were all the rage during the Gilded Age. Alfred enlarged Durant's property, originally built as a luxurious family home with only five bedrooms and dining capacity for 12. He added the Wigwam, a major guest facility, a men's entertainment headquarters, flush toilets, hot and cold running water, concrete tennis courts, and a playhouse, and doubled the size of the dining room to accommodate 24 people. His first wife, Elsie, disliked the rustic setting, so the camp went unused from 1903 until their divorce. Margaret, on the other hand, loved the nearby lake and forest and helped Alfred develop Sagamore further. They eventually installed a hydroelectric complex to supply electricity and added a bowling alley, a telephone system, and a large new laundry.[57]

Margaret got away for several days to make a "flying visit" to Baltimore where, accompanied by her step-sister, Daisy, and her husband, James McVicker, she visited her mother and her new husband at her childhood home for several days. As was her usual traveling routine, she made the round trip from New York City in Alfred's private rail car, the *Wayfarer*.[58] Since marrying Alfred, she travelled on the *Wayfarer* in elegance and quiet whenever she could. The car had been part of the Vanderbilts' railroad history that included the building of the New York Central and Grand Central Terminal. "Like her," her grandson Alfred Vanderbilt, III wrote some years later, "it was famous and old, and held mysteries and memories and meanings."[59]

11

Fresh Starts

The *New York Times* reporter who met their ship, the French liner Provence, when it docked in New York, was curious about the new-born. "Was it true," he asked Alfred, if the proud grandfather, Isaac Emerson, had built an entire dairy for his first grandchild? "What, a whole dairy for one baby? What on earth could he do with it?" Vanderbilt replied.[1]

The previous November, Isaac had agreed to purchase Brooklandwood for $400,000 before December 1, 1914. In the meantime, he agreed to pay $25,000 a year in rent. The purchase price was one of the highest in recent years for a property in Maryland's countryside. The 370-acre estate sat in the heart of the Green Spring Valley just north of Baltimore.[2] After hearing about Alfred's question, Emerson acknowledged to a *Sun* reporter that he had been building a "model dairy" with 100 cows now on the property, with more to come shortly, but that he had not bought the cows with young Alfred in mind. He did, however, allow that the milk and butter from the dairy would suit his grandson and anyone else as well.[3]

By early 1913, the Captain and Anne had moved from the Emerson Hotel to the rolling hills of Spring Valley. In his never-ending pursuit of business opportunities, Emerson soon offered "Brooklandwood Spring Water" for sale to the public by the spring of 1915. Prices ranged from a quarter for a five-gallon bottle to $1.50 for a case of 24 carbonated one-half pints.[4]

The original main house was built in about 1793 by Charles Carroll of Carrollton, the only Catholic signer of the Declaration of Independence and one of the colonies' wealthiest men, for his daughter Polly four years after her marriage to a man of modest means, Richard Caton. They used it as their "summer residence," residing full-time in a Baltimore townhouse, also a gift from Polly's father. The mansion sat on the top of a prominent hill to make the most of cool summer breezes. The estate had changed hands several times, many rooms had been added to the original structure, and a variety of outbuildings now dotted the land. The *Washington Evening Star* called the Captain's newest purchase "the finest estate in Maryland."[5]

A notable change from the urban life-style the Captain had known since coming to Baltimore 32 years earlier, the Valley was home to similar estates and offered its residents rolling, grassy hills with patches of forest. In addition to the dairy, Brooklandwood boasted an array of livestock, including cattle and horses, and all the tools and implements needed to farm the land.[6]

* * *

Isaac and Anne continued their lavish life-style with "parties that were handsome affairs honoring dignitaries and celebrities." In between parties, Emerson added a grass tennis court, a circular pool with a fountain, a five-hole golf course, a swimming pool, and the dairy. Several Rolls-Royces, a Pierce-Arrow, and two yachts provided for their transportation. A staff of servants saw to the cooking and housekeeping.[7] His neighbors owned comparable estates. One, the Wickliffe Castle, for instance, modeled after the Wickliffe Castle in England, was the home of Dr. and Mrs. Walter F. Wickes. After practicing medicine in Baltimore for several years, he moved to Chicago to become a successful stockbroker before returning to the Baltimore area. Like the Captain, Wickes entertained frequently at his estate and maintained a stable of race horses. The Castle sat on a 182-acre estate bordering Brooklandwood. The Wickliffes' home consisted of 23 rooms throughout four stories, three baths, and a four-car garage. Their grounds featured a tenant house, stables, and several outbuildings.[8]

Unique to Emerson's estate, however, was his ownership of a fire engine manned by his crew of servants, which numbered three in the kitchen, three in the pantry, several maids and chauffeurs, and a gardener. The ten-minute blast from a siren mounted on top of the mansion signaled the crew to get cracking for a practice run. The existence of the fire-fighting equipment proved fortunate when two fires erupted on the estate in October 1921. Four automobiles and two horses had to be to be moved when the first fire started in the loft of the combined garage and stable, resulting in minimal damage. The second fire destroyed a large part of the greenhouse and threatened the poultry plant.[9]

* * *

Nationwide attention was drawn to Brooklandwood in May 1913, just six months after the Captain and Anne moved in. Anne's daughter, Ethel, became engaged to Francis Huger McAdoo, the son of William Gibbs McAdoo, President Woodrow Wilson's treasury secretary. The two had known each other since childhood as both sets of parents had homes in Irvington-on-the Hudson.[10]

11—Fresh Starts

They were married on June 21, 1913, at the bride's home, Brooklandwood. The ceremony was memorable on two accounts, the first being the guest list. It was headed by President Wilson, his first wife Ellen, who died the following year, and the two Wilson daughters, Eleanor, whom William McAdoo would marry in 1914, and Jessie. Wilson was the first president to attend a Baltimore wedding since President McKinley attended the wedding of ex-Postmaster General James A. Gary's daughter, Lillian, 13 years earlier.

President Wilson and family arrived by automobile, whose chauffer lost his way near Hyattsville, Maryland, and had to repair two tire blowouts, delaying the party's arrival until just before the ceremony was to begin. Other members of Wilson's cabinet and their wives, including Secretary of State William Jennings Bryan, Secretaries of Interior, Agriculture, and Labor, Attorney General James McReynolds, and Vice President Thomas R. Marshall, also attended. At the insistence of the Secret Service, charged with protecting the president, mounted police from the Baltimore city force patrolled the grounds and stood at all entrances to the mansion, demanding to see the invitation card of each guest.[11]

A torrential downpour drenched the grounds at 4:00 p.m. just as the wedding party was starting toward the pergola, a structure of wooden columns that supported a roof of wooden beams and rafters, where the couple had planned to exchange vows. A gust of wind blew it to the ground. Seeing that an outdoor wedding was impossible, Anne quickly arranged for an indoor ceremony that went off flawlessly, followed by a buffet luncheon. Grape juice was the only beverage served at Wilson's table. The president congratulated the newlyweds and mingled with other guests before departing for the White House, but not before presenting the couple with a tall, silver vase monogrammed with Ethel's initials. Wilson, from his knowledge of Francis as a student in one of his Princeton classes, assured Anne that her new son-in-law was both dependable and ambitious. Shortly after Wilson's departure, several ushers drove the newlyweds in a car bedecked with white ribbons to the waiting *Margaret*, on which they spent the bulk of their honeymoon.[12]

* * *

The Captain continued refurbishing Brooklandwood to his liking and indulged his passions for sailing and horse racing. A month before the wedding, he and Anne attended the Kentucky Derby in style. August Belmont, Jr., a fellow member of the Santee Club, arrived at Churchill Downs in his private rail car with a "group of society people." Belmont joined Emerson and "his group of friends," including several ladies decked out in the fashionable hats seen at the annual Run for the Roses, in cheering mightily for two horses, Ten Point and Donerail. The latter, who went off at odds of 91–1, thrilled the crowd by fighting for the lead at every turn. Donerail announced his presence to racing circles by prevailing by a half length while setting a new record of 2:04 4–5 for the mile and a quarter romp.[13]

Three months after the Derby, the Captain and Anne, along with Margaret and Alfred, arrived at Narragansett aboard the *Margaret*. The Emersons and the Vanderbilts entertained guests at the end of August in Narragansett's Casino. They ate dinners in a ballroom decorated to represent the forest at Versailles. A week later, Newport's casino hosted the 17th exhibition of the Newport Horse Show. Other dignitaries, including the Grand Duke Alexander-Mikhailovich of Russia, James W. Gerard, U.S. Ambassador to Germany, and Mrs. John Jacob Astor, who had survived the sinking of the Titanic a year earlier, which took the life of her multi-millionaire husband, John Jacob Astor IV, joined the Emersons in applauding Alfred's riding performances that earned him several ribbons.[14]

Back at Brooklandwood in mid–September, the Captain set to organizing a race featuring four sloops: one each from yacht clubs in Cambridge and Annapolis, Maryland, as well as the Baltimore Yacht Club and the Corinthian Yacht Club, also in Baltimore. First prize would be a $100 silver loving cup to be presented to the winner by none other than himself. Emerson's entry, *The Eleanor*, took home the trophy. Dinner and dancing followed in the Baltimore Club's dining room.[15]

The winter months, as usual, found Isaac and Anne at Arcadia. Among the invited quests over the Christmas holidays was Secretary of the Treasury, William G. McAdoo, whose son had married the Captain's step-daughter, Ethel, just six months earlier. McAdoo was so taken with the plantation that he recommended it to President Wilson. After reading in the papers that Wilson found the weather and lack of privacy at Pass Christian, Mississippi, where he and his family were vacationing, problematic, McAdoo, in a "Dear Governor" letter, advised, "I have never visited a more charming and ideal spot. It is a real Arcadia. So if you want to break your return journey and spend a week here, Cap't Emerson says that he will be very happy to turn the place over to you."[16] Wilson stayed on in Mississippi.[17]

* * *

As 1913 turned into 1914, the Captain and Anne continued life at Brooklandwood, entertaining in their accustomed grand style, operating the dairy and spring water distribution businesses, and making plans to host steeplechase tournaments over their property.

By the summer and fall of 1914, Europe was a tinderbox with the start of World War I. America did not declare war on Germany until 1917, but the U.S. government did sell arms and munitions to Germany's enemies, including Great Britain. British ships transported the war supplies across the Atlantic, which prompted the German Embassy to issue a warning "that those sailing in the war zone on ships of Great Britain or her allies do so at their own risk." The warning appeared in newspapers the day before the British Liner, the *Lusitania*, two-thirds of whose cargo consisted of war materials, was to leave New York for Liverpool, England. Its route would take it through the war zone. Alfred Vanderbilt would be one of the ship's first-class passengers.[18]

He could have booked passage on another ship, perhaps one flying the American flag, but the Lusitania's exceptional speed, touted as sufficiently faster than German U-boats, and its first-class suites appealed to him and the other wealthy people on board. Mahogany, satinwood, and veneered walnut paneling surrounded inlaid desks, wardrobes, and dressing tables. Alfred appreciated his private, marble-walled bathroom with wash basin and toilet rimmed in gilt. A personal steward, Walter Wood, would be at his disposal for the duration of the voyage.

Alfred's mother, Alice, had seen the German warning and called her son in the early morning of May 1, asking him to cancel his trip. He received another warning, a telegram handed to him by his valet, Ronald Denyer, that read "Have it on good authority *Lusitania* is to be torpedoed. You had better cancel passage immediately." The message was mysteriously signed "Morte," the French word for death.[19] Thirty-eight-year-old Vanderbilt brushed the warnings aside as "absurd." On the morning of May 1, 1915,

Dressed to the nines with top hat, watch chain, gloves and a cane, Alfred could cut a striking figure. LC-USZ62-118342. Prints and Photographs Division, Library of Congress, Washington, D.C.

he dressed in his customary charcoal-grey suit with a pink carnation in his lapel and a tweed cap, bid farewell to Margaret, Alfred Jr. and George Washington Vanderbilt III, born September 23, 1914, and with Denyer set out for New York City's Pier 54 to board the ship.

Others prominent Americans ignored the warnings as well. Bookseller Charles Lauriat, who survived the *Lusitania*'s sinking, said later, "Like many other passengers I gave the notice no serious thought." Another survivor, theatric scenic designer Oliver Bernard, said he was "not seriously perturbed" by the German warning. He saw it as a gesture meant "to embarrass the United States Government and create further consternation in England."[20]

While at sea, Wood handed Alfred a telegram from a British woman, Mary Barwell, that read, "Hope you have a safe crossing. Look forward very much to seeing you soon." Some fellow passengers, hearing of the telegram, wondered if Barwell was the latest of Alfred's mistresses. "Everyone," historians Greg King and Penny Wilson write, "knew that few women resisted his charms—and he, theirs."[21] The two never got together.

At 2:10 p.m. on May 7, as she was sailing just off the coast of Ireland near Queenstown, one of the ship's lookouts, Leslie Morton, shouted thorough his megaphone, "Torpedoes coming!" Eighteen minutes after the first

An artist's illustration of the German torpedo striking the *Lusitania*'s hull. LC-USZ62-21728. Prints and Photographs Division, Library of Congress, Washington, D.C.

torpedo slammed into the "Queen of the Ocean," as she was known at the time, on the starboard side, she was seen no more.[22] Of the 1,959 souls on board, 1,198 lost their lives, including Alfred. His body was never found, despite Margaret hiring tugboats and divers for two weeks to search the waters where the ship went down. A reward offered by Walter Webb-Ware for its recovery went unclaimed. (The amount of the reward was variously reported at the time to be 400 pounds, or $1,000 and $5,000.) In efforts to motivate fishermen to recover bodies in the area of the ship's sinking, the Cunard Line, which had built the ill-fated luxury liner, offered a reward of $5 for the recovery of every body, while the American consulate offered a $10 reward for each American body recovered.[23]

Alfred, who could not swim, met his impending doom with sacrifice and aplomb. Oliver Bernard recalled Alfred saying with his characteristic grin as the ship was listing, "Well, they got us this time." Bernard saw Alfred give up his life belt to a woman, 25-year-old, second-class passenger Alice Middleton, load children into life boats, and tie life jackets to babies floating out of the ship's nursery, until he too was swallowed up by the sea.[24]

Bernard also reported seeing a large purple leather jewel case that Alfred held in his right hand. He speculated that it may have belonged to Lady Mackworth, a member of the Thomas party whose members Alfred had spent time with during the voyage. "Perhaps," Bernard said, "he had volunteered to save her gems."[25] Alfred's grandson, Alfred G. Vanderbilt, III. in a 1999 article for *Forbes Magazine*, reports that his research found that his grandfather held a similar case, but that the case contained the jewels that he bought at the auction of Mary Ruiz's property. If the grandson's account is true, it raises interesting questions of why Alfred had the jewels with him and what he planned to do with them in England.[26]

While the contents and owner of the jewel case may never be known for sure, the manner in which Alfred met his death was considered heroic by many. Typical of the plaudits accorded Alfred and printed in papers across the country was the one by fellow passenger Mrs. Stanley Lines of Toronto, Canada. "People." she said, "will not talk of Mr. Vanderbilt in the future as a millionaire sportsman and a man of pleasure. He will be remembered as the children's hero and men and women will salute his name."[27]

Not all were as effusive in their praise for Alfred. The *Chicago Daily Tribune* editorialized that his death "closes one of the most conspicuous careers of folly, pleasure, scandal, and divorce that ever came out of the rich set of New York and Newport society."[28]

Upon hearing the tragic news, Isaac joined Margaret in New York. Alfred's sister, Mrs. Harry Payne Whitney, and his brother Reginald said, after a short visit with Margaret, that "she was bearing up bravely."[29] After the Captain concluded that the lack of news could only mean that Alfred was lost, he asked the manager of the Vanderbilt Hotel to lower its flag in mourning. Margaret, however, continued to hold out hope. "I will not believe Alfred is dead until I see the body," she insisted. "I have a feeling," she continued, "that he has been picked up, perhaps unconscious and unable to give an account of himself and that his identity will be made known in a short time."[30] Her hopes were boosted momentarily when an article in the Philipsburg, Pennsylvania, paper *The Daily Journal* reported that an English paper, *The Daily Mail*, reported that his body had been found on the English Coast and was on its way to Queenstown.[31] The report proved false. Making no mention of the *Lusitania*, the Vanderbilt family finally announced on May 21 that Alfred had died at sea on May 7.[32] Margaret took some comfort from the reports that Alfred had died a hero's death.[33]

* * *

Alfred's death meant changes for Margaret. His first wife Elsie, though divorced, had been restored to the full enjoyment of the highest social position she enjoyed while married to him and "became the dominant personage in the house of Vanderbilt of the younger generation." Elsie's ascension meant a considerable diminishment of Margaret's social standing. Extensive social campaigns underway by the widow in New York and England had to be abandoned.[34] Alfred's will, however, made Margaret a wealthy woman. She received $8 million, $3 million in cash and a $5 million trust fund, the interest and dividends from which she received for the rest of her life. She also inherited most of his real estate, including the 1,526-acre Sagamore Lodge, where he had gone to relax while his first marriage was deteriorating and where he had returned to share memorable times with Margaret, the 1,030-acre Camp "Kill-Kare," and his 2,000-acre tract known as "Moose River Tract." The one property she did not inherit, but which she wished she had, was Oakland Farm in Portsmouth, Rhode Island. Alfred considered Oakland Farm his primary residence. That went to his first son, William.[35] Margaret made a last and nostalgic visit to the farm in September, gathering up her belongings, saying farewells to the staff, and recalling the many good times she shared with Alfred and others there.[36]

She then took her sons Alfred and George to Arcadia to be with her father and childhood friend and now step-mother, Anne McCormack Preston Emerson. There the Captain bestowed on her yet another gift, a piece of land on which, with the help of William Parker, who had overseen construction of the Emerson Hotel and the Bromo-Seltzer Tower, she planned to build a $100,000, 30-room "bungalow" which the local paper predicted "would be perhaps the finest private residence in the State." The house, she expected, would allow her to remain close to her father during his winter sojourns to Arcadia while providing her boys with a warm winter climate where they could learn the skills of sportsmanship so prized by their father.[37]

* * *

Sportsmanship was a theme prized by the Emerson clan. Both the Captain and Margaret took to yachting, hunting, automobile and horse racing. So it came as no surprise that the Bromo-Seltzer King's next donation to his alma mater would be an athletic stadium and field. The current venue was rocky, uneven, and lacked any drainage, limiting play to exhibition games and contests with small nearby colleges. Games with major rivals, such as the University of Virginia, could never be played at home. Emerson changed that with a gift to UNC-CH of $40,000 in the fall of 1915 to build a modern facility. Modeled after Homewood Field at Baltimore's Johns Hopkins University, Emerson Field, "smooth and level as a floor," had room for a football gridiron, baseball diamond, and running track deep enough in cinders to be used year-round. Fifty-two hundred spectators could view the action from newly-built stands. The clubhouse had adequate space for both the home and visiting team to change and shower in marble lined bathrooms. Emerson bought and shipped to Chapel Hill 1,500 Amur River Privets, a green shrub, to surround the concrete stadium wall, "to prevent the field from looking like the yard of a state prison or reformatory."[38]

The first UNC-CH conference game ever played in Chapel Hill, a baseball game against arch-rival University of Virginia, christened the Emerson Athletic Field on Monday, April 3, 1916, before more than 5,000 people, many of whom arrived on special trains from "various sections of the Old North State."[39] Emerson, though invited and eagerly awaited by many, sent a letter of regret from Arcadia, saying family business prevented him from attending.[40] In response to an earlier letter to him from university officials who effusively thanked and praised him for his donation, Emerson, after noting he was about to leave for Europe, offered a hurried acknowledgment in his customary low-key manner.

> I trust that my efforts to provide a suitable athletic field for the students at the University to which I am directly indebted for what little I have been able to accomplish, will be a more fitting reply than any words which are now at my command. With assurances of my highest person esteem, and unfaltering interest in the dear old university, believe me, Faithfully yours.[41]

12

Building, Divorcing and Marrying

At age 58 in 1916, Isaac Emerson showed no signs of slowing down. The idea of retirement never entered his mind. In addition to helping Margaret through the pain of Alfred's death, starting the process of building a house for her and the boys at Arcadia, all the while settling into his new home at Brooklandwood, he had embarked on another major construction project: an eight-story apartment house, The Emersonian.

In keeping with his taste for the luxurious, the complex, again designed by Sperry and supervised by Parker, consisted of 28 3,260-square-foot units. Each featured four bedrooms and three baths, Greek-inspired columns, a carved marble fireplace mantel and wood paneling in the living room, a spacious kitchen, rooms for two maids with a bath in between, a trunk room, a storage room, a linen room, and 12-foot-high ceilings painted with the seal of Baltimore. Tenants would find a physician's office on the ground floor.[1] Also on the ground floor would be a 2,500-square-foot drug store with two entrances. In case of fire, an unlikely occurrence given that the construction was done with all fireproof materials, an opening to a spiral fire escape, into which tenants would sit and glide to the ground, was installed in each unit.[2]

Emerson believed he could find 28 families in Baltimore who would appreciate quarters that emulated the finest in suburban living, something, he said, "a little different and be willing to pay for it." As usual, he was right in such business judgments. Nine units were taken before a single spade had broken ground. Eighteen were spoken for before the complex was half completed.[3]

The Emersonian was one of five luxury apartment buildings in the Druid Park area. Others included the Riviera, the Esplanade, the Marlborough, and Temple Gardens. Each attracted a German-Jewish clientele, many of whom had built successful businesses in East Baltimore and "migrated" to the Eutaw Place-Druid Park area.[4] Buyers of Emersonian units

12—Building, Divorcing and Marrying 125

included Louis Blaustein, founder of the American Oil Company, and department store magnate Max Hochschild. Joseph Castleberg, a Baltimore jeweler, claimed the Emersonian's penthouse for a ten-year lease at $6,000 a year, which would help defray the building cost of about $250,000.[5]

Castleberg, unfortunately, would not live to see the end of his lease. He died in an elevator accident in the building in 1921. The 17-year-old African American operator, Dorothy Vogel, was cleared of any charges in the accident after the police determined that Castleberg had tried to enter the elevator after it started moving. Vogel was fined $51.45 for operating an elevator without experience. Emerson paid her fine and a weekly salary until she found another job that didn't involve an elevator.[6]

Emerson built his apartment house on the land that once held his famed Italian garden next door at 2500 Eutaw Place. Before construction began, he moved all plants and sculptures to his Brooklandwood estate. The apartment building's location, the back wall of which was a mere six feet from his former mansion and blocked the glorious view of Druid Park Lake, gave rise to an urban legend. The story goes that he built the apartments to spite his ex-wife by "effectively blocking Mrs. Emerson's precious view of the lake and leaving her to stare out her window at cold brick walls six feet away." The location, the story continues, also allowed Isaac and Anne literally to look down on Emilie.[7] As we have seen, however, by 1916 Emilie was single, her second husband had died, and Emilie had moved away from Baltimore. Isaac and Anne now resided in Brooklandwood. If anyone was to be looked down on from the heights of The Emersonian, it would have been Henry J. Matthews, who bought the Eutaw Place mansion from Emilie.

Construction of the Emersonian coincided with another of the Captain's projects, the building of Margaret's "cottage" at Arcadia. The day after work began on digging a canal from the Waccamaw River to Margaret's home site, a report in the *Greenville News* noted, "This is good news to Georgetown. It means the circulation of large sums of money locally." Acknowledging that the agricultural culture of the lowcountry was now a thing of the past, the report continued, "This economically is the best disposition to make of them [the aging plantations]. The expenditures of such places are greater than could be realized by planting the lands."[8]

For some, managing two construction projects while maintaining an active social life would be fulfilling as their golden years approached. Not quite for the Captain. By 1918, the Bromo-Seltzer legend had established a herd of Guernsey cattle which he took great pride in showing. At the 1918 Timonium Fair, held in Timonium, Maryland, not far from his Brooklandville estate, the new breeder's bull, Brooklyn Wood Warrior, who took his name from the Captain's dairy, Brooklyn Wood Dairy, and known as one of the show places in the fashionable Green Spring Valley, won the blue ribbon for his classification.

Encouraged by that showing, Emerson took his entire herd to Shreveport, Louisiana, in the fall of 1920 to show them at the annual National Jersey Cattle Show. His competition included those of other millionaires such as lumber baron R. A. Long of Kansas City, C. I. Hood of Hood's Sarsaparilla Company in Lowell, Massachusetts, Ed C. Laseter of Falfurrias, Texas, Minstrel Al G. Fields, "and others of note." The herd also provided the buttermilk, milk, cream, and ice cream for Emerson's dairy. Most of the output went to the Hotel Emerson's kitchens, but the amount made available to the public lured many Baltimorean families out for a Sunday drive in the country to stop by Brooklandwood.

All was going well with the Captain's various projects at Brooklandwood until, in what could have been a disastrous setback to his herd and dairy, an outbreak of anthrax in July of 1922 was successfully contained. One of the Captain's cows had died from the poison, prompting local health officials to inoculate the entire the herd and close down the dairy until no further traces of the poison were found.[9]

* * *

By now the Hotel Emerson was well established. The demand for space had become so great that by 1922 the Captain embarked on yet another building project. He added a new ballroom and a banquet hall. On the land adjoining the hotel on East Baltimore Street, he built a two-story addition measuring 40 by 103 feet, with a seating capacity of 500 people, making it one of the largest hotel banquet rooms in the city. Civic organizations such as the Civitans and Kiwanis held their weekly luncheons in the new banquet room. As was by now common practice for all of Emerson's construction projects, be they for business or pleasure, Sperry drew up the plans and Parker managed the operation.[10]

Emerson's hotel was in the news again in 1924. Knowing that the Army-Navy football game would be coming to town on November 29 and that existing hotel space would not accommodate all of the thousands of out-of-town spectators, the Captain hastened to add a 12-story annex to his hotel. The fast pace of the construction to have the addition ready by game time resulted in building code violations in August, the corrections of which slowed progress.[11] As the building neared completion, complaints of gouging reached Mayor Howard W. Jackson in mid–October that the Emerson, and only the Emerson, had raised its rates—$10 for a double room with bath in place of the advertised $6.50—and that advance payment was now required. The hotel's manager, William Parker, defended his decisions, saying the room rates were "capacity rates" and that there was no limit on the number of people allowed in a room. Payment in advance was necessary because, he said, "we know many making reservations won't attend."[12] Mayor Jackson settled the matter in early November of 1924 by saying no exorbitant rates would be charged by any hotel. He did not comment on the Emerson's advance payment requirement.[13] Army prevailed, 12–0, at Municipal Stadium in front of 80,000 spectators including President Calvin Coolidge.[14]

* * *

With her father engaged in his projects, Margaret returned to living the life of the wealthy and socially connected. Her "cottage" was built, but little money flowed locally from it as the *Greenville News* had predicted. Nor did she spend much time at Arcadia. A friend introduced her to a resort community, Lenox, Massachusetts, in the Berkshires. Adjacent to Stockbridge in western Massachusetts, Lenox was a gathering spot for the well-to-do, who built expansive houses designed by famous architects including William Adams and Chester Holmes, who drew up the plans for Margaret's house. Known as "society architects," their reputations were made by designing "sumptuous city clubs, classical town houses, and tasteful country houses."[15] Her neighbors included the novelist Edith Wharton, whose estate, The Mount, bordered hers, and industrialist George Westinghouse. From his son, George Jr., she bought a house that sat on 300 acres with a mile-long shore front on Laurel Lake, razed it, and built a mansion she called Holmwood, no doubt named after an area of the same name in England where Alfred had raced his horses and coaches. The property featured ornate stone bridges spanning lagoons, winding drives flanked by tall pines, stables for 20 horse-drawn vehicles, previously owned by Alfred, and a gymnasium. She also constructed a roadside memorial to him.[16]

As comfortable as her Lenox surroundings were, Margaret would spend only a few weeks there during the summer where she, nevertheless, maintained an active social schedule. Among her annual entertainment venues at Holmwood was a symphonic festival performed by the Boston Symphony Orchestra and conducted by Serge Koussevitzky. In August of 1936, President Franklin D. Roosevelt's mother, Sara Delano Roosevelt, the United States Ambassador at Large, Norman Davis and his wife Mackie, and President Calvin Coolidge's widow, Grace, headed the guest list.[17]

It was at Holmwood that she reconnected with Raymond Baker, who had lovingly seen her off to the Far East after representing her in her Reno divorce from Smith Hollins McKim. On June 12, 1918, she married Baker, recently appointed Director of the United States Mint by President Wilson. Previously Baker had been a mining engineer, the warden of the Nevada State Prison, and a bank president in Reno. Nevada U.S. Democratic

A sportily dressed Raymond T. Baker (left) talking with Virginia's Democratic Senator Claude A. Swanson in 1919, a year after he and Margaret were married. LC-DIG-Lec-12193, Prints and Photographs Division, Library of Congress, Washington, D.C.

12—Building, Divorcing and Marrying 129

Senator Key Pittman served as his best man. Her father gave Margaret away for the third time. A small but prominent group, including a number of Vanderbilts, Maryland Senator James D. Phelan, Rear Admiral Cary T. Grayson, and secretary to President Wilson, Joseph P. Tumulty, attended the ceremony. The president, who had been invited but did not attend, sent a book of his writings as a gift to Baker.

Baker gave his bride a gift of Liberty Bonds, the proceeds from which went to support the Allied Troops. The bonds were loans to the government by citizens to be repaid to the buyer with interest. Purchasing Liberty Bonds was seen as a patriotic act. After leaving the reception in her limousine for a Camp Sagamore honeymoon, the couple traveled west through Denver and San Francisco, where Baker inspected the government mints. They made their home in Washington, D.C. Isaac and Anne returned to Brooklandwood.[18]

Margaret soon found Washington's social protocol stifling. By one account, she would be obliged to make 300 calls on people in the nation's capital "in whom she had not the slightest interest, and whom, upon the whole, she preferred not to know." Her solution was to travel extensively in the West, where "she could put the breadth of the continent between her and Washington."[19] The breadth of the continent also kept her separated from Baker.

* * *

Another socially notable marriage of a family member took the Captain and Anne to Asheville, North Carolina, for the wedding of Anne's son, Frederick Clarke McCormack, to wealthy Virginia socialite Virginia Ritchie Harrison from Brandon-on-the-James. Parts of her family home, which fronted the James River, were reputed to have been designed by Thomas Jefferson. McCormack, who had been living with the Emersons at Brooklandwood, was in his last semester at Princeton University. The *Washington Herald* described the ceremony, held on December 12, 1919, to its readers as being "an out-of-town wedding of interest to society in the National Capitol, Maryland, and Virginia."[20]

Also of interest was the Captain's gift to his step-son. In his tradition of bestowing large real estate gifts on family members, he conveyed the Emersonian Apartments, estimated to be worth several hundred thousand dollars, to Frederick. The newlyweds honeymooned at Arcadia before returning to Brooklandwood, where the Captain's largesse continued. Using Virginia's childhood home as a model, he built a three-story brick structure containing 50 rooms near Brooklandwood, that he named Brandonwood, for the McCormacks to call home.[21]

* * *

Ever since arriving at Brooklandwood, the Bromo-Seltzer King used his wealth to gain entrance into the Green Spring Valley society. Just the purchase of the property in itself was not a guarantee of acceptance. Never shy about displaying his wealth, high-priced cars, notably Rolls Royces, a 12-cylinder Packard, and a Pierce-Arrow graced his stable. Two chauffeurs drove the Emersons to church every Sunday in the largest Rolls. He and Anne entertained lavishly. Large tents with wooden floors allowed for dancing during the innumerable parties they hosted. Japanese lanterns lit the grounds. Guests seated at small tables feasted on buffet suppers.[22] Valet parking was provided for those who arrived without chauffeurs.

Bill Tilden, considered one of the tennis greats of all time, played an occasional match on the court the Captain had installed. Gene Sarazen, one of the world's top golfers in the 1920s and 1930s, was no stranger to the five-hole golf course at Brooklandwood. As he had done years earlier at his Eutaw Place mansion, Emerson and the current Mrs. Emerson, on December 10, 1927, invited guests to an indoor musicale with professional artists including Miss Dorothy Speare, a soprano with the Washington Opera Company. She was accompanied by Mrs. Mary Muller Fink, a harpist, and the pianist, Sol Sax. Entertainment moved outdoors in warm weather.[23]

To insure enough Scotch would be available for his guests, the Captain had the foresight to import 30 barrels of the libation from Europe before Prohibition became law in 1920.[24] He had gone on record opposing prohibition while the amendment was making the rounds of the states. "It would," he said during a 1918 dinner at the Willard Hotel in Washington, D.C., "injure business and put a check on the growth and activities of the city, in my opinion."[25] Prohibition would also, he no doubt realized, put a damper on the Washington galas he enjoyed. He was a regular at dinners given by the Gridiron Club, such as the one in 1917 as one of 300 invited guests, including President Wilson, members of his cabinet, "and others," as the *Sun* observed, "prominent in government and business life of the nation."[26]

Another example of the Bromo-Seltzer King mingling with the well-connected was the opening of the grand opera festival of the Washington (D.C.)'s Opera Company on December 5, 1927. A golden horseshoe exemplifying "the wealth and power of the country" greeted audience members as the opening curtain rose. Headliners included Luella Mellus, an American prima donna, Dorothy Speare, whom Emerson would engage to sing at Brooklandwood a few days later, and who had just completed a successful operatic tour of Italy, and Maurice Capitaine of France.

Ambassadors, wives of cabinet members, senators, and representatives; four children of U.S. presidents; and editors from leading maga-

12—Building, Divorcing and Marrying

zines such as *Collier's Weekly* and the *Saturday Evening Review* attended. "Other parties," the *Washington Post* reported the day before the event, "are due to arrive in private cars." Two of the parties were "Isaac Emerson of Baltimore" and "Mrs. Ray Baker of New York."[27]

* * *

Not all Americans were living a life of ease and luxury during the last years of the 20th century's second decade. The twin tragedies of a worldwide influenza epidemic and World War I brought suffering and death to millions. Margaret took time out from building Holmwood to volunteer with the Red Cross in several ways. She served in the Red Cross's canteen corps at the embarkation center in New York. There she worked to bolster the spirits of American doughboys on their way to Europe. She found a way to combine socializing with supporting the Red Cross by attending a masquerade ball in Philadelphia in 1918. All money raised was donated to the Red Cross. Others in attendance included Alfred's first wife, Elsie French Vanderbilt, and Margaret's father and step-mother. Perhaps a hatchet of sorts had been buried.[28]

* * *

The war turned Isaac's attention to the navy once more. He gave Alfred's luxurious steam yacht, the *Adroit*, which he purchased from his son-in-law's estate, to the government on the condition that it be used only to patrol Maryland waters. The navy readily agreed and sent the yacht to one of its shipyards to be fitted out with guns. Unlike his service as commander of the Maryland National Militia during the Spanish-American War, Isaac took no active role, but two of his son-in-laws did. Francis McAdoo and Frederick McCormack both served as officers aboard the *Adroit*.[29] The Captain also dispatched his beloved yacht *Margaret* to the navy in return for $104,000 in October 1917. Instead of simply pocketing the money, the Bromo-Seltzer magnate put almost all of it into Liberty Bonds. Emerson's purchases led the *Sun* to praise him in the fall of 1918, saying, "In the parlance of the populace, let it be recorded that Captain Isaac E. Emerson, in addition to being one of the foremost citizens of Baltimore, is 'one real sport.'"[30]

The *Margaret* joined a fleet of similar civilian craft to confront German's newest military threat, submarines. The navy had only destroyers, which took a long time to build, with which to fight the new menace. As a supplemental measure, the navy reconfigured about a thousand existing boats of various types: yachts like the *Margaret*, tug boats, river steamers, tankers, and freighters. They could be quickly modified and armed. Some, but not all were up to the fight ahead. Of the crafts donated to the navy, author Prosper Buranelliu wrote, "Scores were not fit to make a sea voyage, let alone engage in any warfare. They limped, broke, and covered themselves, some with glory, others with pathetic ridicule."[31]

The *Margaret* fell into the latter category. Captained by 32-year-old Lieutenant Frank Jack Fletcher, a Naval Academy graduate and Medal of Honor recipient during the United States occupation of Vera Cruz, Mexico in 1914, and crewed by 61 men with little to no experience at sea, the reconfigured *Margaret*, whose top speed was slower than that of her supposed prey, met an inglorious end. On her first day at sea in the Atlantic Ocean, 59 of the 61-member crew got seasick and could barely keep her on course. The backrush from her guns on the first test firing caused damage to the ship and flooded the enlisted men's sleeping quarters. After three days at sea, the engine ceased to work. She had to be towed into port. After repairs, Fletcher and crew sailed forth once more, only to run out of coal and be towed into port once again.

Other reconditioned yachts in the *Margaret's* armada encountered similar setbacks, earning them the moniker "the Suicide Fleet." A German submarine commander delivered the final insult when he said he had sighted the *Margaret* but held his fire because she wasn't worth a torpedo. The Captain's former pleasure craft eventually made it to the Azores Islands, where she was tied up at a mooring buoy in the harbor of Ponta Delgada. Instead of fighting German subs, she became the venereal station where doctors diagnosed and treated sailors for gonorrhea and syphilis. After the Armistice, she was towed back to the States in 1920, bought by an Italian firm for scrap, and towed back across the Atlantic to meet her final fate in Genoa.[32]

Fletcher's fortunes, on the other hand, would improve dramatically with the start of World War II. He commanded the destroyer *USS Benham* at the start of the war, a considerable step up from the *Margaret*. From 1942–1945, he commanded U.S. Naval Forces in the North Pacific.[33] One of the *Margaret's* crew members, Raymond Davis Borden, kept a detailed log of the yacht's wartime escapades that resulted in his humorous book, *Maggie of the Suicide Fleet*.[34]

* * *

Three years after "The War to End All Wars," ended with the signing of the Versailles Treaty in Paris in 1919, rumors of a split between Ray and Margaret began to be heard. They were fanned by Margaret's 1922 trip to France. Upon her return in May, after a three-month stay with sons Alfred and George and daughter Gloria Baker now two years old, she insisted that she went for health reasons and not to establish residency in Paris for divorce. She told reporters, "If a woman happens to go to Paris without

12—Building, Divorcing and Marrying 133

her husband it's as bad as taking up a residence in Reno."[35] Her husband backed her up at the time of her departure for France. Baker said then there was no truth to the separation rumors and that she'd normally go to Palm Beach, Florida "this time of year (January)," but being in mourning over the death of her mother, "she had decided to go to a quiet place in the south of France."[36] The Captain met her at the pier in New York on her return in May and accompanied her to his estate in Brooklandville. Alfred and George travelled on to Newport to stay with relatives, while Gloria visited cousins in San Francisco. Baker stayed in Washington.[37]

Whatever Margaret's reasons for visiting Paris, speculation about her motives was not unfounded. From 1920–1927, American couples could obtain a divorce in Paris more easily, with less publicity, and more joie de vivre than a Reno divorce entailed. Unlike Reno's six-month residency requirement, Paris courts had a residency requirement but did not specify a time period. The proceedings were kept secret. The press could not attend the hearings. Witnesses were rarely called. Documents were sealed. A couple, after one of them had lived in the City of Lights for a period of time, merely had to tell a judge that reconciliation was impossible. Grounds for divorce in Paris could include drunkenness and nagging, especially if the nagging was done in public.

Historian Nancy Green noted that Paris gave Reno a run for its money "with its gay lights, sleek gigolos, its secret courts, and its discreet lawyers." American state courts recognized Paris divorces as long as the reasons were compatible with those required in a state court. As a result, many Paris divorces used adultery, whether true or not, as the reason. A Paris divorce was an option only for the wealthy. The cost could run as high as $10,000, considering transportation, housing, living expenses, and payments, some above board and some below, to lawyers, judges, and document preparers.[38]

Margaret's mother, Emilie A. Basshor, had died of heart problems in August of 1921 in Atlantic City, New Jersey, four months before Margaret sailed for France. Margaret took her mother's body to Lenox for a funeral service conducted at Trinity Church. She was buried in the Church on the Hill Cemetery in Lenox. Her gravestone reads, "Peace, Perfect Peace."[39]

To the extent a mother's relative affection for her children can be judged by what she leaves them in her will, it appears that Emilie favored her biological daughters, Lillie and Daisy, over Margaret. After naming Daisy—Mrs. James McVickar—the principal beneficiary of her $90,000 estate and leaving $10,000 to Lillie—Mrs. W. W. White—and her Atlantic City property to her chauffer, Richard Armstrong, she left a portion of her silverware to Margaret.[40]

* * *

Two years later, during July of 1923, with Baker still in Washington, Alfred and brother George arrived at Newport from Narragansett Pier with their grandfather aboard his boat, the *Adroit*, which the navy had returned to him minus the armaments of war. Margaret departed Holmwood with Gloria for Newport to join them. All would spend a week as guests of Alfred's mother at her Newport "cottage," The Breakers.[41] It still stands as a symbol of the Vanderbilts' enormous wealth and social standing at the time. The Breakers, with its 70 rooms, furnishings, and decorations, was modeled after the 16th-century palaces of Genoa and Turin, Italy.[42]

Margaret and Baker remained married, if more in name than in reality, for another five years before they called it quits officially. Margaret received her second divorce decree in Reno, Nevada, this one from the man who had represented her in her first divorce proceedings there. The latest divorce, on October 2, 1928, did not surprise friends. Baker, no lon-

Margaret and her fourth husband, Charles M. Amory, watching the races at Pimlico Race Course in Laurel, Maryland, shortly after their marriage in New York City. Author's collection.

ger director of the Mint, a position he left in 1922, had returned to Reno and a bank presidency. The *Chicago Daily Tribune* reported that Margaret was too busy with her horses, an interest first encouraged by Alfred and recently taken seriously by her, to bother about a divorce except when she took part in the Palm Beach, Florida social season. There, Nancy Randolph, society editor for the *Chicago Daily Tribune* commented, "one simply gasps at the magnificence of her jewels."

Rumors had surfaced shortly after their 1919 wedding that frictions existed between the two. She, the stories went, wanted Baker to give up politics, pursue a business career, and attend social affairs. He preferred politics. In 1926, Baker would run unsuccessfully against Nevada's incumbent Republican U.S. Senator, Tasker L. Oddie. At the same time, he developed a relationship with Dodge automobile heiress Delphine Dodge Cromwell, daughter of Horace E. Dodge who, with older brother John, founded the Dodge Motor Company. Desertion was given as the grounds for the divorce.[43]

From Reno she went for a visit to San Francisco, where she declared her decision never to marry again. "I am not thinking of marrying," she said on October 8, "and besides three marriages are enough.... I intend to devote my life to my children." She wanted to rebut the whispering that had her engaged to Charles Minor Amory, whom she referred to as "a dear friend of mine and a fine man."[44]

Her vow to remain single lasted the better part of three weeks. Even though Margaret and Baker were just months from divorcing in June of 1928, they hosted a dinner party in Lenox at Margaret's Holmwood estate. Charles Amory joined five other dinner guests there.[45] A Harvard graduate, Amory, six years Margaret's junior, had a membership in two Boston Hunt Clubs and several sporting clubs in New York. His first marriage had ended in a Paris divorce. He and Margaret had seen a lot of each other before the dinner. As Randolph reported, "For several winters one thought of Margaret and Charlie as inseparable. Wherever Margaret went in Palm Beach, there Charlie was to be found, her faithful companion."[46]

They tied the knot on October 24, 1928, just three weeks after her divorce from Baker, at Charlie's sister's house in New York City. This time Margaret walked herself down the aisle, wearing "a simple black velvet afternoon gown and a small black velvet turban." There was no wedding party. Following a short honeymoon and residence in New York's Ambassador Hotel, they opened a villa for the upcoming Palm Beach social season.[47] The two would remain inseparable, at least for awhile.

Six weeks later, Baker and Cromwell, who had obtained a Reno divorce on the grounds of cruelty from New York banker James H. R. Cromwell on September 28, 1928, exchanged vows on December 4, 1928, at the Ambassador Hotel, from which Charles and Margaret had recently left.[48]

* * *

While the Bakers were divorcing and remarrying, another Emerson family divorce and marriage were in the works. Ethel McCormack McAdoo, Anne Emerson's daughter and the divorced wife of Francis McAdoo, whom she had married in front of President Wilson and members of his cabinet in 1913, married a second time at Brooklandwood on April 25, 1929. She had been granted a divorce decree from McAdoo by a tribunal in Paris in 1923 after ten years of marriage. To meet French residency requirements, she leased an apartment for several months but never set foot in it. The couple attended two required reconciliation sessions which lasted a total of eight minutes, during which Francis refused to discuss the matter.

Ethel's new husband, Walter Winchester Keith, was a familiar figure in Brooklandville. He was well known in hunting and social circles as a member of the Green Spring Valley Hunt Club. He fought with the British Royal Flying Corps in World War I. He had obtained a divorce from his first wife just five months before the wedding. Captain Emerson walked Ethel down the aisle a second time as family and friends from Baltimore, New York, New Orleans and Illinois looked on.[49]

13

New Projects

In the midst of the family marital events, the Bromo-Seltzer King took up a keen interest in the sport of kings. Mint julep in hand, he watched the horses run at nearby Pimlico Race Course in Laurel, Maryland. He played every race, usually betting a horse to show. After the last race, he would settle his bill and divide his winnings; he usually came out ahead, with his two attendants, a chauffeur and a footman.[1]

In 1923, he introduced his ten-year-old grandson, Alfred Gwynne Vanderbilt, Jr., to the horses by taking him to Pimlico to see the Preakness, the second jewel of racing's Triple Crown, on May 12. Some years later Alfred, who would go on to make a name for himself in the sport, remembered that he bet on Tall Timber "because I liked the name."[2] Tall Timber started strong but finished in fifth place.[3]

Emerson further indulged his equine interest by opening his grounds to drag hunts and steeplechases. Similar to a fox hunt, where horse-mounted riders follow hounds chasing a fox, drag hunts feature riders behind a pack of hounds who have been trained to follow a trail of aniseed, a flavoring used in liquors, or another strong smelling substance, spread over a distance of three miles. Like a steeplechase, drag hunt riders' horses must jump fences and occasional water hazards along the route. The Green Spring Valley Hunt Club sponsored the drag races for groups of about 20 riders. Spills were not uncommon, but injuries to riders were rare.[4]

Anne's son, Frederick McCormack, and his wife, Virginia, now lived on the estate in the house built for them by the Captain. In 1925, the two men hosted the 24th running of the Grand National Point-to-Point steeplechase race, in April. The event attracted out-of-town spectators. The following year they hosted the same race but, with their wives, preceded it with a luncheon for invited guests.[5] Before 7,500 spectators, 25 steeds, thought to be the largest "timber jumping" field in Maryland to date, set an unusually fast pace that caused the death of one horse and serious injury to its rider.[6]

The Emerson turf saw the same race again in April of 1928. By now the race, first run in obscurity in 1899 as a pony race for the lads of Green Spring Valley, had grown in stature to be one of the premier steeplechase races in the East. As testament to its exalted status among equestrian aficionados, 2,000 drenched spectators braved a relentless downpour for the six minute and 39 second 1928 race.[7] On a drier April day in 1930, 10,000 spectators arrived at Brooklandwood to witness 11 riders again guide their mounts over the 16 "stiff as iron" post and rail fences that dotted the three-mile course.[8] While most spectators were from the Baltimore area, many came from New York, Philadelphia, Boston, Wilmington, Washington, D.C., and Virginia. The younger set was well represented. Many pretty girls and young men were reported emerging from sports roadsters and limousines in high spirits.[9]

During the same time, Emerson dabbled in Democratic Party politics. Five days before the running of the 1926 National Point-to-Point, Emerson arranged a formal reception on April 12 at Brooklandwood for Virginia's 39-year-old Governor, Harry Flood Byrd. Byrd came to Baltimore to address the Southern Maryland Society. Army troops escorted Byrd and his party of 25 Virginia officials from their arrival at Mount Royal Railroad Station to the Southern Hotel. There he addressed 600 members and guests of the Society by giving a detailed account of Virginia's suffering during the Civil War and the Commonwealth's concerted and successful efforts toward recovery since. He ended his speech by endorsing the importance of state rights. He touched on "the menace of Federal encroachment," asserting that "local self-government remains a right to be guarded jealously." Byrd would go on to national prominence as a conservative U.S. senator staunchly opposed to integration.

Following his speech, mounted police and reservists escorted Byrd's party through crowds of spectators lining the streets of Baltimore to the Maryland Club, where Maryland Governor Albert Ritchie welcomed the entourage with warm words and refreshments. From there, state and city motorcycle police led Byrd and his party to Brooklandwood, where mounted troops guarded the approach to Emerson's estate. A 17-gun salute and a flag-raising while five National Guard airplanes circled overhead completed the welcoming activities. Remarks by the governor and a lavish dinner followed.[10]

* * *

Four months after Byrd's visit to Brooklandwood, Margaret struck paydirt at the 1926 Hopeful Stakes in August at Saratoga Springs, New York. With the state's governor, Al Smith, and his wife, Catherine, in the stands, Margaret's two-year-old Lord Chaucer, who went off at 40–1 odds, carried her stable's white blocked and cerise (a deep, reddish-pink color) silks, colors not dissimilar to those Alfred had used on his coaches, to victory. She claimed $48,850 in prize money.[11] "Baltimore's leading sportswoman," as the *Sun* referred to her, had earlier seen her Rock Man take the show position in the May 1926 Run for the Roses at Churchill Downs.

Her ever-indulgent father liked what he was seeing. Several months after her Saratoga win, he presented her with the Russ Farm, 250 acres in Worthington Valley about 15 miles northwest of Baltimore and not far from Brooklandwood. There she would establish a breeding farm, racing stables for 60 horses, and a one-mile outdoor track with all the equipment and personnel required to sustain the operation.[12] She named the land Sagamore Farm after the camp by the same name she and Alfred used as a retreat for themselves and guests in the Adirondacks. Shortly after conveying the property, Isaac build a quarter-mile covered track so her horses could train at full speed despite the winter weather, thereby getting a training jump on less-protected mounts before the start of the spring racing season. Along with the land and the track, her generous father gave Margaret his stable of thoroughbreds.[13]

By April of 1928, 29 thoroughbreds were trained and stabled at Sagamore Farm. One of them, Black Wrack, was the property of 16-year-old Alfred Jr., now eschewing formal education to follow in his father's equine footsteps. His mother continued to make her mark throughout Maryland's racing venues with horses like Scotch and Soda and Night Life that she entered at Pimlico, Laurel, Aberdeen in Maryland, and Belmont and Saratoga Springs. They were no strangers to finishing in the money.[14] She also entered her second and final horse in the Kentucky Derby—Don Q, who finished seventh in 1928.[15] By the spring of 1930, Sagamore Stables was being touted by *Sun* reporter Edward Sparrow as a showplace for thoroughbreds "that probably has no equal anywhere in the United States and Canada."[16]

* * *

The Emersons enjoyed the Captain's fortune, but at the same time were not indifferent to the needs of others. In March of 1928, Anne made a $3,000 contribution, matched by her husband, toward the improvement of the Eudowood Sanatorium, a hospital for patients with tuberculosis. In addition to her financial contribution, Anne became a vice-chairman of the fund-raising campaign. She joined, among other vice-presidents, Robert Garrett, grandson of long-time Baltimore and Ohio Railroad president John Garrett, and a gold medalist for the discus throw at the 1896 Olympics; and Frank A. Furst, an engineer who led the digging of the Cape Cod Ship Canal and the draining of portions of Florida's Everglades.[17]

Emerson himself, as we have seen, made contributions to his alma mater. The Captain again combined his interest in philanthropy and sports by offering, in 1925, to build a new football stadium for UNC-CH. He conditioned his offer on the school's 11 defeating the University of Maryland's squad in their October 31, 1925, game in College Park, Maryland. He made his offer at a pre-game lunch following the Tar Heels' trip to College Park from Baltimore, where they had been Emerson's guests at his hotel. The offer stunned UNC-CH coach Bill Fetzer, who said, "I cannot say anything that would do justice to how I feel, consequently I can't say anything." An unnamed UNC-CH player, in a statement his English professor might have blushed at, said simply, "Say, ain't he the real stuff." The Tar Heels held up their end of the deal, shutting out the Terps, 16–0.[18]

Emerson's offer, however, went for naught. He proposed expanding the concrete stand on one side of the field, which he had donated the funds for in 1915, into a horseshoe stadium. The university decided that, given the immense popularity of football (16,000 fans had somehow crowded into the 5,200-seat Emerson Field for a game between the Tar Heels and the arch-rival Cavaliers of the University of Virginia), a larger stadium than what Emerson had proposed was needed. William Rand Kenan, Jr., an 1894 graduate of UNC-CH and a member of the football team, stepped forward with an offer to fund a 24,000-seat stadium as a memorial to his parents. Rand had built a fortune by helping to found Union Carbide and aiding Henry Flager in developing Florida's east coast. Like Emerson, Kenan, retained strong ties to his alma mater. The resulting stadium became known as Kenan Stadium. Emerson Field continued to be used for baseball games and track meets.[19] In 1927, the university did accept Emerson's offer of enough Bromo-Seltzer stock to establish a chair in Biological Testing and Drug Assaying.[20]

Another offer that was gratefully accepted was his $40,000 gift to the campaign for the Hospital for the Women of Maryland made in June of 1930. Edgar Allan Poe, a nephew of the poet and chairman of the advisory committee, said Emerson's donation to the Baltimore Hospital brought the campaign to the point where construction of the new facility could begin.[21]

The Captain's generosity extended to members of his Brooklandwood staff as well. He paid for the college education of the sons of two of his chauffeurs, Robert Ricketts and Emerson Gerhardt, both of whom graduated from Carnegie Institute of Technology. He covered the hospital charges for the birth of another son of a chauffeur, John Calvin Laslett.[22]

Not all Brooklandwood staff were so deserving. A housekeeper, Marie Leslie, 63, in July 1928, bought $400,000 worth of jewelry from Wanamaker Department Stores in Philadelphia and New York, using a letter of credit from the Emersons to buy household goods. She altered

13—New Projects

the letter to include permission to purchase jewelry. The jewels included a marquise diamond weighing 3.2 carats, a 95-carat diamond clasp worth $110,000, and a pearl rope necklace valued at $90,000. Leslie sold the bulk of the jewels to a New York jeweler, Harry Winston, for $60,000, and disposed of others at several pawn shops. Suspicious of the large purchase, a Wanamaker manager cabled Anne in Europe, asking if the purchases were authorized. Learning they weren't, Wanamakers involved the police, who arrested Leslie and Winston. A sheriff deposited the jewels in his safe and later returned them to Anne. Most of the jewels left at pawn shops were also returned to her. Leslie was admitted to a sanitarium in Connecticut and later sentenced to three to six years in prison on a charge of grand larceny after her 1930 trial. Winston was cleared of any wrongdoing. He later became well known for donating the Hope Diamond to the Smithsonian Institution in 1958 after owning it for a decade. Marilyn Monroe helped him along the road to notoriety when she sang the line "Harry Winston, tell me about it," in the 1953 film *Gentlemen Prefer Blondes*.[23]

The Emersons had arrived in Europe shortly before receiving the Wanamaker's telegram, to take possession of the Captain's magnificent new yacht. This pleasure craft he named for his wife, calling it the *Queen Anne*. The 180-foot-long, sea-going yacht, built by the German firm, the Krupp Shipbuilding Corporation, was designed to take the Captain, Anne, invited friends, and a crew of 20 to many parts of the world in style and comfort. Its diesel engines could take it 6,000 miles without refueling. Passengers were accommodated in six double staterooms, lounging decks, and a large saloon. After a summer cruise in the North Sea and the Mediterranean and a return to Baltimore in November, the *Queen Anne* set out three months later for southern waters with stops in Savannah, Georgia, and the Panama Canal.[24]

* * *

As the Emerson Drug Company continued its profitable ways, its owner received many offers to sell. He turned them all down. The most notable offer came from E. C. Carrington, a New York City attorney turned financier with substantial corporate holdings in New York, Chicago, and Santa Barbara, California. In response to Carrington's 1926, $10 million offer, Joseph Hindes, the drug company's president, speaking for its chairman of the executive committee who was wintering at Arcadia, said, "The Captain has received offers in the past from several financiers, and he has given them the same answer—the company is not for sale. He has instructed me to answer all offers in a similar manner."[25]

* * *

When at Arcadia, as we have seen, Emerson led a busy life—hunting, entertaining, and making improvements to the property. By the time of Carrington's offer, he was also immersed in another commercial project, this one in Narragansett, Rhode Island, a favorite summer and fall haunt. In September 1920 he, now 62, had assumed the presidency of the Narragansett Improvement Association (NIA). The NIA issued stock to finance its mission which, as described in the charter, was to "correct deplorable conditions on the beach." Once a place where it "was a delight to bathe," the beach, the charter continued, had been transformed by "a most undesirable excursion element that litter the beach with lunch boxes, tonic bottles ... and parade the beach in bathing suits that would hardly be permitted at Coney Island." Citing a lack of interest by property owners and voters, the NIA proposed to buy stretches of the affected beach, remove "unsightly shacks," and improve selected bath houses and hotels. Parts of the beach would be reserved for association members. Other parts would be open to the public but under the association's management. The group's proposed ordinances would prohibit dressing or undressing in automobiles and crossing any street in a bathing suit, and would regulate the parking of vehicles. Special police would be hired to enforce the ordinances should the town council adopt them.[26]

By improving the area's appearance and facilities, the NIA hoped to attract a clientele willing to pay enough for the Association to turn a profit and pay a six percent dividend to investors. Emerson offered instructions on the type of people he preferred to use the new facilities. In a March 9, 1925, letter, he informed T. G. Hazard, a leading citizen of Narragansett and the project's secretary/treasurer, that the woman leasing a bath house from the Association "is to have the privilege of renting rooms that have not been taken by Association members to any persons or person—excluding certain nationalities." He did not elaborate.[27]

Emerson supervised the operation closely. When not in Narragansett, he communicated by telegram, night letters, and telephone with Hazard. In them, Emerson conveyed instructions to Hazard on, among other topics, conditions for leases, placement of fences and boardwalks, paint colors, layout of buildings, stock allocations, special rental rates for members of the Association, and payment of bills to various contractors.

The Burnside Hotel was an early project. Two employees of the Emerson Hotel, William Parker, the manager and long-time Emerson confident, and a clerk, Ralph A. Wells, proposed to lease, improve, and manage the Burnside. Emerson orchestrated letters of recommendation for both to the Association's Board of Directors from himself, Baltimore's police commissioner and mayor, and the presidents of the Western Maryland Railroad and the National Bank of Baltimore. With such weighty references, the Board accepted the two men and the changing of the name to Hotel de la Plage, French for Hotel by the Beach, perhaps inspired by the Captain's visits to France.[28] The hotel did well until destroyed by fire in 1925.[29]

Other initiatives did not go as well. The Association's attempt to purchase The Casino, a site for dining, dancing, and illegal but ongoing gambling, fell through due to an inability to obtain a clear title.[30] Emerson still visited The Casino, nevertheless. While he may or may not have gambled, he did watch others engage in games of chance. A police raid of the premises in September of 1923 resulted in the indictment of ten men on gambling charges. Emerson and several others were named as material witnesses and each released on a $100,000 bond. The judge assessed the bond only to insure the men's appearance at the gamblers' trial. The men got their money back when they appeared in court.[31]

Income from the renovated properties failed to keep pace with Emerson's expectations. For several years, he used his own money to buy back stock from investors who wanted out as well as to pay bills. The Association's president stopped the buyback practice when the Rhode Island Hospital Trust Company, on behalf of a client, wanted to redeem shares in May 1927. Emerson wrote Hazard, "Because I now own more than half of the entire stock issue, I am in accord with your suggestion that we do not offer to buy the stock of the Mather Estate."[32]

The NIA and Emerson's patience would soon expire. On December 13, 1928, Emerson informed the Board by letter from Arcadia, "Apparently the Association is insolvent and I respectfully ask each of you to write me ... your recommendation regarding the steps we should take.... Something must be done at once otherwise a receivership shall be necessary." He vented his frustration as he continued,

> I accepted the Presidency of the Association reluctantly. The leading promoters at the time assured me that they "would do all of the work" and finance the project. Those who were most insistent that I should take the presidency have long since deserted me in my efforts to make the beach a fit place to bathe and even worse have started an opposition project further up the beach and still more contemptible have resorted to methods not generally expected of gentle and fair minded business people by trying to engage the employees that I engaged to run the Bathing and Swimming establishment during the past season during my absence abroad.[33]

By January 11, 1929, only four of the 20 directors had responded. Only one, Herbert Caswell, offered a suggestion other than bankruptcy. He proposed opening the bath houses and small restaurants to the public. Emerson rejected Caswell's proposal out of hand, saying in a letter to Hazard, "To do this our original object to break up the public nuisance of public bath houses, which was a disgrace to Narragansett, would be completely thwarted." "You of all men," Emerson continued, "know to what extent I was forced to make investments from time to time to carry out the original plan, and now for one of the Directors to start a competitive establishment ... is beyond my idea of fair treatment." He closed his letter with "With sincere regards and thanks for your efforts in trying to make the association a success, believe me." He added a P.S.: "I am sailing for a few days to the West Indies."[34]

The NIA problems were occurring at the same time the Emersons were dealing with their servant's illegal jewelry purchase and subsequent trial, preparing for the 30th running of the Grand National at Brooklandwood, and the marriage of Anne's daughter Ethel to Walter Keith.[35] A trip to the West Indies no doubt looked very appealing to both.

On April 10, 1929, Hazard informed Emerson, since returned from the West Indies, by telegram that "The Wakefield Trust Company is expecting payment on his note of $15,298.30. Please advise what action I shall take." By return telegram two hours and 15 minutes later, Emerson advised, "Company is insolvent. Have no suggestions except to consent to receivership."[36]

The failure of the NIA in 1929, while disappointing to the Captain, did

A front view of the Captain's expansive, ocean-front mansion, Whitehall, sitting on a 12-acre tract of land in Narragansett, Rhode Island. Author's collection.

13—New Projects

not dissuade the Emersons from continuing to summer at Narragansett. They had a home there. In 1917 Emerson had built Whitehall, a mansion in keeping with the style of "The Big House" at Arcadia, his Eutaw Place home in Baltimore, and his estate at Brooklandville. The 30-room mansion sat on 12 acres fronting the Atlantic Ocean.[37] The son of one of the Captain's chauffeurs, John Percival Laslett, John Calvin Laslett remembered his father telling him that "partying was always in" at Whitehall until it was sold in 1947. The father often drove young women, soon to become debutantes, to the house, including President John F. Kennedy's future wife, Jacqueline Bouvier. Clambakes were a favorite at Whitehall. A local fisherman made the preparations, putting lobsters, clams, fish, corn-on-the cob, and potatoes amongst layers of steaming seaweed heated by a fire that had been built to heat rocks laid by the side of the swimming pool. After two hours of steaming under a large tarp, the feast would be ready.[38]

* * *

The couple passed the winter of 1929–1930 at Arcadia as had long been their custom. John Laslett, who was five years old in 1929 and accompanied his father to Arcadia, in later years remembered the Captain at the time as "an imposing figure. When I saw him ... he would wear a rather round grey Homberg hat, had a clipped white mustache, was slightly on the portly side but always very erect and very distinguished."[39] From Arcadia the couple cruised on the *Queen Anne* to Palm Beach, where they stopped for a visit with Margaret and her fourth husband, Charles Amory. A party of friends then joined the Captain and his wife for a sail to the West Indies and home to Baltimore.[40]

Upon his return, he kept busy by joining forces with Mrs. Henry Barton Jacobs, who owned a villa in Newport and had been married to Robert Garrett, and C. Wilbur Miller, a prominent lawyer and businessman and neighbor of Emerson's in Worthington Valley, to participate in Baltimore's first flower and garden exhibit. Emerson's entry, managed by his head gardener, covered 300 square feet and included violets, cineraria, pineal, azaleas, palms, and ferns. His display took first place.[41]

Shortly after the garden show, the Captain suffered a mild stroke which cost him the almost complete loss of the use of one arm and a leg. By late October 1930, the news had turned more promising. He had regained partial use of his arm and leg but still needed help getting around. He thought himself on the mend and made plans to celebrate Christmas at Arcadia. His condition suddenly worsened ten days before he planned to leave Brooklandwood. He died from a massive brain hemorrhage on January 23, 1931. Margaret had been "almost constantly at his bedside" for two weeks. His *New York Times* obituary, in addition to noting his

The interior of the Emerson Vault on the second floor of the Green Mount Cemetery's mausoleum. Emerson's coffin is on the right; Anne Preston McCormack Emerson's coffin is on the left. Her son, Frederick, is interred in a crypt just beyond the coffins. Author's collection.

many accomplishments, commented that "Captain Emerson and his second wife, Mrs. Anne Preston McCormack Emerson, were widely known in American society and also in the capitals of Europe."[42] Frank P. Graham, president of his alma mater, sent a telegram to his widow saying, "Trustee, faculty, and student body desire to pay tribute of respect and affection to a loyal son, a good friend, and a wise benefactor."[43]

Following a funeral service held at his home, his body was interred at the mausoleum in Baltimore's Green Mount Cemetery, a historic resting place for the famous and infamous including Johns Hopkins, founder of the city's world-class university; John Wilkes Booth, who assassinated Abraham Lincoln; Allen Dulles, former CIA director; Enoch Pratt, founder of Baltimore's Enoch Pratt Free Library; the Abells, founders of the *Baltimore Sun*; the Garretts of Baltimore and Ohio Railroad fame; an entire West Point class of generals, both Union and Confederate; former mayors and governors, and Margaret's first husband, Dr. Smith Hollins McKim.[44] In death as in life, the Captain remains in the company of the prominent and the well-known.

14

Those Marrying and Unmarrying Emersons

The inventor of Bromo-Seltzer left an estate worth $20 million. Anne received the Brooklandwood property and Whitehall in Narragansett. He willed the Worthington Valley property to Margaret for life and, upon her death, to his grandson, Alfred Vanderbilt, Jr. Margaret also received title to the mansion in Lenox. Knoll Wood went to Anne's daughter, Ethel. Francis McCormack's wife, Virginia, was given title to Brandonwood. George Vanderbilt received the rights to Arcadia. The *Queen Anne* was to be sold. He had set up a trust to handle his controlling stock in the Emerson Drug Company, the Maryland Glass Corporation, and the Emerson Hotel to generate income for family members and business associates. The bulk of the income went to Anne. Gloria Baker received 12,000 shares of stock to be held in trust for her by her mother.[1]

The Emerson Drug Company continued its founder's philanthropy. Black Thursday, October 24, 1929, which brought the stock market down and helped the country's descent into the Great Depression, had occurred 15 months before the Captain's death. Many of the nation's well-to-do stepped forward with contributions to relief funds that had sprung up across the country. John D. Rockefeller, Jr., gave $1 million to New York City's Unemployment Relief Fund. Cyrus H. McCormick, Jr., son of the inventor and a Chicago businessman, contributed $100,000 to the Illinois Joint Emergency Relief Committee, as did William Wrigley, Jr., chewing gum manufacturer who held a minority stake in the Chicago Cubs baseball team, and the estate of Marshall Fields, Chicago department store magnate. Similar gifts came from donors in Pittsburgh and Cleveland. The Emerson Drug Company led the way in Baltimore with a November 1931 gift of $300,000 to the Baltimore Community Fund. Other Baltimore firms and individuals pitched in but at much lesser amounts, $4,000 to $80,000.[2]

Continued brisk sales of its product during those trying financial times were one reason for the firm's generosity. The effects of the Depression no doubt increased the frequency of headaches and upset stomachs. Some of these ill effects were brought on by the overindulgence in food and drink, especially alcohol of dubious quality, like the prodigiously produced bathtub gin. Joseph F. Hindes, still the company's president, reported in December of 1931 that the company "had held its own" during the year and that enough money was its coffers that stockholders could expect larger distributions in the near future than the $0.50 quarterly dividend recently announced.[3] That dividend was "an extra" one, not just the expected quarterly dividend. While Bromo-Seltzer was prospering, many other concerns that had thrived during the Gilded Age and for years afterwards, including railroads, were struggling. The New York, New Haven and Hartford, the Boston & Maine, the Missouri Pacific, the Texas and Pacific, and the Colorado & Southern Railroads omitted their regular quarterly dividends.[4]

On an individual financial note, Smith Hollins McKim's second wife, Mary Lenora McKim, let it be known on the occasion of Dr. McKim's death, September 26, 1932, that he had received only a $4,000 annuity for dropping his alienation of affection suits against Margaret, her father, and Alfred Vanderbilt in 1911. Newspapers accounts had since widely reported the amount as $7,500. "I think," she said, "this is a propitious time for the truth.... The amount was conspicuously brought to the notice of the public ... that Captain Emerson fixed things up by handing his son-in-law $50,000 cash and an annuity of $7,500 a year." She did not comment on the cash total. The discrepancy in the annuity figures may not, however, have been a financial hardship for the McKims. After their 1922 marriage, Dr. McKim practiced his orthopedic skills on the Riviera, near Monte Carlo, until ill health forced his return to Baltimore in 1928.[5]

* * *

"Those marrying and un-marrying Emersons," as the *San Francisco Chronicle* had referred to the family in 1911, continued to keep newspaper society writers busy. After 14 years of marriage and one daughter, Margaret Emerson McCormack, Virginia filed for divorce in Reno in March 1933, charging Frederick McCormack with cruelty. The couple had been separated for several months. Frederick continued to live at Brandonwood after Virginia and daughter Margaret moved out.[6] Frederick re-married in May 1934. It was his bride's, Margaretta McNeal Davis, third marriage. Considered a "socially prominent horsewoman of Devon, New Jersey," she was the former wife of the artist Peter Arno, who would contribute 99 covers and many cartoons to the *New Yorker* magazine.[7]

A week before his wedding, 18-year-old college student Rosemary Leahy sued McCormack for $50,000. Leahy claimed she met him at a night club in April, where he gave her a fountain pen. The pen exploded as she was handling it in her dorm room, burning her hand and arm. An infection developed, sending her to the hospital. The case was settled out of court.[8]

Frederick, whom the Captain had appointed as an assistant to him when he married Frederick's mother, rose to the position of Vice-President with the Emerson Drug Company by 1947. He had become an avid yachtsman, racing his yacht, *Zara*, in many races including the Newport-Bermuda race. He commuted between his official residence, Karong, an estate in Stevenson, Maryland, and an apartment penthouse in New York City. It was in the penthouse that a maid found him dead of a self-inflicted gunshot behind his right ear from a .38 caliber revolver on December 4, 1947. Business worries and Margaretta's instigation of divorce proceedings were put forward as possible reasons. He left no note. Margaretta claimed he gave her only $160 a week allowance from the $90,000 annual payment he inherited from Emerson's estate.[9]

Prior to Frederick's suicide, his older sister, Ethel, filed for her second divorce in 1934. She charged her husband of five years, Walter Keith, with cruelty. When she realized that he would never be able to deliver upon his promise to become sober. At his suggestion, she went to Reno but stayed there only three weeks after he made repeated requests over the phone for her to return home. The end came when he terrified Ethel and her mother, Anne Emerson, one June night in the Brooklandwood home. Announcing that he could "take it no more" and telling Ethel she "could go to hell," he produced a pistol from his jacket pocket and waved it around. When Ethel screamed, Keith told her, "Don't worry, it's not for you. It's for me. But don't speak out of turn. I might have to use it on you."

Anne subsequently told the judge that Keith became "noisy and troublesome and destroyed property, sometimes smashing windows" during sessions with the bottle. After threatening Anne and the night watchman, Anthony, both of whom had rushed to the living room after hearing Ethel's scream, he suddenly quieted down. "I'm through," he said, and walked out of the house. Judge C. Gus Grason granted Ethel a partial divorce in December 1934.[10] (A partial divorce is granted in states that do not recognize legal separations. It allows the couple to live apart while the marriage remains legally intact.)[11] Further attempts at reconciliation failed. Edith returned to Reno, where she received an absolute divorce from Keith in August 1935.[12]

Six months after Keith terrorized Anne and Ethel, another threat came Anne's way in the form of an anonymous letter in January 1935. The letter informed her that she was the target of a kidnapping plot. The writer said he could tell her about the plan in return for a price, rumored to be

$5,000. Baltimore Police Commissioner Charles D. Gaither launched an investigation to find the author of the letter, ordered flood lights installed on the outside of the mansion and outbuildings, and posted armed, private detectives at the entrance gate to check the credentials of all visitors. Nothing further was heard about the plot. Gaither concluded, "there is no threat here," and life soon returned to normal at Brooklandwood.[13] As with many events involving an Emerson, the *New York Times*, the *Chicago Daily Tribune*, and the *Baltimore Sun* all ran the story.

A year after the kidnapping scare in January 1936, Keith entered into his third marriage. Elizabeth Atterbury tied the knot with him in a quiet ceremony in the Belvedere Hotel, where her mother lived. The bride's father, the late Gen. William Wallace Atterbury, had been president of the Pennsylvania Railroad. The couple made their home in Philadelphia and on Keith's plantation near Georgetown, South Carolina, not far from Arcadia.[14] Ethel's third marriage would not occur until April 30, 1940, when she married Matthew J. Looram, a retired New York City stockbroker, in a ceremony attended by family members. The newlyweds made their home in Brooklandville.[15]

* * *

A month before Edith's partial divorce, Margaret filed for her third divorce after a six-year marriage to Amory, in West Palm Beach. She charged him with "habitual intemperance." She resumed use of her maiden surname and once again said she would not marry again. This time she meant it.[16] She maintained her real estate holdings, including her villa in West Palm Beach, not far from that of Joseph P. Kennedy, father of John F. Kennedy.[17] There she kept up an active social schedule. Just before Christmas on December 21, 1935, for instance, she entertained 15 for dinner. Guests included two of her children, Alfred and Gloria, as well as Mrs. Arthur Somers Roche, recently widowed by noted mystery writer Arthur Roche, and Herbert Bayard Swope, Jr., son of the famous journalist and editor, Herbert Swope, the first to win the Pulitzer Prize for reporting. She had hosted a luncheon earlier in the day.[18]

Her love of travel led her on a trip to England and Italy with 16-year-old Gloria in the summer of 1936. This was not Gloria's first trip to Italy. Many reports circulated about her romantic interest in a Roman lad she'd met in Rome the previous summer. A highlight of the 1936 trip was being hosted by Benito Mussolini, Italy's prime minister who had started his megalomaniac rise to power by bringing Ethiopia to her knees a year earlier.[19]

Shortly after returning from Italy, she sold her Holmwood property at auction, having been unable to find a buyer. She had lost interest in Lenox and moved to Sands Point, Long Island. Her Cedar Knoll estate, a 24-room home in Sands Point, allowed her to be closer to Alfred and George, who owned adjoining estates. Originally built by John Wesley Harper, a member of the Harper and Brothers publishing empire, her new estate served as another of Margaret's entertainment sites.[20] A notable example was the coming-out party, estimated to cost $50,000, she put on for Gloria in September 1937. Over 1,000 guests attended, including Count Kurt Haugwitz-Reventlow and his wife, the Woolworth dime store heiress Barbara Hutton, former Secretary of the Treasury Ogden Mills, and playwright George S. Kaufman.[21]

Following the party, Gloria embarked on a round-the-world trip in the spring of 1938. She got as far as Honolulu, where she became ill and leased an estate for her recovery. Margaret sailed to Honolulu not only to be with Gloria, but also with son George and his wife, who now lived in Hawaii. Upon her return to the States, Gloria, at times touted in the press as "Society's Glamour Girl," married Henry Topping, Jr., brother of Daniel R. Topping, future president of the New York Yankees baseball team, in the drawing room of her mother's Palm Beach villa in December 1938. Henry had been granted a divorce just the week before.[22] He was the first of Gloria's three husbands. She died in 1975 at the age of 54, the mother of two children and the grandmother of four.[23]

Margaret continued entertaining at Cedar Knoll until a massive fire of mysterious origin fought by more than 300 firemen and Coast Guardsmen, who laid 1,200 feet of hose from Long Island Sound to the fire, destroyed the mansion on the evening of August 20, 1942. Only the charred external walls were left standing. Margaret was attending the races at Saratoga Springs at the time and flew back immediately to assess the damage.[24]

She rekindled a relationship with Long Island in January of 1947 with the purchase of the Rynwood Estate in Old Brookville, just six miles from an estate that son Alfred had recently bought in Syosset. The *New York Times* called Rynwood "one of the best known of North Shore estates."[25]

At the time of the fire, World War II was well underway. As she had done during World War I, Margaret interrupted her social life to volunteer with the Red Cross in 1944, this time as Assistant to the Director of the American Red Cross in the South Pacific, where both of her sons were now in the navy. She ordered her Red Cross uniform before leaving. After putting it on and standing in front of a mirror, she grimaced, "I look like the grandmother of all Western Union Boys." She was now 60 years old.[26]

The South Pacific evidently agreed with her. She bought an estate on Kahala Avenue in Honolulu, which by the end of World War II was well on its way to replacing Nuuanu Valley as the social center of the island. The Bromo-Seltzer heiress tired of the island several years after the Japanese surrendered and sold her estate to the industrialist Henry Kaiser, of Kaiser Aluminum and Kaiser Steel.[27]

After the war, she continued as a society leader in New York City, on Long Island, and in West Palm Beach. She kept up her interest in horse racing and was often seen with Alfred at Sagamore Farms and in his box at race tracks throughout the East. She continued to buy horses to race and later use for breeding. An early purchase had been War, son of Man o' War, for whom she paid $45,000. She financed a staff of 30 to operate the farm under the watchful eye of J. H. (Bud) Stotler. Between 1925 and 1934, Stotler's efforts paid off to the tune of 240 winners and winnings of $415,000.[28]

A heart attack took her life on January 2, 1960, in her Fifth Avenue apartment. A requiem mass was held at St. Patrick's Cathedral in New York City on January 2, 1960. The *New York Times* obituary referred to her "as one of the last surviving social leaders of the gilded era preceding World War I." She was buried in a private ceremony in the Gate of Heaven Cemetery in New York State's Westchester County, also the resting place of Babe Ruth, on January 5. The cemetery was then and still is available to people of all religious faiths as long as the deed holder to the burial plot is Catholic. The deed to Margaret's plot is in her name, supporting Gloria's statement that, even though she was divorced three times, the Catholic Church had reinstated Margaret at some time after her excommunication at the time of her divorce from Smith Hollins McKim.[29]

* * *

Margaret's sons, Alfred Vanderbilt, Jr., and George Vanderbilt III, took different paths in lives. Margaret, deciding not to wait for her death, gave Sagamore Farm to Alfred on his 21st birthday in 1933. A year later, he had three horses nominated to run in Kentucky Derby, one of whom, Discovery, placed second in the Derby and third in the Preakness.[30]

Alfred became one of America's best-known horsemen. Joseph Durso's obituary of him in the *New York Times* stated, "He was the elegant symbol of the sportsman in high society when he was the impresario of horse racing and the pillar of one of America's most aristocratic families." "He was," in the words of Snowden Carter, editor of *The Maryland Horse Magazine*, "one of the really big, big men in racing of all time, in racing, breeding, and management." By age 25, he was president of Pimlico Race Track where, on November 1, 1938, 40,000 spectators saw one of the sport's most memorable contests. Seabiscuit upset Triple Crown winner War Admiral. He made improvements to the starting gate subsequently used at all tracks, and invented the photo-finish camera. Alfred was the nation's top-earning owner in 1935 and 1953, helped found and

Margaret and 23-year-old son Alfred on their way to the opening day races at Belmont Park on Long Island, May 11, 1936. Author's collection.

led the New York Racing Association that operated Belmont Park, site of the Belmont Stakes, the third leg of the Triple Crown, in 1940 and 1941. He served as chairman of the New York Racing Association from 1970 to 1974.

His most famous horse, Native Dancer, won 21 of the 22 races he started, losing by only a neck in the 1953 Kentucky Derby, and was named "Horse of the Year" in 1954, a year after he won both the Preakness and the

Belmont Stakes. His most famous client among the rich horse owners who brought their prize horses to Sagamore was England's Queen Elizabeth. She kept a broodmare at Sagamore during its heyday.

Alfred served aboard a Navy P.T. boat in World War II, earning the Silver Star. A strong believer in the cause for world peace, he was active with the United World Federalists. Like others in the Emerson family, he was no stranger to marriages and divorces—three of each. He had three sons and three daughters. He sold Sagamore Farm in 1987, 12 years before he died at age 87 in his sleep November 12, 1999, at his home in Mill Neck, New York, after returning from his daily visit to Belmont Park.[31]

George married four times, owned, at various times, extensive estates on Long Island, California and Hawaii; traveled the world as a big game hunter, deep-sea fisherman and yachtsman; established the George Vanderbilt Foundation for Marine Biology in Palo Alto, California; and served as a lieutenant on a P.T. boat in World War II, earning the Legion of Merit. He kept up an active interest in Arcadia, usually visiting in the winter to hunt and entertain friends from California, New York, and Hawaii. Guests included film star and Fred Astaire's dancing partner, Ginger Rogers. Another prominent guest, President Franklin D. Roosevelt, went bass fishing at Arcadia one day in mid–April 1944, just a year before his death.

On treks to Panama, the South Seas, and Africa on his yacht the *Pioneer*, George brought back thousands of species of mammals, reptiles, fishes, and birds for the Philadelphia Academy of Natural Science. On July 6, 1938, George's only child, Lucille (Lulu) Vanderbilt, was born in Honolulu to his first wife, Louise "Lulu" Miriam Parsons, whom he had married in 1935. In addition to Arcadia, he owned a 32-acre estate near his mother's on Long Island from 1935 to 1945. In 1946 he bought a 1,500-acre estate that he named Shadow Valley Ranch near Northern California's Shasta-Trinity National Forest. Movie stars John Wayne, Audrey Hepburn and Spencer Tracy were frequent overnight quests.

His fourth wife, Louise Mitchell Paine from New York City, was on the board of the Children's Cancer Fund of America when they wed on March 23, 1961, in Scottsdale, Arizona. She reported him suffering from depression. Three months later, the 47-year-old leapt to his death from a tenth-floor suite in San Francisco's Mark Hopkins Hotel, on June 25, 1961. He was buried in a private ceremony at Arcadia. His daughter, known by all as Lulu, inherited the property from her father. She has owned the estate ever since. As of 2015, the well-maintained estate ranked as one of South Carolina's most beautiful plantations. In 1978, Arcadia was added to the National Register of Historic Places.[32]

Margaret's childhood friend and the Captain's widow, Anne Preston McCormack Emerson, continued in residence at Brooklandwood while

"The Big House" at Arcadia as it appeared when the property was placed on the National Register of Historic Places in 1978. HABS SC,22-GEOTO, v, 5-2. Prints and Photographs Division, Library of Congress, Washington, D.C.

entertaining friends and family in grand style both at Brooklandwood and in Narragansett. She contributed generously to charities. She held season tickets to the opera and other musical performances at the Lyric Theater in Baltimore, whose preservation and improvement took much of her time. She died on May 5, 1946, and was interred next to husband in the Emerson Vault in Green Mount Cemetery.

Daughter Ethel inherited Brooklandwood along with her mother's jewelry, clothes, automobiles, livestock, and farming implements. She established a trust to manage her Bromo-Seltzer stock. Son Frederick inherited Whitehall with the proviso that it be sold upon his death and the proceeds made available to his daughter, Margaret Emerson McCormack.[33] Antonio F. Totelli, an ice, real estate, and liquor dealer in Providence, Rhode Island, purchased Whitehall for $60,000 at a public auction on July 12, 1948, shortly after Frederick's death.[34] The structure was deemed an eyesore and torn down in 1971. Sea Grace, an 11,000-square-foot mansion, was built on the site in 2005. It went on the market in July 2018 for $18 million. The sales material noted the area's legacy for being a summer retreat for some of the nation's wealthiest families, and that Jay Leno and Taylor Swift had recently purchased estates nearby.[35]

* * *

Hot summer nights and Sunday afternoons in the 1930s and 1940s saw Baltimoreans flock to what became known as Emerson Farms at Brooklandwood, drawn by the cooler temperatures and a much-enlarged diary. Lillian Jenny, who sold the firm's products, said, "We opened at nine in the morning and didn't close until eleven at night, seven days a week. We had so many customers it took six and seven in help." Visitors sought out the Farm's ice cream, buttermilk, chocolate milk and cottage cheese, all considered the best for miles around because "we made everything fresh daily from our own cows," explained Linwood Tinsley, a herdsman on the farm.[36]

15

Changes Come to Bromo-Seltzer

As the Emerson kith and kin continued with their lives, the product that made them all possible continued to churn out substantial profits, even as the Great Depression brought despair and hardship to millions. Two events in the 1930s, however, changed the company's visibility and its product's formula.

In 1936, the revolving, four-story high, 20-foot-wide, replica blue bottle of Bromo-Seltzer, with its 596 electric lights that sat atop the Bromo-Seltzer Tower, disappeared. *Baltimore News American* columnist Lou Azrael informed the city on March 10, 1936, that "today was the day the bottle came down." City engineers had determined that the bottle's revolutions were causing cracks to appear throughout the 13-story building. They ordered it removed. The clock tower and office building remained. The bottle's removal and the number of tall buildings built in downtown Baltimore since Emerson built the tower in 1911 combined to diminish Bromo-Seltzer's visibility throughout the city.[1]

Criticism of patent medicine drugs in general and Bromo-Seltzer in particular had grown steadily after passage of the 1906 Pure Food and Drug Act. Linette A. Parker, a nurse and faculty member at Columbia University's Teachers College,[2] said in 1921, "The American people are only 50% healthy," for which she blamed "impure water, alcohol, caffeine, nicotine and our awful and absurd use of drugs and patent medicines." As for Bromo-Seltzer, she wondered, "How many people who take Bromo-Seltzer frequently at soda fountains [where they would not have labels to read nor control over the amount dispensed] know that they are taking acetanilide, a habit forming drug?"[3]

A year later, in a company-produced booklet detailing the meticulous manufacturing and distribution details adhered to in order to deliver a safe and effective product to consumers, the company briefly addressed the acetanilide issue. Acknowledging, in a master stroke of understatement, "that much has been said and written" about acetanilide, the company defended its use by citing findings from the United States

Pharmacopoeia and the National Formula. Both organizations, charged with setting standards of purity and dosage for drugs, said the average dose for acetanilide when given alone was three grains, and three and a half when mixed with other substances such as caffeine and bromide of soda, both found in Bromo-Seltzer. A teaspoon dose of Bromo-Seltzer, the booklet reported, contained "about an average dose of acetanilide (three and three-fifth grains)" as well as "about an average amount of caffeine, and about half the Pharmacopoeial dose of bromide of soda." The company noted that all Bromo-Seltzer ingredients were well known to the two organizations, but pointed out that physicians might exceed the recommendations. In the case of Bromo-Seltzer, however, the booklet stated, "Our experience of about thirty-four years has convinced us that every ingredient in Bromo-Seltzer is in proper proportion."[4]

In another unfavorable review of Bromo-Seltzer, Nurse Margaret O. Fadds, in 1932, noted that Emerson had applied for a trademark on Bromo-Seltzer, but not a patent. The reason, she explained, was that a patent required a product be new and useful. A trademark merely protected the name, so no one else could legally call their patent medicine Bromo-Seltzer even if they used the exact ingredients. A trademark, Fadds noted, had the advantages of being good for 20 years and could be renewed indefinitely, while patents expired after 17 years. "Thus," she concluded, "it is that Bromo-Seltzer has probably come to be worth millions, not by virtue of the product, but because the name has become known to nearly every American."[5]

To keep the name in front of the public while assuring users of its safety and effectiveness, the Emerson Drug Company kept up its advertising blitz. In 1937, a four-page circular appeared. It contained endorsements from everyday people such as a salesman, a stockbroker, a telephone operator, and a radio announcer. Each endorsement was accompanied by the person's name and a photograph. An accompanying statement claimed that a group of doctors, who, by contrast, went unnamed, found Bromo-Seltzer "relieved morning after headaches faster than any other they tested." Another unnamed doctor was quoted as saying "certain pain relieving drugs (like the one used in Bromo-Seltzer) have done more to give relief ... than any other discovery of ancient and modern time." A statement on the boxes in which bottles of the potion were shipped simply read, "A Balanced Compound of Several Medicinal Ingredients for Headaches and Neuralgia." Giving an international aura to its product, the company gave directions for its use in English, French, Spanish, German, Yiddish, Italian, and Polish.[6]

A person who was disinclined to provide a testimonial for Bromo-Seltzer was Katherine Tupper Marshall, wife of the army's General George

Marshall. While General Marshal, Chief of Staff for the War Department in 1940 and later author of the Marshall Plan, was expanding the army's manpower and capabilities, Katherine Marshall was preparing for their daughter Molly's wedding to be held on Christmas Day, 1940. She used Bromo-Seltzer to relieve "a tight feeling in the back of her head." George disapproved. He took advantage of the Christmas Eve party following the wedding rehearsal to make his feelings known to all present. The general presented her with a large box elegantly wrapped in silver paper and tied with a festive Christmas ribbon. Inside was a foot-high bottle of Bromo-Seltzer. Its appearance caused "a roar of laughter" among the party goers. "I was," Katherine said, "made the complete butt of the party." She promised revenge.[7]

* * *

Public dissatisfaction with the loopholes in the 1906 Act that enabled harmful food and drugs to remain in interstate commerce finally culminated in the Federal Food, Drug, and Cosmetic Act of 1938. The final straw came the year before when an untested drug labeled "elixir of sulfanilamide" killed scores of people across the Midwest including many children, as soon as it hit the market.[8] FDA Administrator W. G. Campbell ordered his entire staff of 240 to fan out across the country and seize as many bottles of the potion as they could find. Chemists discovered that an ingredient, diethylene glycol, was the guilty party. The manufacturer had broken no law, because all ingredients were truthfully listed on the label. The use of the term "elixir," however, led to a charge of misbranding, the only charge the FDA could level. The term elixir was reserved for drugs containing ethanol, which the elixir of sulfanilamide did not. "It is unfortunate," Campbell lamented, "that under our present inadequate law ... the FDA is obliged to proceed ... on a technical and trivial charge of misbranding." The new Act, however, expanded Campbell's powers by giving the FDA the power to monitor the safety, as well as the accurate listing of ingredients, of foods and drugs.[9]

Armed with the authority of the new Act, Campbell again sent his staff forth in early 1939 to seize drugs thought to be harmful. Dispensers of Bromo-Seltzer in New York City, Atlanta, Knoxville, and Greensboro, N.C., received visits in March. Agents seized thousands of bottles of various sizes. The seizures came to the attention of U.S. Democratic Congressman William P. Cole, Jr., who represented Maryland's second district, which included downtown Baltimore. In a March 10, 1939, letter, Campbell assured Cole "that no more seizures are planned if the company cooperates."[10]

When analyzed, investigators found uneven amounts, some higher than considered safe, of acetanilide and bromide among the samples. The FDA had determined that frequent or continued use of acetanilide "may be dangerous, causing serious blood disturbances, anemia, collapse, or a dependence on the drug." Bromides, the FDA warned in the same publication, when used frequently "may lead to mental derangement, skin eruptions or other serious effects." In addition, as the FDA warned about the use of acetanilide, it said of bromides, "Do not take more than the dosage recommended."[11]

While the FDA found no fault with Bromo-Seltzer's listing of ingredients and instructions for use on its labels, the FDA, which based its warnings on the fact that consumers could not be assured that safe amounts of acetanilide and bromide were present in every dose, filed a suit in Federal court charging the Emerson Drug Company with failure to inform users of the potential hazards.[12]

Executives of the Emerson Drug Company were not pleased. The company offered a variety of defenses. "The manufacturer," an Emerson Drug Company spokesperson asserted, "has had many clinics conducted and has obtained scores of opinions from nationally recognized medical and technical experts which support its claim that its product is not dangerous." As was the company's practice, the spokesman did not identify the clinics or the experts, a far cry from the company's practice of identifying people featured in the testimonials cranked out by the advertising department.[13]

The company also challenged the constitutionality of the seizures. Since the new law empowered any employee of the department of agriculture to seize any drug, without a hearing, that the employee deemed to be "dangerous to health," the company was deprived of the benefit of the due process clauses in the 4th and 5th Amendments to the Constitution. The Agriculture Department's 100,000 employees were deemed by the Emerson Drug Company to "have no technical knowledge of drugs." The company also raised the issue of fairness. "For a product to be permitted to be sold for half a century," the spokesperson continued, "with no indications by the Federal authorities that it is any degree dangerous, and then suddenly, without warning, [be] subjected to arbitrary procedure seems most unfair."[14] Citing these objections, the company asked Federal District Judge John Knox, in the Southern District of New York, to dismiss the suit. He refused.[15]

Fair or not, FDA inspectors had gathered evidence for the suit through extensive investigations. The company's assertion that employees knew nothing about drugs aside, Campbell's agents went to work. In Knoxville, for instance, Inspector Edward L. Holmes, posing as a customer, asked "for a dose of Bromo-Seltzer" from a "soda clerk" in 13 pharmacies. Some doses came from a mechanical dispenser, others were dispensed by hand. The doses, obtained on March 2, 1939, varied in weight from a low of 4.519 grams to a high of 17.83 grams. Of concern to the FDA was the fact that the different weights meant customers were ingesting differing amounts of acetanilide and bromide without knowledge of the potential harm to them. Another investigator, C. F. Bruening, analyzed "one heaping teaspoon," the amount suggested as a dose on the powder's packaging. He, as might be expected, found little variance in the samples' weights. He also found each sample contained 3.88 grains of acetanilide, 6.34 grains of bromide, and lesser amounts of caffeine, citrates, carbonates, sodium, and sugar. He concluded that, based on the amount of acetanilide and bromide in each teaspoon Bromo-Seltzer should be "considered a dangerous drug."[16] Bruening's assessment mirrored that of U.S. Surgeon General Dr. Thomas Parran, Jr., who, in a March 11, 1939, speech to New York City's Chamber of Commerce, declared acetanilide a dangerous drug.[17]

By the fall of 1939, both the FDA and the Emerson Drug Company believed they would prevail at the upcoming trial. On October 1, 1939, however, Bromo-Seltzer, finding the FDA's findings potentially troubling, voluntarily changed the formula. Future production would conform to a new tolerance limit set by the FDA, 2½ grams of acetanilide and 7½ grains of bromide per tablet, tablets now replacing powder as the distribution mode.

In light of the company's change, Judge Knox proposed that the FDA and Emerson Drug Company sign a consent decree in place of a time-consuming and expensive trial. Both parties agreed.[18] The decree stated that the powders seized could have been harmful if used according to suggestions on the package, but that the new product conformed to the Federal Food, Drug, and Cosmetic Act.[19] The decree was entered "without prejudice," meaning either party could initiate future litigation over the same issue.[20] The decree allowed the Emerson Drug Company to extract the citric acid contained in the 34,469 containers in the FDA's possession for future use. The remaining ingredients "were drained into city sewers."[21]

The federal government's issues with Bromo-Seltzer did not end there. In 1942, the Federal Trade Commission (FTC), whose mission was to see that a firm's advertising of a drug conformed to the claims made on a drug's label, charged the Emerson Drug Company and two other firms selling headache remedies, Miles Laboratory and Capudine Chemical Company, with false and misleading advertising. The FTC challenged the advertised claim for Bromo-Seltzer that it "alkalizes i.e., reduces the excess acidity caused by overindulgence." "Overindulgence," the FTC asserted, "in food or drink will not cause acidity ... and use of the preparation will not counteract the effects of overindulgence ... and will not reduce acidity throughout the body."

15—Changes Come to Bromo-Seltzer

Eight years later in 1950, the FTC, on a 2–1 vote by its commissioners, dismissed the charges against the companies, all of whom promised to mend their advertising ways. Emerson Drug Company executives agreed to use the word "alkalize" in its ads to mean the potion only reduces acidity in the stomach and nowhere else in the body. The company's president, Kenneth A. Bonham, noted that the order called for no change in Bromo's labeling but applied only to words used in the company's ads. He thanked the Commission for "a new cooperative approach ... in settling the proceedings harmoniously," perhaps a not so subtle criticism of the FDA. FTC Commissioner William A. Ayres voted against the agreement, saying, "at best it will have no binding effect and cannot be enforced in the event of violation."[22]

The public now had greater assurances that Bromo-Seltzer and similar FDA-approved drugs were safe to take, but users still had to rely on statements from the manufacturers of patent medicines that the curative claims for their products were true. Not until 1962, in the form of the Kefauver-Harris Amendments to the 1938 Act, which President John F. Kennedy signed into law on October 10, 1962, would the FDA have the authority to require proof from the manufacturer that a drug was effective as well as safe.[23]

The new law did not sit well with many pharmaceutical companies, several of whom challenged its constitutionality and argued that the courts and not agencies of the federal government should rule on a drug's effectiveness. It took 11 years for the issue to reach the Supreme Court. In four unanimous decisions in June 1973, the Court gave the FDA "sweeping authority" to force ineffective drugs off the market.[24] In refuting the drug makers' complaints, Justice William O. Douglas wrote, "If the control over drugs is to be efficient, they must be exercised with dispatch. Only paralysis would result if case-by-case battles in the courts were the only way to protect the public."[25]

Shortly before the Court's ruling, the FDA, in April 1973, reported the findings from a panel of scientists. The labels for over-the-counter antacids, such as Bromo-Seltzer and the newcomer on the block since 1931, Alka-Seltzer, should, the panel recommended, say they were only useful for granting relief from a headache, or for a headache and acid indigestion. The panel proposed that the FDA ban other antacids which claimed relief from such ailments as morning sickness, nervous or emotional disturbances, excessive smoking, and cold symptoms. The panel found Alka-Seltzer and Bromo-Seltzer to be "safe and potentially effective" and excluded both from the proposed ban.[26] The FDA accepted the panel's recommendations.

Nine years later in 1982, the FDA further refined its constraints for

Bromo-Seltzer, Alka Seltzer, and Pepto-Bismol as well, saying that they were safe and effective, but that the labeling claims such as "fast relief ... or any other term that non-specifically relates to the speed of action are misleading." At the same time, the FDA said love potions such as Spanish Fly "are unlikely to have the aphrodisiac powers claimed for them."[27]

* * *

While the world-famous headache reliever was successfully navigating the various challenges, the company continued to make a profit, which it had done every year since 1889. Net sales for the first half of 1954 came to $7,164,000. That figure increased to $8,151,000 for the first half of 1955. Even with those impressive results, company president Francis H. McAdoo, Jr., a son of Francis and Ethel, agreed to a merger with the Warner-Lambert Pharmaceutical Company in January 1956. Warner-Lambert would add the immensely popular Bromo-Seltzer to its line of products. Bromo-Seltzer, in turn, it was thought, would benefit from Warner-Lambert's well-established, worldwide sales organization.[28]

The merger brought about gradual changes in production. Roughly 18 million bottles and 29 million "pocket packages" continued to flow out of the Baltimore facility each year. That changed in late 1967, when the Emerson Drug Company moved its manufacturing process to Lititz, Pennsylvania, six miles north of Lancaster, where Warner-Lambert had a large manufacturing plant. The company agreed to build a two-story, 116,000-square-foot warehouse for Bromo-Seltzer. "The most logical, practical, and economic approach to fulfilling company needs was to combine the Baltimore operation by expanding facilities there," explained a Warner-Lambert spokesperson.[29]

Not long after the move to Lititz, competition from other products producing relief from headaches and upset stomachs, such as Alka-Seltzer, Pepto-Bismol, and Tylenol, cut into Bromo-Seltzer's market share to the point where by 1994 the remedy was considered to be moribund. One reason for its decline was that by 1971, Miles Laboratory, the manufacturer of Alka-Seltzer, was spending $17.4 million annually to promote Alka-Seltzer. Warner-Lambert's budget for Bromo-Seltzer ads, on the other hand, was a comparative paltry $2.8 million a year.[30] The Captain was turning over in his proverbial grave.

Sales for Emerson's invention plunged from as high as $16 million a year to $1.7 million in 1994, as consumers turned more often to products such as Maalox, Mylanta or Tums. Entrepreneur Jeffrey S. Himmel, chairman of the New York-based Himmel Group, saw an opportunity. Having rejuvenated such "ghost" brands as Doan's Pills and Lavoris Mouthwash, he acquired the rights to Bromo-Seltzer, intending to resuscitate the once popular headache remedy. Himmel's yearly sales goal for Bromo-Seltzer was an ambitious $50 million. His efforts fell far short.

The rights to Bromo-Seltzer then bounced around between several companies until 2006, when they landed with Tower Laboratories in Essex, Connecticut.[31] Market research convinced executives at Tower, a company that specialized in effervescent medicines, that Bromo-Seltzer retained high name recognition. "We did some market research and found that the name recognition among customers over 40, 45 is very high," said Tower's president, Norman Needleman, in 2006. To help boost sales, the Tower Company reformulated and repackaged the remedy in an attempt to attract users. Ingredients were reduced to three, aspirin, citric acid, and sodium bicarbonate. Acetanilide had been eliminated entirely in 1984, nine years after the bromides were withdrawn.[32] Packets in packages replaced the traditional blue cobalt bottle that had contained Bromo-Seltzer in granulated form.[33] The Tower Company experimented with targeting cities with populations of older people, such as Providence, R.I., and Fort Myers and Tampa, Florida. A television advertising campaign known as the "Bromo burp" featured a person burping on air and then extolling the benefits of Bromo-Seltzer.[34]

Several years before Tower's campaign, *New York Times* writer Gina Barreca had sounded Bromo's decline in 2001. She included Bromo-Seltzer on a long list of products "that once seemed essential to life that no longer captures the public imagination." Among the items she grouped with Bromo-Seltzer were "hair nets that ladies actually slept in, big plastic curlers, baked Alaska, flash cubes, and clothes brushes."[35]

Despite the energetic efforts of the Tower Company, Bromo-Seltzer today is a faint shadow of its former self. A search of CVS's and Rite Aid's websites in 2018 turned up no results. The CVS website advised "Search instead for Alka-Seltzer." Packets of 20 Bromo-Seltzer tablets manufactured by Tower can be found on Amazon. The labeling promises "Fast Effervescent Action for Relief of acid indigestion, upset stomach, heartburn with head ache, and body aches and pains." The fast action claim merely means the tablets dissolve quickly in water. Unlike the earlier versions which attracted so much unflattering commentary from government and medical critics, detailed usage recommendations and warnings abound on the Tower packages.[36]

Epilogue

Some notable structural reminders of Bromo-Seltzer and the Captain remain in Baltimore. The Emersonian Apartments, following a long period of decline, were refurbished and re-opened for occupancy, along with the neighboring Riviera and Esplanade Apartments, in 1996 by the Roizman Development Corporation of Plymouth Meeting, Pennsylvania.[1] The Bromo-Seltzer Tower still stands. Artists now pursue their work in spaces where Bromo-Seltzer employees once did. A museum including a

The Captain's Eutaw Place mansion and the Emersonian Apartments looming over it, as they appeared in 2018. Author's collection.

large collection of vintage Bromo-Seltzer bottles occupies the top floor. The Captain's Eutaw Place mansion with the two stone lions still guarding the front entrance stands but is in need of repair. The Emerson Hotel remains alive in the memory of many Baltimoreans but was closed in 1969 and demolished in 1971. Brooklandwood is now the site of St. Paul's School, a private Episcopal school for grades 1–12. Sagamore Farm continues as a prime horse racing facility now under the leadership of Kevin Plank, a former linebacker and running back for the University of Maryland in the 1990s and the founder of the sporting clothing company, Under Armour.

Relatively little is known about the man by people in Baltimore today. Francis O'Neill, forty plus years a reference librarian with The Maryland Historical Society said in a 2019 interview that Emerson, "Is not a name on the tip of anyone's tongue today. He was a successful industrialist. People know the tower, and there may be some senior citizens who remember going to Emerson's Farm for ice cream." O'Neill added, "He wasn't the nicest person in the world for the way he treated his first wife. He's not anyone I'd like to hang out with."[2] In a 1996 letter to the Maryland Club in Baltimore, Edward Emerson Murray described his great uncle as "being of the age, fancy, free, and a man who lived his life with the cup full!!"[3] Edward Murray's son, Andrew Murray, said in a 2018 interview, that Emerson suffered from the three worst afflictions a man could have namely "slow horses, fast women, and bad whiskey."[4]

Chapter Notes

Preface

1. Edward Emerson Murray to Board of Governors, The Maryland Club, Baltimore Maryland, January 25, 1996.
2. Interview with Andrew Murray, September 20, 2018.
3. Telephone conversation with Mitch Whiteley, May 22, 2018.

Introduction

1. http://courses.lumenlearning.com/boundless-ushistory/chapter/thegildedage/. Accessed March 9, 2018.
2. 1870 and 1890 U.S. Census Reports.
3. Antero Pietila, *Not in My Neighborhood: How Bigotry Shaped a Great American City* (Chicago: Ivan R. Dee, 2010), 9.
4. *Chicago Daily Tribune*, Display Add, pg. 33, October 29, 1929.
5. "Isaac E. Emerson to be Buried Today," *Baltimore Sun*, January 25, 1931.
6. Ibid.

Chapter 1

1. Marjoleine Kars, *Breaking Loose Together: The Regulator Rebellion in Pre-Revolutionary North Carolina* (Chapel Hill: University of North Carolina Press, 2002), 1–3.
2. http://www.ncgenweb.us/chatham/militia.htm. Accessed November 27, 2016.
3. Although most sources place Emerson's birth in 1859, and this book follows that convention in its title, there is some evidence that he was born a year earlier. John H. Emerson, a great-nephew of Emerson who has researched the family extensively, reported to the author that the date 1858 appears in the Bible of Isaac's sister, Laura Emerson. John H. also noted that the 1860 census of Middle Division, Chatham County, NC, has Isaac listed as age 2 in the household of his father, Robert Jehu Emerson. The census enumeration date was July 18, 1860. Isaac's birth date was July 24. There is no doubt, John H. concluded, that Emerson was described as age two by either his mother or father. Emerson himself seemed unsure of his birth year. A review of his frequent passport applications shows that he entered 1859 on some of them and 1858 on others, but always with the same birth date, July 24.
4. "Captain Isaac E. Emerson," *The Pharmaceutical Era* LXIV, no. 8, New York: August 1927. 209.
5. Louis H. Manarin, ed., *North Carolina Troops 1861–1865: A Roster of Volume II Cavalry* (Wilmington, NC: Broadfoot, 1989), 207. As quoted in Family Group Record-8. Prepared by John H. Emerson.
6. Ibid.
7. "J. W. Emerson, Jr., Celebrates His 75th Birthday Saturday," *Chatham News*, October 25, 1935.
8. http://www.civilwar.org/education/history/end-of-war/johnston-surrenders.html. Accessed February 28, 2017.
9. "J. W. Emerson, Jr."
10. Family Record Group-8. Prepared by John H. Emerson, 12
11. "Waddell at Durham," *Semi-Weekly Messenger* (Wilmington, NC), November 8, 1898.
12. Ibid.
13. Northcarolinahistory.org. Accessed June 27, 2017.

14. North Carolina Marriage License on Ancestry.com. Accessed April 17, 2017.
15. Interview with John Hudson Emerson, Cary, NC, February 8, 2017.
16. James Vickers and Thomas Scism, *Chapel Hill: An Illustrated History* (Chapel Hill, NC: Barclay, 1985), 104.
17. "Members of the Class of '79," *Sunday Citizen* (Asheville, NC), June 2, 1929.
18. John Hudson Emerson interview.
19. http://docsouth.unc.edu/true/dialectic/dialectic.html Accessed March 24, 2017
20. "Sordid crime and punishment in Old Chapel Hill," *Daily Tar Heel* (Chapel Hill, NC), August 19, 1985.
21. Vickers and Scism, 108.
22. 1894 passport application on Ancestry.com. Accessed April 17, 2017.
23. Vickers, 108.
24. "Horner-Emerson," *Baltimore Sun*, April 23, 1896.
25. John Hudson interview. The 1870 Census gives her age in 1870 as 16
26. "Captain Isaac E. Emerson," *The Pharmaceutical Era*, Vol. LXIV, 209.
27. Vickers, 108.
28. Marjorie Spruill Wheeler, *New Women of the New South: The Leaders of the Woman Suffrage Movement in the Southern States* (New York: Oxford Press, 1993), 88.
29. 1880 Census.
30. Baltimore City Court of Common Pleas (Marriage Licenses) Isaac E. Emerson and Emma A. Duner [sic], book 1873–1880, 124, 10/20/1879 {MSA C213–3; 03/01/01/003].
31. Mary Claire Engstrom to Dr. Watson, November 14, 1952. Charleston Historical Society.
32. https://sha.org/bottle/pdffiles/Bromo-Seltzer.pdf. Accessed July 18, 2017.
33. "Rise of Drug Clerk Emerson," *Charlotte Observer*, June 29, 1902.
34. Dr. Joe Schwarcz, *The Fly in the Ointment: 70 Fascinating Commentaries on the Science of Everyday Life* (Toronto, ON, Canada: ECW Press, 2002) 210.
35. *Baltimore City Directories*, 1882–1891. Library of Congress. Washington, D.C.
36. "Death of an Old Soldier: Brief Locals," *Baltimore Sun*, June 6, 1888.
37. Gilbert Sandler, "I Remember ... A Real Old-Time Drug Store," *Baltimore Sun*, December 1, 1957.
38. Robert J. Brugger, *Maryland: A Middle Temperament 1634–1980* (Baltimore: Johns Hopkins University Press, 1988), 363, as cited in *London Daily Chronicle* (reprinted in *Baltimore Sun*, January 6, 1984), quoted in Sherry H. Olsen, *Baltimore: The Building of an American City* (Baltimore, John Hopkins University Press, 1980), 198.
39. H. L. Mencken, *Happy Days: 1880–1892* (New York: Alfred A. Knopf, 1936), 55.
40. Sherry H. Olsen, *Baltimore: The Building of an American City* (Baltimore: Johns Hopkins University Press, 1980), 175–193.
41. *Ibid.*
42. Baltimore City Directories, 1882–1891. Library of Congress, Washington, D.C.
43. Olsen, *Baltimore*, 55.
44. "DIED," *Baltimore Sun*, July 6, 1883.

Chapter 2

1. David L. Cowen and William H. Helfand, *Pharmacy: An Illustrated History* (New York: Harry N. Abrams, 1990), 146–150.
2. https://schools.studentdoctor.net/school/unc-pharm/0/university-of-north-carolina-chapel-hill-eshelman-school-of-pharmacy?gclid=Cj0KCQjwvqbaBRCOARIsAD9s1XD6HT5bXN_PbtcORsXaRlLp6pbWbwn3NGP0plGcRZfczV7Jse3YTlsaAoeHEALw_wcB. Accessed July 14, 2018.
3. William S. Powell, ed., *Dictionary of North Carolina Biography*, Vol. 2, D-G. (Chapel Hill: University of North Carolina Press, 1986), 155.
4. Durham County Historic Architecture Inventory, Northwest Durham Quadrant, NW6-NW7, as quoted in Family Group Record-8, 17.
5. E-mail to author from John H. Emerson, July 3, 2017.
6. Powell, 155.
7. *Druggist Circular & Chemical Gazette* 33, no. 7 (July 1, 1889), 168.
8. Emerson Drug Co. stationary. Isaac

E. Emerson Papers, Manuscript Department, Wilson Library of the University of North Carolina at Chapel Hill. Southern Historical Collection.

9. Clayton Coleman Hall, ed., *Baltimore: Its History and Its People*, Vol. III (New York: Lewis Historical Publishing, 1912), 874.

10. "President Goucher's Trip Postponed," *Baltimore Sun*, May 12, 1893; *The Atlantic Reporter*, Vol. 29. (St. Paul, MN: West Publishing, 1894) 586–587.

11. "What a Man and His Industry Are Doing for Baltimore," *Wall Street Journal*, May 24, 1912.

12. http://www.hagley.org/online_exhibits/patentmed/history/history.html. Accessed May 24, 2018.

13. http://www.learnnc.org/lp/editions/nchist-newcentury/5088. Accessed March 6, 2017.

14. *Wilson Mirror*, April 18, 1891.

15. http://www.hagley.org/online_exhibits/patentmed/history/history.html

16. "Peruna and the Bracers," *Collier's Weekly*, October 28, 1905, 71.

17. The Warshaw Collection. Patent Medicines, Box 9, File 13, Smithsonian Institution, National Museum of American History, Archives Center, Washington, D.C.

18. One *Los Angeles Times* ad appeared on August 25, 1893, below the article "Canadian Pacific Won't Come." A *San Francisco Chronicle* ad appeared on January 6, 1893, below the article "The Flying Flower."

19. "Barber's Bid For Patrons," *New York Times*, July 26, 1903.

20. Advertisement #8. Der Deutsch Amerikanische Naturarzt, February 1899, XII.

21. Warshaw Collection.

22. Charles W. Parsons, ed., *Pharmaceutical Era*, Vol. 10 (Detroit: D. O. Haynes, September 1), 232.

23. "Isaac E. Emerson," *American Druggist and Pharmaceutical Record* 24 (March 22, 1894), 153.

24. "Druggists Have a Banquet," *New York Times*, October 5, 1894.

25. "Proprietary Association," *America Druggist and Pharmaceutical Record*, October 18, 1899, 8, 35, 77.

Chapter 3

1. "Captain Emerson Resigns," *Baltimore Sun*, April 17, 1901.

2. "Naval Reserves," *Baltimore Sun*, January 19, 1894.

3. "The Sloop-of-War Dale," *Baltimore Sun*, January 5, 1895.

4. http://www.ageofsail.net/aoshipns.asp?sletter=sloop;iword=2. Accessed May 7, 2017.

5. "Down Goes the Dale," *Baltimore Sun*, January 7, 1895.

6. Isaac Emerson to Henry Douglas, January 8, 1895. Invoice from Maryland Wrecking Company. Adjutant General Papers, Appendix E, Series S-397, Box 1 and 2, Maryland State Archives, Annapolis, MD.

7. "Auto Case Angers Emerson," *New York Times*, January 22, 1905.

8. "The Maryland Naval Reserves," *New York Times*, June 30, 1895.

9. "The Naval Reserves," *Baltimore Sun*, November 19, 1896.

10. "Reserves Home Again," *Baltimore Sun*, July 9, 1895.

11. "Sailor Lads Will Go," *Baltimore Sun*, November 28, 1895; "Forecast for Baltimore and Vicinity," *Baltimore Sun*, December 7, 1895.

12. Louis R. Harlan, "The Booker T. Washington Papers," Vol. 3 (Urbana: University of Illinois Press, 1974), 583–587; http://historymatters.gmu.edu/d/39/. Accessed June 21, 2017.

13. https://www.britannica.com/event/Atlanta-Compromise. Accessed July 28, 2018.

14. "Naval Militia Association," *Baltimore Sun*, May 2, 1896.

15. "Mr. Emerson's Fine Yacht," *Baltimore Sun*, September 18, 1895.

16. "Naval Military Association."

17. "May Get the Yantic," *Baltimore Sun*, April 9, 1897; "Local Briefs," *Baltimore Sun*, May 5, 1897.

18. "The Naval Reserve," *Baltimore Sun*, November 19, 1896.

19. "To March Behind McKinley," *New York Tribune*, February 24, 1897.

20. "President McKinley: Patriotic and Stirring Scenes," *Washington Post*, March 5, 1897.

21. Katherine Reynolds Chaddock,

Uncompromising Activist: Richard Greener, First Black Graduate of Harvard College (Baltimore: Johns Hopkins University Press, 2017), 106–116.

22. "Great Horse Season," *Baltimore Sun*, October 13, 1901.

23. "Fifth and Its Vets," *Baltimore Sun*, April 26, 1897.

24. http://www.grantstomb.org/hist4.html. Accessed June 1, 2017.

25. "The Negro Left in the Cold," *Charleston Sunday News*, May 16, 1897, as cited in Chaddock, 116.

26. "Nydia Off for the Newport Cruise," *Baltimore Sun*, July 28, 1897.

27. http://www.historytoday.com/richard-cavendish/sinking-maine. Accessed June 2, 2017.

28. "Maryland Naval Militia," *Baltimore Sun*, February 17, 1898.

29. "Plans for Naval Reserves," *Baltimore Sun*, March 9, 1898.

30. "Consul Lee's Son Returns," *Chicago Daily Tribune*, March 14, 1898.

31. "Steam Yacht," *New York Tribune*, March 14, 1898.

32. Ibid.

33. "Our Sailors Bold," *Baltimore Sun*, January 27, 1897.

34. https://history.state.gov/milestones/1866-1898/spanish-american-war. Accessed June 8, 2017.

35. http://www.spanamwar.com/6thMass.htm. Accessed May 22, 2018; "Welcome the Sixth," *Baltimore Sun*, May 21, 1898; Gene Thorn, "First Civil War Deaths Took Place in Baltimore," *Washington Post*, April 19, 2011.

36. W. C. Payne, *The Cruise of the USS Dixie* (Washington, DC: E. C. Jones, 1899), 6–7.

37. Payne, 75.

38. Isaac E. Emerson to The Adjutant General, Annapolis, Maryland. Report of the Commander, First Naval Battalion, For 1898. December 28, 1898. *Maryland Documents*, Maryland General Assembly, 1900.

39. "A Mosquito Fleet," *Baltimore Sun*, May 4, 1898.

40. "Flags for the Sailors," *Baltimore Sun*, May 20, 1898; "Officers of the Dixie," *Baltimore Sun*, May 24, 1898.

41. https://history.state.gov/milestones/1866-1898/spanish-american-war. Accessed June 8, 2017.

42. "Society Leaders Who Will Fight Spain," *Los Angeles Herald*, June 12, 1898.

43. "The Ship's Stay Prolonged," *Baltimore Sun*, September 13, 1898.

44. "With Open Arms," *Baltimore Sun*, September 13, 1898.

45. "A Celebration Abandoned," *Baltimore Sun*, September 14, 1898.

46. "State Capital," *Baltimore Sun*, May 9, 1900.

47. "What is Doing in Society," *Baltimore Sun*, November 2, 1898.

48. "News of the Shipping," *Baltimore Sun*, December 10, 1905; Neal Cox, *Neal Cox of Arcadia Plantation: Memoirs of a Renaissance Man* (Georgetown, SC: Home House Press, 2003), 31.

49. Julia Brock and Daniel Vivian, *Leisure Plantations and the Making of the New South: The Sporting Plantations of the South Carolina Low Country and Red Hills Region* (Lanham, Maryland: Lexington Books, 2015), 108.

50. "News of the Shipping," *Baltimore Sun*, December 10, 1905; Neal Cox, 31.

51. "I. E. Emerson's Gun Wins Cup," *Baltimore Sun*, February 26, 1904.

52. "I. E. Emerson Wins at Traps," *Baltimore Sun*, February 17, 1904.

53. "Does Well at the Traps," *Baltimore Sun*, February 23, 1906.

54. "Mrs. McKim's Gun Wins," *Baltimore Sun*, February 21, 1907.

55. "The Nydia in a Storm," *Baltimore Sun*, February 22, 1899.

56. Ibid.

57. "Druggists' Convention at Old Point," *Baltimore Sun*, May 23, 1899.

58. "N. W. D. A. Select Old Point Comfort," *American Druggist and Pharmaceutical Record* 38 (January–June 1901), 176.

59. "The Maryland Boys," *Baltimore Sun*, March 5, 1901.

60. "For a Military Club," *Baltimore Sun*, April 12, 1901; "Club Project Abandoned," *Washington Post*, October 14, 1906.

61. "Captain Emerson Resigns," *Baltimore Sun*, April 17, 1901.

62. "Captain Emerson's New Yacht," *Baltimore Sun*, November 12, 1900; "Dr. Emerson Gets New Yacht," *Baltimore Sun*, November 10, 1900.

63. "Emerson's Handsome Yacht," *Baltimore Sun*, April 6, 1901.

Chapter 4

1. Antero Pietila, *Not in My Neighborhood*, 10.
2. Ed Gunts, "Historic Emerson Mansion," *Baltimore Fishbowl*, May 4, 2016.
3. 1910 Census.
4. "To Have Italian Garden," *Baltimore Sun*, May 27, 1903.
5. "Gen. and Mrs. Booth Part," *Washington Post*, April 28, 1909; "Gen. Alfred E. Booth Dies," *New York Times*, May 12, 1914.
6. "Horner-Emerson," *Baltimore Sun*, April 23, 1896.
7. "Verdict Against Mrs. I. E. Emerson," *Baltimore Sun*, December 21, 1896; "Rights of Married Women," *Baltimore Sun*, December 19, 1896.
8. http://www.bach-cantatas.com/Lib/Burmeister-Richard.htm. Accessed May 30, 2017.
9. "For Crippled Children," *Baltimore Sun*, February 6, 1897.
10. "Mrs. Emerson Not Taxed," *Baltimore Sun*, March 1, 1898.
11. "White-Emerson," *Baltimore Sun*, February 17, 1898.
12. "To Aid the Veterans," *Baltimore Sun*, March 21, 1898; "Confederate Relief Bazar, *Baltimore Sun*, February 28, 1898; "Maryland Relic Room," *Baltimore Sun*, March 30, 1898; "End of the Bazar," *Baltimore Sun*, April 23, 1898.
13. "Flags for the Sailors," *Baltimore Sun*, May 20, 1898.
14. "Protectors of Animals," *Baltimore Sun*, May 5, 1899.
15. "Confederate Lawn Fete," *Baltimore Sun*, June 5, 1899.
16. "Notre Dame College," *Baltimore Sun*, June 9, 1899.
17. "Notre Dame Alumni Outing," *Baltimore Sun*, June 21, 1899.
18. "Commander Emerson Home," *Baltimore Sun*, September 18, 1899.
19. "Must Pay for the Pictures," *Baltimore Sun*, September 29, 1899.
20. Bid Sheets dated March 24, 1899, in Emerson Papers.
21. "State News," *The Progressive Farmer* (Durham, NC), July 23, 1895.
22. "Narragansett Pier," *New York Times*, August 26, 1900.
23. "Mrs. Emerson's Fete," *Baltimore Sun*, February 16, 1901.
24. "$2,000 to Play One Piece," *Baltimore Sun*, January 12, 1905.
25. "Mrs 'Bromo-Seltzer' Wins," *Inter-Ocean* (Chicago), February 17, 1901.
26. "To Doctor and Mrs. Emerson," *Baltimore Sun*, March 25, 1903.
27. "Mrs. Reid Gives Xmas Party," *Baltimore Sun*, December 25, 1904; "Mrs. Andrew M. Reid, Gold Star Leader," *New York Times*, May 12, 1937; "Society News," *Baltimore Sun*, March 6, 1910.
28. "Box Holders at the Opera," *Baltimore Sun*, October 24, 1911.
29. "Mrs. Emerson Uses Pistol," *Baltimore Sun*, January 19, 1901.
30. "Burglar at Dr. Emerson's," *Baltimore Sun*, April 18, 1900.
31. "A Daring Burglar," *Baltimore Sun*, December 10, 1897; "Davis Is Recognized," *Baltimore Sun*, December 11, 1897.

Chapter 5

1. "Funeral of Mr. Garrett," *Baltimore Sun*, September 29, 1884.
2. "McKims Agree to Part," *Baltimore Sun*, May 22, 1909.
3. "Miss Margaret Emerson," *Baltimore Sun*, October 30, 1902.
4. "The Stuyvesants of New York City," *Louisville Courier-Journal*, August 2, 1903.
5. Advertisement for B. B. Kirkland & Co. that appeared in the *Hartford Courant* (Connecticut) on July 2, 1886.
6. "What is doing in Society," *Baltimore Sun*, May 17, 1901.
7. https://www.britannica.com/biography/Henry-Charles-Keith-Petty-Fitzmaurice-5th-marquess-of-Lansdowne. Accessed August 9, 2017.
8. "Globe Girdler Home," *Baltimore Sun*, June 12, 1902.
9. "Yacht Margaret in Port," *Baltimore Sun*, July 7, 1902.
10. "Globe Girdler Home."
11. "Yacht Margaret in Port."
12. Emerson papers.
13. "Whiskey and Wine at Auction," *Baltimore Sun*, April 25, 1900.
14. "Auto Run to Washington," *Baltimore Sun*, September 9, 1902.
15. "Carriage Without Horses," *Baltimore Sun*, December 20, 1898.

16. "Fast Time in Auto," *Baltimore Sun*, October 20, 1902.
17. "High Surf Stops Autos," *Baltimore Sun*, January 28, 1905; "Barney Oldfield," *New York Times*, October 6, 1946.
18. "Board Accepts Withdrawal," *Baltimore Sun*, November 14, 1903; "Auto Case Angers Emerson," *New York Times*, January 22, 1905; "Mrs. Emerson Settles," *Baltimore Sun*, March 22, 1905.
19. "Miss Margaret Emerson," *Baltimore Sun*, October 30, 1902.
20. *Ibid.*
21. "Dr. Smith H. McKim Dies in Baltimore," *Baltimore Sun*, September 21, 1932.
22. "McKim-Emerson," *New York Times*, December 31, 1902.
23. "Miss Emerson a Bride," *Baltimore Sun*, December 31, 1902.
24. "Studied Fine Gardens," *Baltimore Sun*, June 2, 1903.
25. *Ibid.*
26. Michael P. Reed, "The Intrepid Mrs. Sally James Farnham: An American Sculptor Rediscovered," *Aristo*, https://www.aristos.org/aristos2.htm, November 2007, Accessed June 18, 2018.
27. "Julia Farnham Wed To Police Captain," *New York Times*, September 16, 1932.
28. Sally James Farnham to "My dear Captain Emerson," 7 January 1904. Emerson papers.
29. "The Intrepid Mrs. Sally James Farnham."
30. Isaac E. Emerson to "My dear Mrs. Farnham," January 12, 1904, Emerson papers.
31. "Julia Farnham Wed To Police Captain."
32. *Ibid.*
33. "Dr. Isaac E. Emerson's Magnificent Italian Garden, Filled with Splendid Statuary and Works of Art, Are Now Complete," *Baltimore Sun*, May 29, 1904.
34. "Lions in the Emerson Crest," *Baltimore Sun*, October 8, 1911.
35. "Society News," *Baltimore Sun*, May 29, 1904.
36. Henry Louis Mencken, *Newspaper Days* (New York: Alfred A. Knopf, 1941), 282, as cited in Robert J. Brugger, *Maryland: A Middle Temperament 1634–1980* (Baltimore: Johns Hopkins University Press, 1988), 416.

37. "Office of the President," Emerson papers.
38. *Ibid.*
39. Correspondence in Emerson papers.
40. https://www.revolvy.com/topic/Rol and%20B.%20Molineux&item_type=topic. Accessed November 10, 2017.
41. John O'Dell, "This Headache is Killing Me," *The Readex Report* 4, no. 4 (November 2009).
42. *Ibid.*
43. "Mr. Emerson Testifies," *Baltimore Sun*, February 6, 1900.
44. http://www.informationfrance.com/Trouville-sur-Mer.php. Accessed August 13, 2017.
45. "Dr. Emerson is Home," *Baltimore Sun*, September 15, 1904.
46. "Shot Dead With His Own Weapon," *The Farmer and Mechanic* (Raleigh), November 29, 1904.
47. Family Group Record-8, 16.
48. "J. Ed. Murray Dies in Canada of Pneumonia," *Baltimore Sun*, August 15, 1938.
49. "Millions in Bromo-Seltzer," *New York Times*, July 2, 1903.
50. Display Ad, *The Afro-American*, November 7, 1903.
51. https://candyprofessor.com/2010/03/15/cascarets-candy-cathartic/. Accessed March 10, 2017.

Chapter 6

1. "Finds Elder Guilty," *Chicago Daily Tribune*, May 28, 1892; "Netcher Pays Big Rental," *Chicago Daily Tribune*, September 22, 1899; "A. P. T. Elder Pays A $500 Fine," *Chicago Daily Tribune*, February 9, 1900.
2. William D. Mann, ed., *Fads and Fancies of Representative Americans at the Beginning of the Twentieth Century, Being a Portrayal of Their Tastes, Diversions and Achievements* (New York: Town Topics Publishing, 1905),vii.
3. Abram P. T. Elder Papers, Manuscript Division, Library of Congress, Washington, D.C. Box 4, Folder 1.
4. "Mr. Burden Describes 'Fads and Fancies' Call," *New York Times*, December 29, 1905.
5. https://msu.edu/~graye/emma/mann_obit.html. Accessed June 8, 2018.

Notes—Chapter 6

"Mr. Burden Describes 'Fad and fancies' Call."

6. Finding Aid, Abram P. T. Elder Papers.

7. "Old Main Artifacts," posted on March 28, 2013, at https://oldmainartifacts.wordpress.com/2013/03/28/bromo-seltzer-emerson-drug-co-baltimore-md/. Accessed March 30, 2017.

8. *The Pharmaceutical Era*, Vol. 22 (New York: D. O. Haynes, 1899), 678.

9. "Pure Food Investigation," *New York Times*, May 12, 1899.

10. H. W. Wiley, "The Harmful Effects of Acetanilide, Autipyrin, and Phenace," Farmers' Bulletin, U.S. Department of Agriculture, July 5, 1909.

11. L. F. Keebler, F. P. Morgan, and Philip Roth, "Harmfulness of Headache Mixtures," Farmers' Bulletin, U.S. Department of Agriculture, September 28, 1909.

12. S. H. Adams, "The Great American Fraud," *Collier's Weekly*, October 7, 1905, 3.

13. Collier's October 7, 1905, 6.

14. Ibid., 4.

15. "Bane in Patent Medicine," *Chicago Daily Tribune*, March 11, 1906.

16. https://www.fda.gov/aboutfda/whatwe do/history/centennialoffda/harveyw.wiley/default.htm. Accessed April 24, 2017.

17. "Taft Hits Drug Frauds," *Baltimore Sun*, June 22, 1911; "The Big Stick," *Chicago Daily Tribune*, June 12, 1911.

18. William J. Mayo, "The Medical Profession and the Issues Which Confront It," *Science* 23, no. 598 (June 15, 1906), 899.

19. William J. Robinson, MD, "Impotence Caused by the Excessive Consumption of Bromo-Seltzer," *Journal of the American Medical Association* XLVII, no. 2 (August 15, 1906), 508.

20. Henry Bixby Hemenway, "Clinical Notes," *Journal of the American Medical Association* XLVII, no. 6 (December 29, 1906), 2, 158.

21. "Sultry Weather Hints for Hard Working Men," *Chicago Daily Tribune*, July 2, 1907.

22. W. A. Evans, "How to Keep Well," *Chicago Daily Tribune*, June 12, 1919. W. A. Evans, "How to Keep Well, *Chicago Daily Tribune*, August 13, 1929.

23. "Dr. Wiley Seeks New Law," *Washington Post*, October 27, 1911.

24. "Dr. Wiley Attacks 'Quacks,'" *Washington Post*, May 22, 1911.

25. "Harvey W. Wiley: Pioneer Consumer Activist," *FDA Consumer magazine*, The Centennial Edition, January–February 2006, 2.

26. Tim Daly, *Daly's Bartenders' Encyclopedia: A Complete Guide* (Worcester, MA: T. Daly 1903), 98.

27. "Chicago Cat Show Closes," *Chicago Daily Tribune*, December 11, 1898.

28. "Police Must Sober 'Drunks,'" *New York Times*, May 29, 1904.

29. "Seventy Years of the Scientific American," *Scientific American*, 112, no. 23 (June 5, 1915), 590.

30. F. Scott Fitzgerald, *This Side of Paradise* (New York: Charles Scribner's, 1920), 214.

31. "Baseball Brevities," *Chicago Daily Tribune*, February 10, 1920.

32. "A.B.C.'s Big Bowling Tourney Opens," *Chicago Daily Tribune*, February 24, 1924.

33. "Wed Two Hours Then Deserted; Gets Divorce," *Chicago Daily Tribune*, April 14, 1922; Elizabeth C. B. Pratt, "The Many "Date Keepers" of New York," *New York Times*, June 25, 1922.

34. "Gunmen Hold Up Drug Store," *New York Times*, January 14, 1923.

35. H. L. Mencken, "On Encyclopedias," *Chicago Daily Tribune*, May 16, 1926.

36. Will Rogers, "Challenges the World," *Washington Post*, April 24, 1927.

37. A. William Dunn, III, "How to Have a Good Time Doing Lil' Old New York," *Afro-American*, June 6, 1929.

38. Alice-Leone Moats, *No Nice Girl Swears* (New York: Knopf, 1933), 24.

39. "To Head Peking College," *Baltimore Sun*, January 10, 1921.

40. George N. Slattery to Capt I. E. Emerson, n.d., Emerson papers.

41. "To the Stockholders of the Emerson Drug Company of Baltimore City," Emerson papers, File 5.

42. Editorial, *Journal of the American Medical Association* XLVII, no. 1 (July 8, 1906), 286.

43. Elder Papers, Box 4, Folder 7.

44. Henry C. Fuller, *The Story of Drugs: a popular exposition of their origin, preparation, and commercial importance* (New York: The Century Company, 1912), 40.

45. "Proposal by Edgar M. Noel," Emerson papers.
46. https://sha.org/bottle/pdffiles/Bromo-Seltzer.pdf. Accessed May 21, 2018.
47. "What a Man and His Industry Are Doing for Baltimore," *Wall Street Journal*, May 24, 1912.
48. Fuller, 40.
49. *Ibid.*
50. Gilbert Percival, MD, "Money Spent for Patent Nostrums," *Health* (January 1907), 19.
51. Americanhistory.si.edu/collections/search/object/nmah/715_714. Accessed July 15, 2018.
52. Clayton Coleman Hall, ed., *Baltimore: Biography* (Baltimore: Lewis Historical Publishing,1912), 874.

Chapter 7

1. Charles Joyner, *Down By the Riverside: A South Carolina Slave Society* (Urbana:, University of Illinois Press, 1984), 12.
2. Interview with Lee Gordon Bockington, Senior Interpreter, HobCaw Barony, Georgetown, South Carolina, May 17, 2017.
3. William Oliver Stevens, *Charleston: Historic City of Gardens* (New York: Dodd, Mead, 1939), 302.
4. "Get Some Yankee Money," *Georgetown Daily Item*, February 17, 1908.
5. Julia Brock and Daniel Vivian, 73.
6. "Thems Our Sentiments," *Georgetown Times*, January 12, 1907, as cited in Jennifer Betsworth, *Then Came the Peaceful Invasion of Northerners: The Impact of Outsiders on Plantation Architecture in Georgetown County South Carolina.* Master's Thesis, University of South Carolina, 2011. 23.
7. Julia Brock and Daniel Vivian, 63.
8. Registrar of Deeds Records, Charleston, South Carolina. Examined May 18, 2017.
9. *Neal Cox of Arcadia*, 29.
10. https://www.merriam-webster.com/dictionary/arcadia. Accessed August 21, 2017.
11. "News of the Shipping," *Baltimore Sun*, October 18, 1907. In later years, the Captain replaced the *Gardenia* with newer boats, including the *Alligator*, manned by a "Negro" named Alonzo Grate. Emerson also bought the *Perch*, a 30-foot boat with an open cockpit, that he used once a day every day between Arcadia and Georgetown for errands (*Neal Cox of Arcadia*, 24–25).
12. Brockington interview.
13. "Holiday Deer Hunting," *Gaffney Ledger*, January 6, 1920.
14. Brockington interview.
15. "Emersons to Move Away," *Baltimore Sun*, January 27, 1907.
16. "Emerson's Southern Home," *Georgetown Times*, February 9, 1907.
17. "Wealthy Hunters Sport in Georgetown Country," *Times and Democrat* (Orangeburg, SC), December 18, 1913; "Taken for Vanderbilt," *Baltimore Sun*, December 20, 1913.
18. "Emerson Hunting License Controversy," *Georgetown Times*, December 20, 1913.
19. *Ibid.*
20. "Prospect Hill," *Georgetown Times*, March 6, 1907; *Neal Cox of Arcadia Plantation*, 32.
21. "Prospect Hill."
22. *Ibid.* The spelling of her last name appeared in newspapers as McCormick and McCormack. I have chosen to use the latter spelling as it conforms with the name she used on her marriage license.
23. *Neal Cox of Arcadia*, 32.
24. "Behind the Old Homes of Waccamaw is a Story," *Florence Morning News*, October 20, 1957.
25. Alberta Morel Lachicotte, *Georgetown Rice Plantations* (Georgetown, South Carolina: Georgetown County Historical Society, 1993), 18.
26. "Behind the Old Homes."
27. http://www.latimes.com/business/hollywood/la-fi-ct-oscars-red-carpet-20170224-htmlstory.html. Accessed August 20, 2017.
28. Harlow Giles Unger, *Lafayette* (New York: John Wiley and Sons, 2002), 31.
29. Bernard M. Baruch, "Bernard Mannes Baruch to Gladys Newman," September 14, 1936, WWP 16843, Cary T. Grayson Papers, Woodrow Wilson Presidential Library and Museum, Staunton, VA.

30. "Lafayette Story Untrue," *News and Courier*, August 23, 1936. A corroborating account can be found in Stanley J. Idzerda, *Lafayette in the Age of the American Revolution: Selected Letters and Papers, Vol. 1* (Ithaca, New York: Cornell University Press, 1977), 6,60-61.
31. "The State of South Carolina, County of Georgetown," In the Court of Common Pleas Decree: Isaac E. Emerson, Plaintiff vs. Robert Grate and Andrew Alston and other persons whose names are unknown," *Georgetown Times*, December 26, 1930.
32. Records of Registrar of Deeds, Georgetown, SC. Accessed May 18, 2017.
33. *Neal Cox of Arcadia*, 64.
34. *Ibid.*, 32–34.
35. Julia Brock and David Vivian, 44; "Arcadia Featured on Prince Georges Historic Tour," *Georgetown Times*, April 3, 1975.
36. Daniel J. Vivian, "The Leisure Plantations of the South Carolina Lowcountry," Doctoral Dissertation, The Johns Hopkins University, 2011, 116.
37. *Neal Cox of Arcadia*, 54–55.
38. *Ibid.*, 58.
39. *Ibid.*, 67.
40. "Cap't Emerson Home," *Baltimore Sun*, December 4, 1911; "Cap't Emerson in Peril," *Baltimore Sun*, December 3, 1911.

Chapter 8

1. "Son-in-Law Sues Emerson," *New York Times*, September 11, 1907.
2. *Ibid.* "Sued by Son-in-Law," *Afro-American*, September 11, 1907.
3. "Dr. Emerson to Pay $500," *Baltimore Sun*, December 21, 1908.
4. "Mrs. Horner Again a Bride," *Baltimore Sun*, January 5, 1909; "Saved Mrs. Horner's Life," *Baltimore Sun*, January 3, 1909.
5. "Husband Fights Wife's Move to Annual Divorce She Secured," *Baltimore Sun*, July 27, 1924.
6. Wife Sues Major Hanson," *Baltimore Sun*, August 19, 1909; "Major Hanson Dead; Wife at Point Loma," *Baltimore Sun*, December 16, 1910; "Mrs McVickar As 'Boss,'" *Baltimore Sun*, October 26, 1911.
7. http://www.the towersri.com/our-past/. Accessed September 4, 2017.
8. "She May Be Ruler of '400,'" *Baltimore Sun*, November 16, 1908.
9. "Mrs. Smith Hollins McKim," *Oakland Tribune*, January 15, 1909.
10. "Some Tea Table Confidences," *New York Times*, October 4, 1903.
11. "Social Sets of Other Cities," *Washington Post*, September 23, 1910.
12. Beverly Bridges, *Great Camp Sagamore* (Charleston, SC: The History Press, 2012), vii.
13. "McKims Agree to Separate," *Baltimore Sun*, May 22, 1909.
14. "Church to Modify Divorce Stand, Predicts Reno Judge," *Baltimore Sun*, October 8, 1922; "Cables News to Parents," *Baltimore Sun*, December 18, 1911.
15. http://people.howstuffworks.com/question741.htm. Accessed September 4, 2017.
16. "Ray Baker in News Again," *Reno Evening Gazette*," April 3, 1917.
17. "Mrs. McKim Surprised," *Baltimore Sun*, June 12, 1910.
18. http://knowledgecenter.unr.edu/digital_collections/exhibits/johnson_jeffries/default.aspx. Accessed September 4, 2017.
19. "Incident of McKim Divorce," *San Francisco Call*, June 29, 1913.
20. "Mrs. McKim Helps Boys," *New York Times*, May 16, 1910; "Ray Baker in News Again," *Reno Evening Gazette*, April 3, 1917.
21. "Mrs McKim Off to Japan," *Washington Post*, August 18, 1910; "Mrs. McKim Off for Hawaii," *Baltimore Sun*, August 16, 1910.
22. "Tea at Narragansett," *Washington Post*, July 24, 1910.
23. http://www.narragansetthistoricalsociety.com/mathewson-hotel/ Accessed September 8, 2017.
24. "They Thought It a Joke," *Baltimore Sun*, August 9, 1910.
25. "Mrs. Emerson is Home," *Baltimore Sun*, August 12, 1910.
26. "Mrs. McKim Not Even Betrothed," *Richmond Times Dispatch*, October 30, 1910.
27. "Fashion's Fads and Fancies," *Washington Post*, November 11, 1910.
28. https://airandspace.si.edu/collec

tion-objects/international-aviation-meet-belmont-park-photographs-1910. Accessed September 6, 2017.
29. "Fashion's Fads and Fancies."
30. "Mrs. McKim Causes Stir," *Baltimore Sun*, November 15, 1910.
31. "May Call It Emerson," *Baltimore Sun*, November 5, 1909.
32. https://www.philadelphiabuildings.org/pab/app/ar_display.cfm/81494. Accessed September 7, 2017.
33. "Sperry Obsequies To Be Held Today," *Baltimore Sun*, August 8, 1930.
34. "May Call It Emerson."
35. Gil Sanders, "Coatless in Baltimore," article e-mailed to author. A similar account appears in "For Rent: Emersonian's 'mansion in the sky,'" *Baltimore Sun*, August 11, 1985.
36. Emerson papers.
37. "To Be Like a Palace," *Baltimore Sun*, February 11, 1911.
38. "Chesapeake Room Plan," *Baltimore Sun*, April 22, 1911. http://baltimorestyle.com/10258/baltimore_marble_and_mirrors_jf11/ Accessed November 8, 2016.
39. "No Tips for Iced Water," *Baltimore Sun*, September 5, 1911.
40. "Markets Here Ample, He Says," *Baltimore Sun*, August 31, 1911.
41. "Major League Ball Pays," *Baltimore Sun*, May 31, 1911. https://www.baseball-reference.com/register/team.cgi?id=de960238. Accessed May 31, 2018.
42. "Chesapeake Room Plan," *Baltimore Sun*, April 22, 1911.
43. "No Tips for Iced Water."
44. "Mustaches Ordered Off," *Baltimore Sun*, November 3, 1911.
45. Kemp C. Gatling, "Remember…the live frogs at the Emerson," *Baltimore Sun*, April 18, 1971; "Baltimore_Marble_and Mirrors_JF11," *Baltimore Style*, http://baltimorestyle.com/10258/baltimore_marble_and_mirrors_jf11/. Accessed November 8, 2016.
46. Sister Madeline Doyle, "Early Twentieth Century Baltimore: The Art of James Doyle, Jr. (1880–1952)," *Maryland Historical Magazine* 82 (Winter, 1987), 307.
47. "Emerson Like a Palace," *Baltimore Sun*, October 31, 1911.
48. "Hotel as City Boomer," *Baltimore Sun*, May 3, 1911.
49. http://rmccivilwar.blogspot.com/2012/09/benjamin-lyons-farinholt-student-1855.html. Accessed November 15, 2017.
50. "Gives $500 for Lee Memorial," *Baltimore Sun*, January 19, 1912. https://Twitter.Com/HistoryNet. Accessed December 15, 2017.
51. "Emerson Opens Tonight," *Baltimore Sun*, October 30, 1911.
52. "Capt Emerson Dined," *Baltimore Sun*, November 10, 1911; "Emerson Guest Tonight," *Baltimore Sun*, November 9, 1911; "Ready for Emerson Dinner," *Baltimore Sun*, October 7, 1911.
53. Pietila, *Not In My Neighborhood*, 14.

Chapter 9

1. "Will Work for Emerson," *Baltimore Sun*, February 11, 1912.
2. "Men of Millions Here," *Baltimore Sun*, April 24, 1912.
3. *The JHU Gazette*, August 18, 2008; Stan M. Haynes, "When Baltimore was convention central," *Baltimore Sun*, June 28, 2012; "After Rooms Ready," *Baltimore Sun*, January 10, 1912.
4. Neil A. Grauer, "Ah, what a grand do was the 1912 convention," *Baltimore Sun*, June 27, 1982; Urey Woodson. *Temporary Roll of Delegates and Alternates to the Democratic National Convention, Baltimore, MD, June 25, 1912* (Baltimore: Day Printing, 1912); "Wilson Lived Here," *Baltimore Sun*, June 29, 1912.
5. "Forward! Is Cry," *Baltimore Sun*, January 26, 1912.
6. "Tars Outline Plans," *Baltimore Sun*, January 31, 1912.
7. "All Hail Capt. Emerson," *Baltimore Sun*, October 6, 1912.
8. "West Measure Knocked Out," *Baltimore Sun*, August 6, 1913.
9. "Baltimore Tries Drastic Plan of Race Segregation," *New York Times*, December 25, 1910.
10. Ibid.
11. Ibid.
12. "West Measure Knocked Out."
13. "Baltimore Race Riot," *Washington Post*, September 26, 1913.
14. "White Headwaiter at Emerson," *Afro-American*, May 9, 1914.

15. "French Chefs 'Fired,'" *Baltimore Sun*, June 30, 1913.
16. "21 Cooks Dismissed From Emerson Hotel," *Afro-American*, May 12, 1922.
17. "Presbyterians Walk Out of Emerson Hotel," *Afro-American*, June 5, 1926.
18. "600 Give Cullen An Ovation Here," *Afro-American*, June 26, 1926.
19. "H.U. Profs Insulted at Emerson Hotel," *Afro-American*, March 10, 1928.
20. "Bar Diners From Hotel Dance," *Afro-American*, February 15, 1941; "Hotel Plans Race Ban on Legionnaires," *Afro-American*, August 2, 1941.
21. Elizabeth Fee, Linda Shopes, and Linda Zeldman. Eds., *The Baltimore Book: New Views of Local History* (Philadelphia: Temple University Press, 1991), 193.
22. "Says 'Welfare' Gives Only Avenue to Segregation," *Baltimore Sun*, January 16, 1924.
23. Gilbert Sandler, "The Big Blue Bottle," *Baltimore Evening Sun*, May 5, 1992; "Big Tower Completed," *Baltimore Sun*, June 24, 1911; Gilbert Sandler, "Where's the Bromo bottle?" *Baltimore Evening Sun*, March 6, 1984.
24. "The Bromo-Seltzer Building," *American Druggist and Pharmaceutical Record*, September 11, 1911, 52.
25. "Carolinians Who Work," *Baltimore Sun*, June 6, 1910.

Chapter 10

1. "Captain Emerson Sues Wife in Baltimore," *Chicago Daily Tribune*, January 20, 1911.
2. "McKim Agrees Not to Sue Vanderbilt," *New York Times*, February 22, 1911. "McKim to Get $7,500 a Year," *Washington Post*, February 23, 1911.
3. "Five Days for Devine," *Baltimore Sun*, June 5, 1900.
4. "Emerson Seeks Divorce," *Baltimore Sun*, January 20, 1911.
5. "A Judicial Indiscretion," *Baltimore Sun*, January 27, 1911.
6. "All Should Be Alike Before the Law," *Baltimore Sun*, January 22, 1911.
7. "Alimony $28,000 A Year," *Baltimore Sun*, May 30, 1911.
8. *Ibid.*

9. "Capt. Emerson Not to Wed," *New York Times*, June 28, 1911.
10. Emerson-McCormack marriage license, Accessed on Ancestry.com January 10, 2018; "Special to the New York Times," *New York Times*, July 6, 1911.
11. "Snapshots at Social Leaders," *Washington Post*, July 17, 1911.
12. "Cap't Emerson and Mrs. McCormack Under the Camera," *Baltimore Sun*, June 22, 1911.
13. "Agog Over Emerson Nuptials," *Baltimore Sun*, July 7, 1911; "Ends Honeymoon Trip of Family," *Detroit Free Press*, September 8, 1911.
14. *Ibid.*
15. "Mr. Emerson at Newport," *Baltimore Sun*, July 15, 1908; "Louis M. Blumstein Dies," *New York Times*, January 27, 1920. Isaac and Margaret had been to Newport five years earlier but only for a short time and also without Emilie. The October 4, 1903, social page of the *New York Times*, "Some Tea Table Confidences," reported that "Mr. Emerson's yacht touched at Narragansett and Newport."
16. "Cap't. and Mrs. Isaac E. Emerson," *Baltimore Sun*, July 7, 1911.
17. "Cap't Emerson and Mrs. McCormack Under the Camera."
18. "Those Marrying and Un-marring Emersons," *San Francisco Chronicle*, July 23, 1911.
19. "Captain Emerson Not to Wed."
20. "Those Marrying and Unmarrying Emersons."
21. "Home with New Ideas," *Baltimore Sun*, September 8, 1911.
22. *Ibid.*
23. "Capt. Emerson Returns," *Baltimore Sun*, September 12, 1911.
24. Edward Emerson Murray to Board of Governors-the Maryland Club, Oil Painting-Madeline Repentante, January 25, 1996.
25. "Mrs. Emerson Weds Today," *New York Times*, August 22, 1912; "Mrs. Emerson Married," *Washington Post*," August 23, 1912.
26. "Capt. Emerson Loses," *Baltimore Sun*, April 26, 1913; "Mrs. Basshor Demurs," *New York Times*, September 12, 1912.
27. "Mrs. Basshor to Move," *Baltimore Sun*, May 4, 1915; "Rayner Place is Sold," *Baltimore Sun*, November 30, 1912.

28. "Garretts Sell Land," *Baltimore Sun*, May 2, 1913. SCL 3179, 228, Baltimore City Land Records, Maryland State Archives, Annapolis, Maryland.
29. "C. H. Basshor Wounded," *Baltimore Sun*, August 20, 1914.
30. " Basshor Dies of Wounds," *Baltimore Sun*, April 23, 1914.
31. *Ibid*.
32. "Mrs. Basshor to Move." https://www.thesevern.com/. Accessed May 22, 2018.
33. "Married," *New York Times*, December 18, 1911.
34. "Bride Cables Her Parents, *New York Times*, December 18, 1911.
35. "Their Pre-Nuptial Divorce Pact," *Salt Lake Tribune*, September 22, 1912.
36. Alfred G. Vanderbilt, Jr., "The End of Innocence," *Forbes*, October 11, 1999, 70–74.
37. Steven H. and Emily Gittleman. *Alfred Gwynne Vanderbilt: Hero of the Lusitania (Lanham, MD: Hamilton Books,* 2013) 6–16.
38. Beverly Bridger. *Great Camp Sagamore: The Vanderbilts' Adirondack Retreat* (Charleston, SC: The History Press, 2012) , 12; "Vanderbilt Left His Wife at Home," *New York Times*, May 8, 1915.
39. http://hovehistory.blogspot.com/2016/10/alfred-vanderbilt-and-his-horses.html. Accessed March 10, 2018.
40. "Vanderbilt Engagement," *New York Times*, April 29, 1900.
41. "Mrs. A. G. Vanderbilt Gives Birth to Son," *New York Times*, September 23, 1912; Alfred G. Vanderbilt, Jr., "Vanderbilt Engagement."
42. "The Missouri Girl Who Disturbs the British Gov't," *St. Louis Post-Dispatch*, July 4, 1909.
43. "Decree of Divorce for Mrs. Vanderbilt," *New York Times*, May 26, 1908.
44. "Cables News to Parents: Both Captain Emerson and Bride's Mother anticipated the Marriage," *Baltimore Sun*, December 8, 1911.
45. Alfred G. Vanderbilt, Jr., "The End of Innocence"; "Decree of Divorce for Mrs. Vanderbilt," *New York Times*, May 26, 1908; "In Fashion's Realm," *Washington Post*, June 13, 1908; Alfred G. Vanderbilt, Jr., "The End of Innocence."
46. "The Missouri Girl."
47. "Life of Vanderbilt Was Marked by Many Climaxes of Moods and Love Affairs," *Greenville News*, May 30, 1915; "The Missouri Girl Who Disturbed the British Gov't."
48. "MME. Ruiz' Suicide Stirs All London," *Chicago Daily Tribune*, June 13, 1909. "Mystery About Suicide," *Baltimore Sun*, June 13, 1909.
49. "Jewels Owned by Mrs. Ruiz Bring $35,000," *St. Louis Post-Dispatch*," December 14, 1909; "Smart Sets in Other Cities," *Washington Post*, December 16, 1909.
50. "$350,000 for Ruiz Gems," *New York Times*, December 18, 1909. While the *Times* reported the figure as $350,000, the *Washington Post* and *St. Louis Post Dispatch* reported $35,000.
51. "Jewels Owned by Mrs. Ruiz Bring $35,000," *St. Louis Post-Dispatch*, December 14, 1909.
52. "The Missouri Girl."
53. "Editorial Pen Points," *Los Angeles Times*, June 12, 1909, as cited in Gittleman, *Alfred Gwynne Vanderbilt*, 47.
54. Greg King and Penny Wilson, *Lusitania: Triumph, Tragedy, and the End of the Edwardian Age* (New York: St. Martin's, 2015), 217.
55. " Vanderbilt Bridal Nest Is the Acme of Luxury," *Farmer and Mechanic*, December 26, 1911.
56. "A. G. Vanderbilts Here," *New York Times*, November 3, 1912.
57. http://greatcampsagamore.org/history. Accessed December 18, 2017.
58. "Mrs. Vanderbilt Here," *Baltimore Sun*, December 15, 1912.
59. Alfred Vanderbilt III, "All Aboard for Sagamore," Special Edition Sagamore E-Newsletter. Received by e-mail from the author, April 2, 2017.

Chapter 11

1. "A. G. Vanderbilts Here."
2. "Takes Brookland," *Baltimore Sun*, December 7, 1911; "$400,000 The Price," *Baltimore Sun*, July 16, 1912.
3. "Vanderbilts Expected," *Baltimore Sun*, November 4, 1912.
4. "Prompt Delivery of Brooklandwood Spring Water and Products," *Baltimore Sun*, May 1, 1915.

Notes—Chapter 11

5. "Pertinent Comment," *Evening Star*, July 16, 1912; Louis Dorsey Clark, "A History of Brooklandville," November 6, 1968, 2, manuscript provided to the author by Jennifer Trone, an administrator at St. Paul's School.

6. "Bonding Co. Wants Lot," *Baltimore Sun*, November 30, 1911.

7. Helen Henry, "The House on the Hill is Full of History," *Baltimore Sun*, December 12, 1971.

8. "Dr. Wickes Dies at 83 at His Home," *Baltimore Sun*, November 9, 1960. "Real Estate Deals and Building News," *Baltimore Sun*, July 22, 1926. https://www.maryvale.com/about-maryvale/history-at-a-glance. Accessed April 23, 2018.

9. "Second Fire This Month on I. E. Emerson's Estate," *Baltimore Sun*, October 30, 1921; "A History of Brooklandville," MS, November 6, 1968, 10.

10. "McAdoo-McCormick," *New York Times*, May 25, 1913.

11. "Francis M'Adoo Weds," *Washington Post*, June 22, 1913; "Becomes Bride of F. H. M'Adoo," *Baltimore Sun*, June 22, 1913; "The President at a Wedding," *New York Times*, November 25, 1913.

12. "Francis M'Adoo Weds."

13. "Unknown Horse Wins on Famous Track," *Daily Gate City* (Keokuk, IA), May 15, 1913. http://www.horsenation.com/2014/04/04/7-horses-that-werent-supposed-to-win-the-kentucky-derby-but-did/. Accessed December 20, 2017.

14. "Baltimoreans Attend Newport Horse Show," *Baltimore Sun*, September 2, 1913; "Narragansett Ball Gay With Costumes," *Baltimore Sun*, August 23, 1913.

15. "Yachts to Race for Cup," *Baltimore Sun*, September 15, 1913; "Eleanor, By Time Allowance, Wins the Baltimore Yacht Club Race," *Baltimore Sun*, September 21, 1913.

16. W. G. McAdoo to "Dear Governor," Georgetown, South Carolina, December 31, 1913, in *The Papers of Woodrow Wilson Digital Edition (*Charlottesville: University of Virginia Press, Rotunda 2017).

17. "Women to Aid Party," *Washington Post*, January 10, 1914.

18. King and Wilson, 5–10.

19. "Disaster Bears Out Embassy's Warning," *New York Times*, May 8, 1915.

20. King and Wilson, 8.

21. *Ibid.*, 111–112.

22. *Ibid.*, 217.

23. Thomas A. Bailey and Paul B. Ryan, *The Lusitania Disaster: The Real Answers Behind The World's Most Controversial Sea Tragedy*. (New York: Free Press, 1975), 193; "Rewards Out for Dead," *Baltimore Sun*, May 14, 1915; "Hunt for Vanderbilt," *Washington Post*, May 11, 1915.

24. Gittleman and Gittleman, 4; http://www.rmslusitania.info/people/second-cabin/alice-middleton/. Accessed January 13, 2018.

25. "Vanderbilt Saved Woman," *New York Times*, May 10, 1915.

26. Alfred Vanderbilt, Jr., "The end of innocence."

27. "Many Children Owe Lives to Vanderbilt," *New York Times*, May 11, 1915.

28. "Alfred Gwynne Vanderbilt," *Chicago Daily Tribune*, May 9, 1915.

29. "Vanderbilt Family All But Hopeless," *New York Times*, May 9, 1915.

30. *New York Herald*, May 10, 1915, as quoted in King and Wilson, 284.

31. "Vanderbilt Body Found," *Daily Journal*, (Philipsburg, Pennsylvania)May 12, 1915.

32. "Give Up Hope of Vanderbilt," *New York Times*, May 22, 1915.

33. "Hunt for Vanderbilt," *Washington Post*, May 11, 1915.

34. " "The Two Mrs. Vanderbilts--The Two Mrs. Astors--And The Strange Results of Two Ocean Tragedies," *Baltimore Sun*, June 20, 1915.

35. Last Will and Testament of Alfred G. Vanderbilt.

36. "Sister-In-Law and Niece of the president will Return to Baltimore," *Washington Post*, September 10, 1915.

37. *Greenville Daily News*, March 4, 1916; "Little Peeps at Smart Life," *Washington Post*, April 18, 1916.

38. "First Big Game Ever Played at Chapel Hill," *Wilmington Morning Star*, April 2, 1916.

39. "Virginia Takes Trip for Southern Games," *Washington Post*, April 1, 1916.

40. "Donator of Athletic Field Cannot Be Here for Virginia Game." *Daily Tar Heel*, April 1, 1916.

41. Isaac E. Emerson to Hon. Josephus Daniels et al, June 28, 1914, courtesy of Andrew Murray on September 20, 2018.

Chapter 12

1. "For rent: Emersonian's 'mansion in the sky,'" *Baltimore Sun*, August 11, 1985.
2. "A $250,000 Home for 28 Families," *Baltimore Sun*, February 8, 1916.
3. Ibid.
4. Gilbert Sandler, *Jewish Baltimore: A Family Album* (Baltimore: Johns Hopkins University Press, 2000), 43.
5. Ibid.
6. "Held for $5,000 Gem Theft," *Washington Post*, November 23, 1911; "Inventory of Debt Filed," *Baltimore Sun*, November 27, 1921; "Elevator Girl is Exonerated," *Afro-American*, September 9, 1921.
7. Gil Sandler, "Emersonian Headache," essay e-mailed to the author. A similar account can be found in "For rent: Emersonian's 'mansion in the sky.'"
8. *Greenville News*, March 24, 1916.
9. "Prize Day at Timonium," *Baltimore Sun*, September 4, 1918; "National Show of Jerseys to be Big Event," *Era-Leader* (Franklinton, LA), October 28, 1920; "Anthrax Closes a Dairy," *New York Times*, July 10, 1922.
10. "Emerson to Expand Along Baltimore St.," *Baltimore Sun*, March 22, 1922.
11. "Says Building Code Has Been Violated," *Baltimore Sun*, August 20, 1924.
12. "Acts on Charge Hotel is Gouging Football Fans," *Baltimore Evening Sun*, October 21, 1924.
13. "No Raise," *Honolulu Star-Bulletin*, November 21, 1924.
14. http://www.baltimoresun.com/sports/college/football/bal—army-navy-baltimore-history-20141212-story.html. Accessed June 16, 2018.
15. Richard S. Jackson, Jr., and Cornelia Brooks Gilder, *Houses of the Berkshires 1870–1930: The Architecture of Leisure*, revised ed (New York: Acanthers Press, 2011), 294.
16. "Will Auction Holmwood," *New York Times*, July 14, 1937. www.holmwoodhistory.com/page12.htm, accessed February 2, 2018.
17. "Washington Society News," *Washington Post*, August 12, 1936.
18. "Mrs. A. G. Vanderbilt Wed to R. T. Baker," *New York Times*, June 13, 1918; "Divorce Granted to Mrs. Amory," *Baltimore Sun*, November 15, 1934.
19. Betsy Patterson, "Betsy Patterson's Social Chatter, *Baltimore Sun*, July 25, 1920.
20. E. C. Drum-Hunt, "Society," *Washington Herald*, December 12, 1919.
21. "Prominent Couple Married at Grove Park," *Twin-City Daily Sentinel*, December 12, 1919.
22. "Musicale At Brooklandwood," *Baltimore Sun*, December 11, 1927; "Society," *Baltimore Sun*, June 10, 1921.
23. "Reflection," John Calvin Laslett. N.d. 6, 8. Received from Charlie Williams, Alumni Director, St. Pauls School, formerly Brooklandwood.
24. "Reflection," 10.
25. "Comment on Passing Events Heard in Washington Hotels," *Washington Post*, March 6, 1918.
26. "Gridiron Men Cheer," *Baltimore Sun*, February 18, 1917.
27. "Notable Audience Will Greet Grand Opera Tomorrow," *Washington Post*, December 4, 1927.
28. "Society, Society, Society," *Washington Post*, November 10, 1918; "Mrs. A. G. Vanderbilt Wed to R. T. Baker"; "Mrs. Emerson Off For South Pacific," *Baltimore Sun*, December 23, 1944.
29. "Former Vanderbilt Boat," *Newport Mercury*, May 25, 1917; "Vanderbilt Yacht Given to US," *Evening Star*, May 18, 1917.
30. "Who'll Buy $50,000," *Baltimore Sun*, October 17, 1918.
31. Prosper Buranelli, *Maggie of the Suicide Fleet: As Written From the Log of Raymond Davis Borden, Lieutenant U.S.N.R*. (New York: Doubleday, Doran, 1930), 2–3.
32. Stephen D. Regan, "When Frank Jack Met Maggie," *Naval History Magazine* 25, no. 1 (February 2011), 2, 52–57; Prosper Buranelli, 274–277.
33. "When Frank Jack Met Maggie." http://www.arlingtoncemetery.net/fj-fletc.htm. Accessed February 6, 2018.
34. Kate Coplan, "The Week at Pratt Library," *Baltimore Sun*, April 27, 1930.
35. "Reported to be Seeking Separation in Paris," *Baltimore Sun*, January 27, 1922.
36. "Mr. Baker Denies Rumor," *Baltimore Sun*, January 27, 1922.
37. "I. E. Emerson's Daughter Denies Separation Rumor," *Baltimore Sun*, May 6, 1922; "Denies Rumor of Divorce," *New York Times*, May 6, 1922.

38. Nancy L. Green, "When Paris Was Reno: American Divorce Tourism in the City of Light, 1920–1927," http://arcade.stanford.edu/content/when-paris-was-reno-american-divorce-tourism-city-light-1920-1927. Accessed March 31, 2018.
39. http://www.townoflenox.com/Public_Documents/LenoxMA_DPW/church%20on%20the%20hill%20cemetery%20burials.pdf. Accessed March 31, 2018.
40. $90,000 Estate Left to Her Daughters by Mrs. E.A. Basshor," *Baltimore Sun*, September 17, 1921; "Mrs. Emilie A. Basshor Dies at Atlantic City," *Baltimore Sun*, August 28, 1921.
41. "Mrs. R. T. Baker at Newport," *Baltimore Sun*, July 29, 1923.
42. http://www.newportmansions.org/explore/the-breakers. Accessed May 28, 2018.
43. "Mrs. R. T. Baker Given Divorce in Reno Court," *Baltimore Sun*, October 2, 1928; Nancy Randolph, "New York Society," *Chicago Daily Tribune*, October 7, 1928; "Raymond T. Baker to Run for Senate," *Baltimore Sun*, March 23, 1926.
44. "Mrs. Baker Not to Rewed," *New York Times*, October 4, 1928; Nancy Randolph, "New York Society, October 7, 1928.
45. "Stockbridge Tennis Won by Miss. Fenno and Mr. Chalfante," *New York Herald Tribune*, June 18, 1928.
46. Nancy Randolph, "New York Society," December 8, 1928.
47. "Mrs. Raymond T. Baker Wed to C. M. Amory By Archbishop Francis at F. Cutting Home," *New York Times*, October 25, 1928.
48. "Meet in Reno, Then They Wed in New York," *Chicago Daily Tribune*, December 5, 1928.
49. "Mrs. Ethel McAdoo Weds W. W. Keith At Emerson Home," *Baltimore Sun*, April 26, 1929; "Mrs. F. H. McAdoo Gets Divorce in Court at Paris," *Baltimore Sun*, November 23, 1923; "Given Partial Divorce from Walter Keith," *Baltimore Sun*, December 27, 1934; "Walter Keith Weds Daughter of Atterburys," *Washington Post*, January 8, 1936; "Divorce Granted to Mrs. Amory," *Baltimore Sun*, November 15, 1934.

Chapter 13

1. *Reflection*, 12.
2. Joseph P. Kelly, "At The Track: Thoroughbred Racing in Maryland, 1870–1973," *Maryland Historical Magazine* (Winter, 2005), 515; 22 Hugh Fullerton, "Salmon Chestnut Colt in Brilliant Victory," *Washington Post*, May 13, 1923.
3. "Virgil Leads Field in Rich Preakness," *New York Times*, May 13, 1923.
4. "Two Spills at Drag Hunt," *Baltimore Sun*, April 20, 1921.
5. "Society: Invitations Are Out for Easter Holiday Events," *Baltimore Sun*, April 5, 1925; "Society: Captain and Mrs. I. E. Emerson to Entertain At Their Valley Home Before Grand National," *Baltimore Sun*, March 22, 1926.
6. "Howard Bruce's Billy Barton Wins National Point-to-Point," *Baltimore Sun*, April 18, 1926; "Society-Spring Steeplechases Will Attract Wide Attention," *Baltimore Sun*, March 21, 1926.
7. "Grand National Captured by Philosopher in Downpour," *Baltimore Sun*, April 22, 1928; "Grand National Will Be Run Today," *Baltimore Sun*, April 21, 1928.
8. Wilf Pond, "Turf, Field, and Ring," *The Spur* 10, no. 45 (May 15, 1930), 168.
9. W. Wilson Wingate, "Chestnut Gelding Captures Grand National," *Baltimore Sun*, April 20, 1930.
10. "Society Reopens List for Dinner," *Baltimore Sun*, April 13, 1926; "Two Governors Voice Message of Democracy," *Baltimore Sun*, April 16, 1926.
11. Henry R. H. Sley, "Lord Chaucer, 40–1, Wins the Hopeful," *New York Times*, August 29, 1926.
12. Will P. Pond, "Turf, Field, and Ring," *Baltimore Sun*, December 16, 1926.
13. "Mrs. Baker has 29 Thoroughbreds Ready for Campaign," *Baltimore Sun*, April 8, 1928; "Views of Readers on Topics of Today," *Washington Post*, November 14, 1926.
14. Robert T. Small, "Bubbling Over Wins Derby," *Baltimore Sun*, May 16, 1926.
15. Telephone call to the author on June 1, 2018, from Chris Goodlett, Director of Curatorial and Educational Affairs, Churchill Downs, Lexington, Kentucky.
16. Edward Sparrow, "Mrs. Amory's

Sagamore Farm is Show Place of Country," *Baltimore Sun*, February 23, 1930.

17. "Capt. And Mrs. Emerson Give $6,000 To Eudood Campaign," *Baltimore Sun*, March 2, 1928; "Garrett, 85, Civic Leader, Banker Dies," *Baltimore Sun*, April 26, 1961; "F. A. Furst Dies," *New York Times*, January 24, 1934.

18. H. C. Byrd, "Tar Heels Get Stadium," *Evening Star*, November 2, 1925.

19. *Ibid.*, https://www.ncpedia.org/biography/kenan-william-rand-jr. Accessed February 8, 2018; David E. Brown, "Southern Beauty," *Carolina Alumni Review* (September–October 2002), 35–40.

20. U.S. School Yearbooks, 1880–2013.

21. "Women's Hospital Fund Now $984,766," *Baltimore Sun*, June 3, 1930.

22. "Reflection," John Calvin Laslett. n.d. 6, 8. Received from Charlie Williams, Alumni Director, St. Paul's School, formerly Brooklandwood.

23. "She Charges $400,000 in Gems to Boss," *Chicago Daily Tribune*, July 25, 1928; "Mrs. Emerson in Court Disavows Gem Deals," *New York Times*, April 30, 1930. https://www.si.edu/spotlight/hope-diamond/history, accessed February 10, 2018; "Woman Gets Jail Term in Charge Account Case," *Washington Post*, July 3, 1930. https://www.si.edu/spotlight/hope-diamond/history, accessed February 10, 2018.

24. "Emerson to Cruise in Big Sea Yacht," *Baltimore Sun*, May 17, 1928.

25. "Offers to Buy Bromo Seltzer for $10,000,000," *Baltimore Sun*, May 1, 1926.

26. "Narragansett Improvement Association, Inc.," Narragansett Pier, R.I., September 15, 1920. Hazard Family Papers, Rhode Island Historical Society, Sub-Group 31, Series 1, Sub-Series 2, Box 1, Folder 15. Subsequent citations of the correspondence will cite only the folder number.

27. Mr. T. G. Hazard from Isaac Emerson, March 9, 1925, Folder 17.

28. William H. Parker and Ralph A. Wells to The President and Board of Directors of the Narragansett Imp. Assoc., Inc., Narragansett Pier, June 7, 1921, Folder 14.

29. *Reflection*, n.d. 6.

30. Thomas G. Hazard to Capt. I. E. Emerson, October 5, 1922, Folder 15.

31. "In Gambling Raid," *Chicago Daily Tribune*, September 21, 1923.

32. Isaac E. Emerson to Mr. Thomas G. Hazard, Jr., May 20, 1927, Folder 17.

33. Isaac E. Emerson to the Board of Directors, December 13, 1928, Folder 19.

34. Isaac E. Emerson to T. G. Hazard, Esq., January 11, 1929, Folder 19.

35. "Grand National Will Be Run Today," *Baltimore Sun*, April 20, 1929; "Alligator Winner in Hunt Cup Race," *Baltimore Sun*, April 28, 1929.

36. Hazard to Emerson and Emerson to Hazard telegrams, April 10, 1929, Folder 19.

37. "Isaac Emerson's 'Whitehall' Is Sold," *Baltimore Sun*, July 13, 1948.

38. *Reflection*, 4.

39. *Ibid.*, 3.

40. "League of Women Voters Planning Benefit Tomorrow," *Baltimore Sun*, March 23, 1930.

41. "To Exhibit Gardens at Flower Show," *Baltimore Sun*, March 17, 1930; "Children Invited to Flower Show," *Baltimore Sun*, April 4, 1930.

42. *Neal Cox of Arcadia Plantation*, 68–69; "Captain I. E. Emerson Dies in Baltimore," *New York Times*, January 24, 1931.

43. "Isaac E. Emerson To Be Buried Today," *Baltimore Sun*, January 25, 1931.

44. Christopher Corbett, "Baltimore's Green Mount Cemetery," *Washington Post*, October 31, 1993; "Rites Tomorrow for Dr. H. H. M'Kim," *Baltimore Sun*, September 21, 1932.

Chapter 14

1. "Captain Emerson Left $20,000,000 Estate," *New York Times*, January 30, 1931. Many newspaper articles reported that Margaret bought the Lenox property, but the fact that Emerson left it to her in his will suggests he may have paid for Holmwood, which would be consistent with his life-long generosity toward his daughter.

2. "Rockefeller's Million Leads Relief in Gifts," *Chicago Daily Tribune*," November 22, 1931.

3. "Earning and Dividends," *Washington Post*, December 9, 1931.

4. "Dividends Omitted by Five Railroads," *New York Times*, December 9, 1931.

Notes—Chapter 14

5. "Dr. McKim's Widow Named Executrix," *Baltimore Sun*, September 27, 1932.
6. "Mrs. F. C. McCormack Seeks Divorce in Reno, Suit Charging Cruelty," *Baltimore Sun*, March 18, 1933.
7. "Mrs. Davis Married to F. C. McCormack," *New York Times*, May 13, 1934.
8. "Friend of Night-Club Singer Sues McCormack For $50,000," *Baltimore Sun*, May 24, 1934.
9. "Emerson Drug Ex-Executive Kills Himself," *New York Herald Tribune*, December 5, 1947.
10. "Given Partial Divorce From Walter Keith," *Baltimore Sun*, December 27, 1934.
11. https://www.liveabout.com/limited-divorce-what-you-need-to-know-1103152. Accessed February 21, 2018.
12. "Mrs. McCormick McAdoo Keith Files Divorce suit in Reno," *Baltimore Sun*, August 17, 1935.
13. "Veiled Kidnap Threat Sent to Emerson Widow," *Chicago Daily Tribune*, January 20, 1935.
14. "Walter Keith Weds Daughter of Atterburys," *Washington Post*, January 8, 1936.
15. "Mrs. Ethel Keith Married," *New York Times*, May 1, 1940; "Invitations Are Issued For An 'At Home,'" *Baltimore Sun*, November 3, 1940.
16. "Divorce Granted to Mrs. Amory," *Baltimore Sun*, November 15, 1934.
17. "Palm Beach Homes Opened by Visitors," *New York Times*, December 2, 1937.
18. "Palm Beach Hosts Have Yule Guests," *New York Times*, December 21, 1935.
19. Nancy Randolph, "Vanderbilts Building Pool at Oakland Farm," *Chicago Daily Tribune*, July 12, 1936; https://www.biography.com/people/benito-mussolini-9419443. Accessed February 26, 2018.
20. "$200,000 Fire Razes Home at Sands Point," *New York Times*, August 21, 1942.
21. "Lavish Party Given for Gloria Baker," *Baltimore Sun*, September 19, 1937; "Long Island Folk Return with Robins and Open Estates," *New York Herald Tribune*, April 4, 1938; "Lady Salvage Sells Long Island Estate," *New York Times*, January 19, 1947.
22. "Miss Gloria Baker Wed to Henry Topping," *New York Times*, December 20, 1938.
23. "Gloria Baker Taylor," *New York Times*, April 27, 1975; "Mrs. Emerson Sails for Hawaii," *New York Times*, June 18, 1938; "Society's 'Glamour Girl' Ill in Hawaii," *Baltimore Sun*, June 20, 1938.
24. "$200,000 Fire Razes Home at Sands Point."
25. "Lady Salvage Sells Long Island Estate."
26. "Mrs. Emerson Off for South Pacific," *Baltimore Sun*, December 23, 1944; Leonard Lyons, "Broadway Potpourri," *Washington Post*, December 8, 1944.
27. Horace Sutton, "Take Sand, Hilton and Stir," *Baltimore Sun*, February 9, 1964.
28. C. Edward Sparrow, "Vanderbilt Has Three Horses for Kentucky Derby Race," *Baltimore Sun*, February 25, 1934.
29. "Mrs. Emerson, 75, Of the '400' Dead," *New York Times*, January 3, 1960; telephone conversation on March 6, 2018, with a gentleman at the cemetery who requested anonymity.
30. C. Edward Sparrow, "Vanderbilt Has Three Horses for Kentucky Derby Race."
31. Tom Keyser, "Racing's Alfred G. Vanderbilt dies at 87," *Baltimore Sun*, November 13, 1999; Robert G. Breen, "Sagamore' Horse School,'" *Baltimore Sun*, August 23, 1963; "Son Born to Vanderbilts," *Baltimore Sun*, December 2, 1949; Walker Childs, "Saving Sagamore," *Baltimore Sun*, May 10, 2009; Joseph B. Kelly, "At the Track: Thoroughbred Racing in Maryland, 1870–1973," *Maryland Historical Magazine* (Winter, 2005), 515.
32. "George Vanderbilt is Killed in Plunge," *New York Times*, June 25, 1961; "Henry Lustig Acquires George Vanderbilt Place," *New York Times*, February 28, 1945; Danielle Reed, "Shadow Valley Ranch," *Wall Street Journal*, November 17, 2000; Neal Cox, *Neal Cox of Arcadia Plantation*.
33. "Emerson Will Bequeaths Estate to Children," *Washington Post*, May 15, 1946; "Mrs. Emerson Succumbs at Valley Home, *Baltimore Sun*, May 6, 1946; "Mrs. Emerson's Will is Filed," *Baltimore Sun*, May 15, 1946.
34. "Pier Estate Sold," *Newport Mercury*,

July 16, 1948; "Isaac Emerson's 'Whitehall' Is Sold," *Baltimore Sun*, July 13, 1948.

35. Kathleen Troost-Cramer, "On the Market," *South County Life Magazine*, July 2018, 54.

36. Gilbert Sandler, *Baltimore Evening Sun*, March 26, 1985.

Chapter 15

1. Gilbert Sandler, "Where's the Bromo Bottle," *Baltimore Evening Sun*, March 6, 1984.

2. "Convention of Trained Nurses," *Buffalo Enquirer*, October 13, 1916.

3. Linette A. Parker, "Unofficial Drugs and Their Control," *The American Journal of Nursing* 21, no. 8 (May 1921), 525.

4. *HEADACHE-The cause of much Discomfort The enemy of 100% Efficiency.* (Baltimore: The Emerson Drug Company, 1922), 33–35.

5. Margaret O. Fadds, "Two Alluring Aspects of Pharmacology: The Patent Medicine Story," *The American Journal of Nursing* 32, no. 2 (February 1932), 140.

6. United States Food and Drug Administration, Notices of Judgements Archives, 1907–1966. Located in Archives and Modern Manuscripts Collection, History of Medicine Division, National Library of Medicine, Bethesda, Maryland; MSC 608, Box 69, Folder 44834-D. Future citations from this source will be limited to NLM, Box #, Folder #.

7. Katherine Tupper Marshall, *Together: Annals of an Army Wife* (London: Brandford Press, 1947), 61.

8. "https://www.fda.gov/AboutFDA/Transparency/Basics/ucm214416.htm. Accessed March 7, 2018.

9. Plea is Made for Federal Law After Drug Kills 14 in West," *Baltimore Sun*, October 30, 1937; Jeff Akst, "The Elixir Tragedy, 1937," *The Scientist* (June 1, 2013).

10. NLM, Box 69, Folder 45051–57-D.

11. Vincent A. Kleinfeld and Charles Wesley Dunn, *Food, Drug, and Cosmetic Act: Judicial and Administrative Record 1938–1949 Federal* (New York: Commerce Clearing House, 1949),577.

12. "Misbranded Sedatives, Pail Relievers, and Headache Remedies," *Notices of Judgement Under the Federal Food, Drug, and Cosmetic Act* (Washington, D.C.: U.S. Department of Agriculture, Food and Drug Administration, May 1940), 33–39.

13. "Bromo-Seltzer Defended," *New York Times*, March 9, 1939.

14. "Pure Food and Drug act Is Attacked in Suit Here," *Greensboro Observer*, March 13, 1939, article found in NLM, Box 69, Folder 45051.

15. "Bromo-Seltzer Defended."

16. NLM, Box 69, Folder 45051–57-D.

17. NLM, Box 69, Folder 44834-D.

18. "Bromo-Seltzer Seizure Fight Is Settled by Consent Decree, Products Returned to Maker," *Drug Trade News* 15, no. 2 (January 15, 1940), 1, 25.

19. "Consent Degree on Bromo-Seltzer," *New York Times*, January 5, 1940.

20. "Bromo-Seltzer Fight is Settled."

21. NLM, Box 89, Folder 59378–80-D.

22. "FTC Files Complaint Against Makers of Various Remedies," *Christian Science Monitor*, October 26, 1942; "FTC Dismisses Drug Charges," *Baltimore Sun*, October 5, 1950.

23. Jeremy A. Greene, M.D., Ph.D., and Scott H. Podolsky, M.D., "Reform, Regulation, and Pharmaceuticals-The Kefauver-Harris Amendments at 50," *New England Journal of Medicine* (October 18, 2012), 1481-1483. The principals were Sen. Estes Kefauver (D-TN) and Rep. Oren Harris (D-AR)

24. "High Court Backs Prescription-Drug Powers of FDA," *Wall Street Journal*, June 19, 1973.

25. *Ibid.*

26. Morton Mintz, "Antacid Headache," *Washington Post-Times Herald*, April 5, 1973; "FDA Asks Ban on 9 Antacids, Label Changes on Rest," *Chicago Tribune*, April 5, 1973.

27. "FDA Panel Frowns on Love Potion Claims," *Baltimore Sun*, October 3, 1982.

28. Carroll E. Williams, "Merger of Drug Firms Planned," *Baltimore Sun*, January 13, 1956.

29. "Bromo-Seltzer Taking a Powder," *Baltimore Sun*, April 16, 1966.

30. "Antacid Headache."

31. Stuart Elliott, "Advertising," *New York Times*, July 8, 1994.

32. Constance M. Park and Ronald Nager, "Sulfhemoglobinemia: Clinical Modular Aspects," *New England Journal*

of Medicine 310, Issue 24 (June 4, 1984), 1579–1584; John M. Goshko, "Report Hits Contents of Brand-Name Drugs," *Washington Post*, August 29, 1975.

33. Stuart Elliott, "The Search for Life in Yet Another Ghost Brand," *New York Times*, September 26, 2006.

34. Ibid.

35. Gina Barreca, "Where Have All the Products Gone? Do We Really Care?" *New York Times*, February 25, 2001.

36. Text on Bromo-Seltzer box of "20 effervescent tablets" sold by the Tower Corporation.

Epilogue

1. Charles Belfoure, "Old Baltimore Inner-City High-Rise Gets a New Life," *New York Times*, June 25, 2000.

2. Telephone interview with Francis O'Neill, August 15, 2019.

3. Edward Emerson Murray to Board of Governors-The Maryland Club, Baltimore Maryland, January 25, 1996.

4. Interview with Andrew Murray, September 20, 2018.

Bibliography

Books

Atlantic Reporter, Vol. 29. National Reporter System: State Series. St. Paul, MN: West Publishing, 1894.

Bailey, Thomas A., and Paul B. Ryan. *The Lusitania Disaster: The Real Answers Behind the World's Most Controversial Sea Tragedy*. New York: The Free Press, 1975.

Betsworth Jennifer. *Then Came the Peaceful Invasion of Northerners: The Impact of Outsiders on Plantation Architecture in Georgetown County South Carolina*. Master's Thesis, University of South Carolina, 2011.

Bridges, Beverly. *Great Camp Sagamore*. Charleston, SC: The History Press, 2012.

Brock, Julia, and Daniel Vivian. *Leisure Plantations and the Making of the New South: The Sporting Plantations of the South Carolina Low Country and Red Hills Region*. Lanham, MD: Lexington Books, 2015.

Brugger, Robert J. *Maryland: A Middle Temperament, 1634–1980*. Baltimore: Johns Hopkins University Press, 1988.

Buranelli, Prosper. *Maggie of the Suicide Fleet: As Written from the Log of Raymond Davis Borden, Lieutenant U.S.N.R.* New York: Doubleday, Doran, 1930.

Chaddock, Katherine Reynolds. *Uncompromising Activist: Richard Greener, First Black Graduate of Harvard College*. Baltimore: Johns Hopkins University Press, 2017.

Cowen, David L., and William H. Helfand. *Pharmacy: An Illustrated History*. New York: Harry N. Abrams, 1990.

Cox, Neal. *Neal Cox of Arcadia: Memoirs of a Renaissance Man*. Georgetown, SC: Home House Press, 2003.

Daly, Tim. *Daly's Bartenders' Encyclopedia: A Complete Guide*. Worcester, MA: Tim Daly Publisher, 1903.

Fee, Elizabeth, Linda Shopes, and Linda Zeldman, eds. *The Baltimore Book: New Views of Local History*. Philadelphia: Temple University Press, 1991.

Fitzgerald, F. Scott. *This Side of Paradise*. New York: Charles Scribner's, 1920.

Hall, Clayton Coleman, ed. *Baltimore Biography*. Baltimore: Lewis Historical Publishing, 1912.

_____. *Baltimore: Its History and Its People*, Vol. III. New York: Lewis Historical Publishing, 1912.

Harlan, Louis R. *The Booker T. Washington Papers, Vol. 3*: Urbana: University of Illinois Press, 1974.

Idzerda Stanley J. *Lafayette in the Age of the American Revolution: Selected Letters and Papers, Vol. 1*. Ithaca, New York: Cornell University Press, 1977.

Jackson, Richard S., Jr., and Cornelia Brooks Gilder. *Houses of the Berkshires 1870–1930: The Architecture of Leisure*, revised ed. New York: Acanthers Press, 2011.

Joyner, Charles. *Down By the Riverside: A South Carolina Slave Society*. Urbana: University of Illinois Press, 1984.

Kars, Marjoleine. *Breaking Loose Together: The Regulator Rebellion in Pre–Revolutionary North Carolina*. Chapel Hill, NC: University of North Carolina Press, 2002.

King, Greg, and Penny Wilson. *Lusitania: Triumph, Tragedy, and the End of the Edwardian Age*. New York: St. Martin's, 2015.

Kleinfeld, Vincent A., and Charles Wesley

Dunn. *Food, Drug, and Cosmetic Act: Judicial and Administrative Record 1938–1949 Federal.* New York: Commerce Clearing House, 1949.

Lachicotte, Alberta Morel. *Georgetown Rice Plantations.* Georgetown, SC: Georgetown County Historical Society, 1993.

Manarin, Louis H., ed. *North Carolina Troops 1861–1865: A Roster of Cavalry Volume II.* Wilmington, NC: Broadfoot Publishing. 1966. As quoted in Family Record Group-8.

Mann, William D., ed. *Fads and Fancies of Representative Americans at the Beginning of the Twentieth Century, Being a Portrayal of Their Tastes, Diversions and Achievements.* New York: Town Topics Publishing, 1905.

Mencken, H. L. *Happy Days: 1880–1892.* New York: Alfred A. Knopf, 1936.

Olsen, Sherry H. *Baltimore: The Building of an American City.* Baltimore: Johns Hopkins University Press, 1980.

Parsons, Charles W. *The Pharmaceutical Era: (Semi-Monthly).* New York: D.O. Haynes & Company, 1893.

Powell, William S., ed. *Dictionary of North Carolina Biography,* Vol. 2, D–G. Chapel Hill: University of North Carolina Press, 1986.

Sandler, Gilbert. *Jewish Baltimore: A Family Album.* Baltimore: Johns Hopkins University Press, 2000.

Schwarcz, Joe. *The Fly in the Ointment: 70 Fascinating Commentaries on the Science of Everyday Life.* Toronto, ON, Canada: ECW Press, 2002.

Stevens, William Oliver. *Charleston: Historic City of Gardens.* (New York: Dodd, Mead, 1939).

Unger, Harlow Giles. *Lafayette.* New York: John Wiley and Sons, 2002.

Vickers, James, and Thomas Scism. *Chapel Hill: An Illustrated History.* Chapel Hill, NC: Barclay Publishers, 1985

Vivian, Daniel J. "The Leisure Plantations of the South Carolina Lowcountry." Doctoral Dissertation, Johns Hopkins University, 2011.

Wheeler, Marjorie Spruill. *New Women of the New South: The Leaders of the Woman Suffrage Movement in the Southern States.* New York: Oxford Press, 1993.

Woodson, Urey. *Temporary Roll of Delegates and Alternates to the Democratic National Convention.* Baltimore: Day Printing, 1912.

Archival Sources

Abram P. T. Elder Papers, Manuscript Division, Library of Congress. Washington, D.C.

Adjutant General Papers. Maryland State Archives. Annapolis, MD. Appendix E. Series S-397. Box 1 and 2.

Baltimore City Court of Common Pleas (Marriage Licenses) Isaac E. and Emma A. Duner [sic], book 1873-1880, p. 124.

Baltimore City Directory

Cary T. Grayson Papers, Woodrow Wilson Presidential Library and Museum, Staunton, VA.

Family Record Group-8. Prepared by John H. Emerson.

Hazard Family Papers, Rhode Island Historical Society, Sub-Group 31, Series 1, Sub-Series 2.

Isaac E. Emerson Papers, Manuscript Department. Southern Historical Collection. Wilson Library of the University of North Carolina at Chapel Hill.

The Papers of Woodrow Wilson Digital Edition. Charlottesville: University of Virginia Press, Rotunda Division.

Registrar of Deeds, Georgetown, S.C.

The Warshaw Collection. Patent Medicines, Smithsonian Institution, National Museum of American History, Archives Center, Washington, D.C., Box 9, File 13.

Newspapers

Baltimore Afro-American
The Baltimore Evening Sun
Baltimore Sun
The Buffalo Enquirer
Charlotte Observer
The Chatham News
Chicago Daily Tribune
Chicago Inter-Ocean
Courier-Journal (Louisville, Kentucky)
The Christian Science Monitor
Daily Journal
The Daily Tar Heel (Chapel Hill, NC)
The Era-Leader (Franklinton, LA)
The Farmer and Mechanic (Raleigh, NC)
The Gaffney Ledger (Georgetown, SC)

Bibliography

Georgetown Daily Item
The Greenville News (Greenville, SC)
Greensboro Observer (Greensboro, SC)
Hartford Courant
Honolulu Star-Bulletin
Los Angeles Herald
Morning News, (Florence, SC)
The New York Herald Tribune
The New York Times
New York Tribune
News and Courier (Charleston, SC)
Newport Mercury (Newport, RI)
Oakland Tribune
Progressive Farmer (Durham, NC)
Reno Evening Gazette
St. Louis Post Dispatch
The San Francisco Call
San Francisco Chronicle
The Salt Lake Tribune
The Semi-Weekly Messenger (Wilmington, NC)
Sunday Citizen (Asheville, NC)
The Times and Democrat (Orangeburg, SC)
Times-Dispatch (Richmond, VA)
The Twin-City Daily Sentinel (Winston-Salem, NC)
The Wall Street Journal
Washington Evening Star
Washington Herald
The Washington Post
Wilson Mirror (Wilson, SC)

Index

Numbers in **_bold italics_** indicate pages with illustrations.
IEE refers to Isaac E. Emerson.

acetanilide: in Bromo-Seltzer 61, 62, 63; Bromo-Seltzer advertising and 18; as dangerous drug, U.S. Surgeon General on 162; eliminated from Bromo-Seltzer 165; Emerson Drug Company on 158–59; FDA testing Bromo-Seltzer for levels of 160–61; as harmful, countering claim of 66
Adams, Henry 10
Adams, Kate 56–57
Adams, S.H. 62
Adroit (Alfred's yacht) 131, 134
advertising: for Alka-Seltzer vs. Bromo-Seltzer (1970s) 164; Bromo-Seltzer 18–19, 159; Bromo-Seltzer Tower 98, **_99_**, 100; Emerson Hotel opening 89; false, FTC charges of 162–63; forms 19–20, **_19_**, **_20_**, **_22–23_**; by Tower Laboratories 165; in white vs. African American newspapers 58–59; at World's Fair (1893) 24–25
African Americans: as Arcadia employees 75–76; Arcadia's Big House refurbished by 72–73; delegate to Democratic presidential nominating convention (1912) 94; as Emerson Hotel guests 97; as Eutaw Place mansion servants 40; Gilded Age and 3; Grant's Tomb dedication and 30; working at Emerson Hotel 96–97; *see also* race relations
Afro-American 59, 66
Alamance Creek, Battle of (1771) 7
alcohol, in patent medicines 18
Alexander-Mikhailovich, Grand Duke, of Russia 118
Algonquin Manor 106
Alka-Seltzer 163, 164
Alligator 176*n*11
Amazon, search for Bromo-Seltzer on 165

American Art School, Baltimore 13
American Bowling Congress 65
American Druggist and Pharmaceutical Record 25, 98, 100
American Medical Association (AMA) 63, 67
American Revolution 7
Amory, Charles M. **_134_**, 135, 151
Amory, Margaret Emerson McKim Vanderbilt Baker: with Charles at Pimlico **_134_**; death 153; divorce 151; IEE's bequest to 148, 184*n*1; IEE's stroke and death and 146; marriage to Charles **_134_**, 135
Annapolis, Maryland, IEE's drug store in 11
Arcadia: African American and other staff at 75–77; approach to the Big House **_73_**; Big House at **_71_**, **_156_**; boats used at 70, 176*n*11; coach stored at **_110_**; family after Alfred's death at 122–23; Frederick McCormacks' honeymoon at 129; historical anecdotes about 74–75; IEE and Anne at 118, 146; IEE's purchase of 70; in IEE's will 148; improvements to 73–74; left by George to Lulu 155; Margaret's attraction to Lenox, Massachusetts and 127; Margaret's cottage at 122–23, 125
Armstrong, Richard 133
Army-Navy football game (1924) 126–27
Askew, Harriet 10
Askew, William F. 10, 12
Associated Press 94
Association of Naval Militias of the United States 28
Astor, Mrs. John Jacob 118
Atlanta Compromise Speech (Washington, 1895) 28
Atlanta Exposition (1895) 27–28

193

automobile racing 50–51; *see also* cars; motor tours
Ayler, Magistrate 44
Ayres, William A. 163
Azrael, Lou 158

Baker, A.W. 76–77
Baker, Gloria 132, 133, 148, 151, 152
Baker, Margaret Emerson McKim Vanderbilt 127, 129, 131, 132–35
Baker, Raymond T. 83, 127, *128*, 133, 134–35
Baltimore: Bromo-Seltzer reminders in 167–68; characteristics of (late 1880s) 14; *City Directory*, IEE's listings in 12; Democratic presidential nominating convention (1912) and 93; Emerson's hotel building plan for 85; fire (1904) 55–56; flower and garden exhibit 146; Green Spring Valley near 115–16; IEE's drug stores in 11; luxury apartments in Druid Park area 124–25; segregation in 91–92, 95–98; Severn Apartments 107; Sixth Massachusetts Regiment honored by 32–33; Spanish-American War veterans parade in 34; *see also* Emerson Drug Company; Emerson Hotel; Eutaw Place mansion; Fayette Street building
Baltimore American 35
Baltimore and Ohio Railroad 14
Baltimore Community Fund 148
Baltimore Orioles 87
Baltimore society: Emersons and 4, 45–46, 52; Greenmount Cemetery and 147; send-off of the *Dixie* and 33, 34; *see also* Brooklandwood property; Green Spring Valley
Baltimore Sun: on Algonquin Manor 106; on Anne's kidnapping threat 151; on *The Dale* 29; on Emerson and hunting 34–35; on Emersons at Arcadia in South Carolina 71–72; on Eutaw Place garden 55; "Glober Girdler Home" article in 48; on housing segregation in Baltimore 95; on IEE entertaining on his yacht 31; on Margaret's horse racing achievements 139; on Margaret's marriage to McKim 52; on McKims' marital strife 81; on McKinley inaugural parade 37; on musicale at Eutaw Place mansion (1901) 45; patent medicine advertisements in 18; on Proprietary Association's members' wealth 93; on sealing Emerson's divorce papers 102
Baltimore Terrapins 87
Baltimore Yacht Club 94–95
Barreca, Gina 165
Barse, William H. 86–87, 89
Baruch, Bernard 71, 74–75
Barwell, Mary 120
baseball, in Baltimore 87
Basshor, Charles Hazeltine 101–2, 106, 107
Basshor, Emilie A. 106–7, 133
Bellevue-Stratford, Philadelphia 89
Belmont, August, Jr. 35, 117–18
Belmont Park Aviation Meet 84
Belmont Stakes 154, 155
Belvedere Hotel, Baltimore 85
Bernard, Oliver 120, 121
Bethlehem Steel 14
bicarbonate, in Bromo-Seltzer 61, 165
Black Thursday (October 24, 1929) 148
Blakistone, George 85
Blaustein, Louis 125
Bollee (big red French automobile) 50–51, 57
Bonham, Kenneth A. 163
booklets, pocket-sized, as advertising 21, *24*
Booth, Alfred E. 40
Borden, Raymond Davis 132
Bouvier, Jacqueline 146
Brandonwood 129, 148
The Breakers, Newport, Rhode Island 44, 108, 134
Brendan, Daniel 44
Bresnan, Timothy 44
Brewster, B.H., Jr. 46
Britannia 26–27
Brock, Julia 70
bromides: FDA testing Bromo-Seltzer for levels of 161; *see also* sodium bromide
Bromo-Seltzer: advertisements for 18–19, 58–59; America's popular culture and 65–66; Baltimore reminders of 167; criticisms 158–59; FDA and "dose" 161–62; FDA on labels for 163–64; FDA seizures and testing 160–61; financial success 16; formula changed for 162; Gilded Age and 4; government scrutiny 61–62, 64; Himmel Group acquires rights 164–65; incentives for selling 20; London office, White and 42; on the *Margaret* 73; misrepresentations 56–57; physicians on harmful effects 63; public appeal 67–68; regulation 4; required descriptive labels of ingredients in 67; sales during Great Depres-

sion 148–49; trademark for 16; *see also* acetanilide; Emerson Drug Company; patent medicines

Bromo-Seltzer bottles: atop Bromo-Seltzer Tower 98; cobalt blue 57; on *The Margaret* 73; Maryland Glass Corporation manufacturing 67; removed from Bromo-Seltzer Tower 158; replicas, on Eutaw Place mansion garden wall 53

Bromo-Seltzer Tower: artists as occupants 167; as Baltimore's tallest building 5; blue bottle removed from 158; Bromo-Seltzer museum in 167–68; building 98; night view **99**; replicas, for Emerson Hotel banquet (1911) 91

Brooklandwood property: in Anne's will for Ethel 156; dairy farming at 115, 116, 118, 125–26, 157; drag hunts and steeplechases at 137–38; entertaining at 130; entertaining at and features of 116; Eutaw Place plants and sculptures moved to 125; Harry Flood Byrd visit to 138; IEE's generosity to staff of 140–41; in IEE's will for Anne 149; kidnapping threat and 151; McCormack–McAdoo wedding at 117; purchase 115; St. Paul's School on 168

Brown, Frank 45; (Maryland governor) 26

Brown v. Board of Education 98

Bruening, C.F. 162

Bryan, William Jennings 94, 117

Buranelliu, Prosper 132

Burmeister, Richard 41

Burnside Hotel: Narragansett Improvement Association and 142–43

Busick, Harry D. 85

Byrd, Harry Flood 138

Calhoun, John C. 74

Camp Sagamore 80, 114, 122, 129

Campbell, W.G. **64**, 160, 161

Capitaine, Maurice 130

Capudine Chemical Company 162

Carlton, Lewis 10

Carrington, E.C. 141

cars 4, 116, 130; Bollee (big red French) 50–51, 57; *see also* automobile racing; motor tours

Carter, John M. 50

Carter, Snowden 153

Cascaret Tablets 59

casino, in Narragansett 79–80, 83, 118, 143

Castleberg, Joseph 125

Caswell, Herbert 143

Catholic Church: Margaret and 153; Notre Dame of Maryland Collegiate Institute for Young Ladies 43, 52

Caton, Polly Carroll 115

Caton, Richard 115

Cedar Knoll estate, Sands Point, Long Island 151–52

Chaboulon, Baroness de 83

Chaddock, Katherine Reynolds 30

Charlotte Journal 12

Chesapeake Bay: Bromo-Seltzer Tower seen from 5, 98; cruising in 32, 43; Maryland Naval Reserves and 26, 27, 29, 31

Chicago: cat show and Bromo-Seltzer-named cat in 65; World's Columbian Exposition (1893) 21, 24–25

Chicago Daily Tribune: on Alfred's death on *Lusitania* 121; on Anne's kidnapping threat 151; Bromo-Seltzer advertising in 19, 21; on IEE and Emilie argument 101; on Margaret's divorce from Baker 135; warning readers to avoid Bromo-Seltzer 63–64

Civil War 3, 8, 26, 32–33

Clampett, F.W. 32

Clark, Champ 94

Cleveland, Grover 35

coaching, Alfred Vanderbilt and 109, **110**, 111

cocaine 17, 18, 24, 62

Cole, William P., Jr. 160

Collier's Weekly 62

Confederate cause, IEE and 90

Confederate Relief Bazar 41

Coolidge, Calvin 127

Cornish, Harry 56–57

cotton plantations 69, 70

Cotton States International Celebration (1895) 27–28

Courier-Journal, Louisville 47

Cox, Neal 76

Cromwell, Delphine Dodge 135–36

Cross, John G. 83

Crothers, Austin Lane 91

Cullen, Countee Porter 97

Cunard Line 121

Custis, Mary Anna Randolph 90

CVS website, search for Bromo-Seltzer on 165

dairy farming: at Algonquin Manor 106; at Brooklandwood 115, 116, 118, 125–26, 157; IEE and 5

The Dale 26–27, 28, 29, 33
Daly's Bartenders' Encyclopedia 65
Daniels, Jonathon 69–70
Darrow, Clarence 66
Dashiell, Milton 96
Davis, Alphonso 10
Davis, John 46
Democratic Party politics, IEE and 138
Democratic presidential nominating convention (1912) 93–94
Denyer, Ronald 119, 120
Dewey, George 33–34
diamonds, Emilie's 41
diethylene glycol, in elixir of sulfanilamide 160
divorce requirements 11, 81, 132–33
Dixie (warship) 33, 34
Dixon, Amzi Clarence 10
Dobler, John 44
Dolan, H. Yale 35
Dooley, Edward J. 65
Douglas, Henry Kyd 26
Douglas, William O. 163
Doyle, James, Jr. 89
Dreyfus, Alfred 43
drug stores *10*, 11, 13, 20
DuBois, W.E.B. 28
Dunn, A. William, III 66
Dunn, Daisy 11; marriage to James McVickar 78–79, 114, 133; marriage to T. Mitchell Horner 40–41, 78
Dunn, Emma Askew 10–11; *see also* Emerson, Emma/Emilie
Dunn, Lillie 11, 42, 43, 50, 51, 133
Durant, William West 114
Durso, Joseph 153

Edward VII, King 113
Elder, Abram P.T. 60–61
The Eleanor (yacht) 118
Elizabeth, Queen of England 155
Elliott, Thomas 41
Emerson, Anna Clark 8, 16
Emerson, Anne Preston McCormack: at Arcadia with family 122; interred at Green Mount Cemetery *147*; as kidnapping target 150–51; later life and death of 155–56; marriage to IEE 103; at Narragansett (1913) 118; *New York Times* obituary of IEE and 148; philanthropic interests of 139; Walter Keith and 150
Emerson, Asenath Hunt Stuart 7
Emerson, Cornelia Lewis 8, 16, 58
Emerson, Cornelia Lewis Hudson 8, 9
Emerson, Emma/Emilie: in car pulled over for speeding 51; court suits by 41; courtship and marriage 10–11; death 133; dinner for Shibusawa and 49; divorce 101–3; The Emersonian and 125; Eutaw Place garden and 55; on gambling raid at Narragansett Club 84; on Horner's suit against Emersons 78; on IEE support for Maryland Naval Reserve 27; IEE's globe girdling adventure and 47; *The Margaret* and 39; musicale at Eutaw Place mansion and 44–45; at National Wholesale Druggists' Association dinner (1894) 25; second marriage 106–7; visits the *Dixie* 33; volunteer work 42–43
Emerson, Isaac E.: Alfred's death on *Lusitania* and 121–22; Baltimore reminders of 167–68; birth date 169*n*3; with Chapel Hill relatives 10; courtship and first marriage 11–12; divorce 101–3; in Druid Park, Baltimore 15; early life 8–9; Elder's biographies of famous men and 60–61; at Emerson Hotel opening banquet *90*; estate 184*n*1; Farnham's sculpture and 54–55; Gilded Age and 3–5; Grant's Tomb dedication and 29, 30; interred at Green Mount Cemetery *147*, 148; Margaret's divorce and 81; Maryland Day at the Atlanta Exposition and 27–28; memberships and social engagement by 4; negative publicity for Bromo-Seltzer and 66–67; oil painting 13, *13*; personal interests of 5; philanthropic interests 140; professional accomplishments 4; profiles 25; remembering 168; second marriage 103; Spanish-American War and 34; stroke and death 145; thrifty nature 43–44; on his Type A personality 100; at UNC-Chapel Hill 10–11; *see also* automobile racing; cars; Emerson Drug Company; horses and horse racing; hunting; Maryland Naval Reserves; motor tours; real estate; sailing and cruises
Emerson, James, Jr. 7
Emerson, James, Sr. 7
Emerson, John 7, 169*n*3
Emerson, John H. 169*n*3
Emerson, John Watson 8–9, 10
Emerson, Julia Booth 9–10
Emerson, Laura White 8, 16
Emerson, Margaret: birth 15; in car pulled over for speeding 51; death 153; father's death and 146; IEE's bequest to 148, 184*n*1; IEE's globe girdling ad-

Index

venture and 47, 49; marriage to Alfred G. Vanderbilt 107–8, 118, 120, 121–22, 127, *154*; marriage to Charles Amory 135, 146, 151; marriage to Raymond Baker 127, 129, 131, 132–35; marriage to Smith Hollis McKim 51–52; musicale at Eutaw Place mansion and 45; as National Wholesale Druggists' Association dinner (1894) 25; postgraduate tour of the Continent by 43; shooting prowess of 35–36; *see also* McKim, Margaret Emerson

Emerson, Ralph Waldo 15

Emerson, Robert Jehu 7–8, 9–10, 12, 169*n*3

Emerson Drug Company: on acetanilide issue 158–59; Atlanta office, Horner and 41, 78; Bromo-Seltzer Tower and 98; challenges to Bromo-Seltzer seizures by FDA 161; changes in Bromo-Seltzer labels by 67, 68; founding 4, 16–17; Frederick McCormack and 150; IEE's death and 148; merger with Warner-Lambert 164; offers to buy 141; philanthropic gifts after IEE's death by 148; profits in 1950s 164; stockholder meeting (1904) 56, 58; *see also* advertising; Bromo-Seltzer; Bromo-Seltzer Tower; Fayette Street building

Emerson Farms *see* Brooklandwood property, dairy farming at

Emerson Hotel 5; additions to 126; African American guests of 97; African Americans working at 96–97; architectural details 87; banquet for IEE at 90–91, *90*, *91*; Democratic presidential nominating convention (1912) and 93–94; European food and 104, 106; gala opening 89–90; IEE's death and 148; Jim Crow culture and 95; *Madeleine Repentante* ("Magnolia Blossom") *105*, 106; outside view *88*; reasons for building 85–86; restaurants 86–87

The Emersonian (apartment house) 5, 124–25, 129, 167, *167*

Eudowood Sanatorium 139

Eutaw Place mansion: attempted burglaries 46; building and staffing of (1895) 40; charitable and social events 41, 44–45; Daisy's wedding reception 40–41; as divorce award to Emilie 102–3; The Emersonian next door to 125, *167*; Emersons at Arcadia in South Carolina and 71–72; garden for 53–55; Margaret's wedding reception at 52; sale 106;

still standing (2018) 168; unsatisfactory photographs 44

Evans, W.A. 63–64

Ewing, Bettie 72

Ewing, George 72

Faber, Edwin 45

Faber, Mrs. Edwin 45

Fadds, Margaret O. 159

Farinholt, Benjamin L. 89–90

Farnham, Sally James Welles 53–55

Faunterloys (Virginia game preserve) 34–35

Fayette Street building 17, 20, 67; *see also* Emerson Drug Company

Fearing, George R. 103

Federal Food, Drug, and Cosmetic Act (1938) 160, 162; Kefauver-Harris Amendments (1962) 163

Federal Trade Commission (FTC) 4, 162

Fetzer, Bill 140

Fifth Regiment (U.S. Army) 34

Fifth Regiment Armory 93

Fink, Mary Muller 130

First National Co-operative Society 67

First Regiment (U.S. Army) 34

The Fisherman & Farmer (Edenton, North Carolina) 20–21

Fitzgerald, F. Scott 65

Fletcher, Frank Jack 132

Florida Gun Club, in Palm Beach 35

The Fly in the Ointment (Schwarcz) 12

Food and Drug Act (1906) 63, 67, 158, 160

Food and Drug Administration (FDA) 4, 160, 161–62; *see also* Campbell, W.G.; Wiley, Harvey W.

Ford, J.W. 77

French scientists, on Bromo-Seltzer 62

Fuller, Henry C. 67

Funderburk, deputy game warden 72

Furst, Frank A. 139

Gaffney Ledger 71

Gaither, Charles D. 151

Gardenia (power yacht) 70, 176*n*11

Garrett, John 139

Garrett, Robert 139

Geer, Edward 28, 31

Georgetown Times 70, 72

Gerard, James W. 118

Gerhardt, Emerson 140

German scientists, on Bromo-Seltzer 62

German submarines 131, 132

Gilded Age 3–5

Gill, M. Gillet 50
Ginger Mint Julep 19, *19*
Goldsborough, Philips Lee 94
Goldsborough, W. Brice 107
Grace, William Russell 29–30
Graham, Frank P. 148
Grand National Point-to-Point steeplechase 137–38
Grant, Frederick 29
Grant Monument Association 30
Grant's Tomb, siting and dedication of 29
Grason, C. Gus 150
Grate, Alonzo 176*n*11
Grayson, Cary T. 129
Great Depression 148
Green, Antoine 97
Green, Nancy 133
Green Mount Cemetery, Emerson Vault in mausoleum of *147*, 148, 156
Green Spring Valley 46, 115–16, 130; *see also* Brooklandwood property
Green Spring Valley Hunt Club 137
Greener, Richard 30
Greenville News 125, 127
Gregg, Maurice 46
Grinnell, Ashbel P. 18

Hall, Edward C. 17
Hanan, Mrs. J.H. 83
Hanriot, Jules Armand 106
Hanson, Cora L. 79
Hanson, J.F. 79
Hapgood, Norman 61
Harkless, J.D. 94
Harper, John Wesley 151
Harrison, Constance Cary 60
Harrison, Virginia Ritchie 129
Hay, John 34
Hazard, T.G. 142, 145
Hearst, William R. 31, 93
Hemenway, Henry Bixby 63
The Herald (Los Angeles) 34
Herzenberg, Charles 56
Heuisler, Charles W. 97–98, 102
Himmel, Jeffrey S. 164
Hindes, Joseph F., Jr. 16–17, 68, 141, 149
Hobcaw Barony (former rice plantation) 71
Hochschild, Max 125
Holmes, Edward L. 161–62
Holmwood, Lenox, Massachusetts 127, 151, 184*n*1
Honolulu property, Margaret and 152–53
Horner, Daisy Dunn 40–41, 78
Horner, Joshua P., Jr. 78

Horner, T. Mitchell 40–41, 56, 78
horses and horse racing: Alfred Jr. and 139, 153–54; Alfred Vanderbilt and 108, 109, 111; IEE's love of 5, 117–18, 137–38; Margaret's interest in 135, 153; Margaret's winnings in 138–39; in Trouville, France 57
Hospital for the Women of Maryland 140
Hotel de la Plage, Narragansett Improvement Association and 143
Houghton, Harry S. 66
Hudson, Isaac 8
Huger, Benjamin, Jr. 74
hunting: after Spanish-American War 34–36; at Arcadia 72, 76; in Italian mountains 48; Margaret's interest in 80, 83; on Waccamaw Neck, South Carolina 69–70

Illinois Joint Emergency Relief Committee 148
immigrants: in Baltimore (late 1880s) 14; European, Gilded Age and 3
influenza epidemic, world-wide 130

Jackson, Howard W. 126, 127
Jacobs, Mrs. Henry Barton 146
James, Edward C. 53
Jarvis, Thomas J. 10
Jeffries, James J. 81–82
Jenkins, Mrs. Edmund P. 47
Jenkins, George 45
Jenkins, Michael 45
Jenny, Lillian 157
jewels, sale of O'Brien's (Ruiz's) 113, 180*n*50
Jews, in Baltimore 14, 92
Jim Crow 14, 28; *see also* race relations
Johnson, Jack 81–82
Journal of the American Medical Assoiation (JAMA) 67
The Jungle (Sinclair) 61
Junior Republic Association for Boys 82

Kaiser Wilhelm der Grosse 47
Karsner, Daniel 35
Kefauver-Harris Amendments (1962), to Federal Food, Drug, and Cosmetic Act (1938) 163
Keith, Elizabeth Atterbury 151
Keith, Ethel McCormack McAdoo 136, 150
Keith, Walter Winchester 136, 150, 151
Kelly, John Jerome 35
Kenan, William Rand, Jr. 140

Kennedy, John F. 163
Kentucky Derby 117–18, 139, 153
Kernan, James L. 85
Kincaid, John J. 96
King, Greg 120
Kirkland, B.B. 47
Knights of Labor 14
Knox, John 161, 162
Ku Klux Klan 9

Ladies Auxiliary of the State Militia 42–43
Lafayette, Marquis de 74–75
Landsdowne, Lord (Henry Charles Keith Petty-Fitzmaurice) 48
Laslett, John Calvin 140, 146
Latrobe, F.C. 45
Lauriat, Charles 120
Leahy, Rosemary 149–50
Lee, Fitzhugh, Jr. 32, 36
Lee, Martha 47
Lee, Robert E. 90
Lenox, Massachusetts: Emilie buried in 133; Holmwood in 127, 151, 184*n*1; Margaret's house among society at 127; move to Sands Point, Long Island from 151–52
Leslie, Marie 140–41
Lexington Market, Baltimore 87
Liberty Bonds 129, 131
Lines, Mrs. Stanley 121
Lisman, Frederick J. 39
Lodge, George Cabot 33
Lodge, Henry Cabot 33
Long, John Davis 26, 28, 29
Looram, Ethel McCormack McAdoo Keith 151, 156
Looram, Matthew J. 151
Lorillard, Caroline 113
Los Angeles Times 18–19, 113
Lowndes, Lloyd, Jr. 30
Lucas, Anthony 65–66
Lusitania 119–21, **120**
Lyric Theater 45–46

Madeleine Repentante ("Magnolia Blossom") **105**, 106
Maggie of the Suicide Fleet (Borden) 132
Magondux, Roger 51
Mahool, J. Barry 91, 95
Maine, sinking of 31, 42
Mallet, William Peter 10
Malster, William T. 33
Manila Bay, the Philippines 33–34
Mann, William D. 60

Margaret (houseboat) 73
The Margaret (yacht) **37**; IEE's divorce and 103; IEE's globe girdling adventure and 47–48; McCormack–McAdoo honeymoon and 117; payroll list for August 1912 **38**; purchase 39; robustness 49–50; summer in Newport, Rhode Island and 79–80; World War I and 131, 132
Marshall, George 159–60
Marshall, Katherine Tupper 159–60
Marshall, Thomas R. 117
Marshall, Walter Harper 89
Maryland Court of Appeals 96
Maryland Glass Corporation 67, 148
The Maryland Horse Magazine 153
Maryland Naval Reserves: Atlanta Exposition (1895) and 27–28; *The Dale* 26–27, 28, 29; Grant's Tomb dedication and 30–31; IEE joins 26; McKinley's inaugural parade and 29; Spanish-American War and 31–33, 34
Mason, William E. 61–62
Mathewson Hotel, Narragansett, Rhode Island 83
Matthews, Henry J. 106, 125
Mayo, William J. 63
McAdoo, Ethel McCormack 118, 136
McAdoo, Francis H., Jr. 164
McAdoo, Francis Huger 116–17, 131, 136
McAdoo, William G. 118
McCormack, Anne Preston: at Arcadia 73; IEE relationship with 103–4; Margaret's divorce and 81; Margaret's second marriage and 107–8; McKim's alienation of affection suit and 101; second marriage 103; spelling of surname 176*n*22; summer in Newport, Rhode Island and 79; traveling with IEE and Margaret 78, 102
McCormack, Cyrus H., Jr. 148
McCormack, Ethel 73; marriage to F.H. McAdoo 116–17, 118, 136; marriage to M.J. Looram 151, 156; marriage to W.W. Keith 136, 150
McCormack, Frederick C. (father) 73, 103–4
McCormack, Frederick Clarke (son) 129; death 150; Emerson Drug Company and 149; interred at Green Mount Cemetery **147**; second marriage 149; steeplechases and 137–38; Whitehall and 156; World War I and 131
McCormack, Margaret Emerson 149, 156

McCormack, Margaretta McNeal Davis Arno 149, 150
McCormack, Virginia Ritchie Harrison 129, 148, 149
McDade, A.J. 10
McDade, Mrs. A.J. 10
McKim, Margaret Emerson: at Arcadia 73; Daisy Dunn Horner moves in with 78; IEE and honeymoon of 52–53; Irvington-on-the-Hudson home of 55; during marriage to McKim *82*; motor tours and 57–58; post-divorce Far East tour by 83; in Reno for divorce 82; rumors of potential marriage to Alfred Vanderbilt 84–85; separation and divorce of 80–81; summer in Newport, Rhode Island and 79–80; *see also* Emerson, Margaret
McKim, Mary Lenora 149
McKim, Smith Hollins: alienation of affection suits filed by 101; Daisy Dunn Horner moves in with 78; death 149; *Dixie* patrols and 33; IEE and honeymoon of 52–53; IEE's globe girdling adventure and 47, 48; interred at Green Mount Cemetery 147; Irvington-on-the-Hudson home of 55; marriage of 51–52; McKinley's second inaugural parade and 37; motor tours and 57–58; musicale at Eutaw Place and 45; separation and divorce by 80–81
McKinley, William 29, 30, 32, 37
McMechen, Anna 95–96
McVickar, Daisy Dunn Horner 78–79, 114, 133
McVickar, James 78–79, 114
Meat Inspection Act (1906) 61
Mellus, Luella 130
Mencken, H.L. 14, 56, 66
Merchants and Manufacturer's Association 94
Meyers, George 97
Middleton, Alice 121
Miles Laboratory 162, 164
Military Club 37
Miller, C. Wilbur 146
Miller, Jacob W. 30
minorities: in Baltimore (late 1880s) 14; *see also* race relations
Moats, Alice-Leone 66
Molineux, Roland B. 57
Monroe, James 74
Monument City *see* Baltimore
Mordecai, George P. 77
morphine 17, 18

Morton, Leslie 120
motor tours: in Europe (1904) 57–58; McKims' honeymoon and 52–53; past Brooklandwood 126; past Grant's Tomb 30; *see also* cars
Murphy, Walter Gibbs 36
Murray, Andrew 168
Murray, Earle 58
Murray, Edward Emerson 105, 168
Murray, J. Edward 58, 106
Murray, Josiah Stockton 58
Murray, W.R. 58
Mussolini, Benito 151

Narragansett, Rhode Island: August of 1913 in 118; Emersons after Margaret's divorce in 83–84; Narragansett Improvement Association (NIA) 142–44; Narragansett Pier Casino 79–80, 83, 118, 143; sailing to 44; *see also* Newport, Rhode Island
Nash, George K. 37
National Association for the Advancement of Colored People (NAACP) 28
National Formula 159
National Jersey Cattle Show 126
National Wholesale Druggists Association 25, 36
Naval Militia Commanders, Washington conference (1898) 32
Needleman, Norman 165
Nevada State Journal 81–82
New Hampshire, U.S.S. 30
New York American Magazine 80
New York City society: Alfred Vanderbilt and 84, 121; Alfred Vanderbilt, Jr., and 153; Four Hundred 80; Gloria Vanderbilt and 152, 153
New York City's Unemployment Relief Fund 148
New York Racing Association 154
New York Times: on Anne's kidnapping threat 151; on dairy for first grandchild 115; Daisy Dunn Horner on Hansons to 79; IEE obituary in 146, 148; on IEE's success 58; on Margaret as Newport hostess 80; on Margaret's marriage to McKim 52; Margaret's obituary in 153; on National Wholesale Druggists Association convention 25; on products no longer capturing public imagination 165; on Rynwood 152; on sale of O'Brien's jewels 113, 180*n*50; on trial for Ward's suit against Emilie 51
New York Tribune 29

Index

Newman, Gladys 74–75
Newport, Rhode Island 80, 103, 179*n*15; cottages 44
Newport Horse Show (1913) 118
The News and Courier, Charleston 75
News and Observer (Raleigh) 12
Nordica, Lillian 44–45
North Carolina, patent medicines manufactured in 18
North Dakota, truthful descriptions of ingredients law in 66, 67
Notre Dame of Maryland Collegiate Institute for Young Ladies 43, 52
The Nydia (IEE yacht): Association of Naval Militias of the United States and 28; cruising aboard 31, 36; Notre Dame preparatory school commencement and 43; reconfigured for civilian travel 35; refurbished for the Navy 32; sale of 39

Oak Hill rice plantation 70
Oakland (Rhode Island) *Tribune* 80
Oakland Farm, Rhode Island 108, **109**, 122
O'Brien, Mary Agnes 111–13, 121
O'Gorman, James 112
Oldfield, Barney 51
O'Neill, Francis 168
opium 17, 18

Palm Beach, Florida 5, 35, 45, 133, 135, 146; *see also* West Palm Beach
Panic of 1893 3
Panic of 1907 68
Paris, grounds for divorce in 132–33
Parker, Linette A. 158
Parker, William H. 98, 122–23, 124, 126–27, 142–43
Parran, Thomas, Jr. 162
Partridge, Ernest S. 50–51
patent medicines: Adams' *Collier's Weekly* articles on 62; *Afro-American* ads for 59; in America (18th and 19th centuries) 17–18; government scrutiny of 62–63, 64; legislation 63, 67, 158, 160; Proprietary Association of America 25, 93; public appeal 67–68; truthful descriptions of ingredients and 66–67; *see also* Food and Drug Act
Payne, W.C. 33
The Peoples Pharmacy 56
Pepto-Bismol 164
Perch 176*n*11
Percival, Gilbert 68

pharmacy, formal educational programs for 16
Phelan, James D. 129
Phelps, Charles E. 41
physicians, on harmful effects of Bromo-Seltzer 63, 67
Pietila, Antero 92
Piffard, Henry G. 61–62
Pimlico Race Course, Laurel, Maryland 137, 153–54
Pittman, Key 129
Pitzer, Anna 94
Plaintiff in Error v. O. A. Johnson (1911) 63
Plank, Kevin 168
Plaza Hotel 79, 80, 81, 109
Poe, Edgar Allan 95, 140
Pope, Anna Clark Emerson 16; *see also* Emerson, Anna Clark
Pope, Jack 16
Porter, Horace 30
Preakness 137, 153, 154
Preston, James H. 89, 91, 94
Price, Calvin W. 107
Pritchell, W.G. 107
Proctor, Ross 50
Prohibition 130
Proprietary Association of America 25, 93
Prospect Hill rice plantation 70, 74–75
Pulitzer, Joseph 31
Pure Food and Drug Act (1906) 63, 67, 158, 160

Queen Anne (yacht) 141, 146, 148

race relations: Atlanta Compromise Speech (Washington, 1895) and 28; in Baltimore (late 1880s) 14; Emerson Hotel and 97; Gilded Age and 3; Harry Flood Byrd and 138; IEE on Narragansett Improvement Association and 142; Jeffries–Johnson boxing match and 81–82; in North Carolina (1870s) 10; segregation in Baltimore and 91–92, 95–96; white supremacy and 9; *see also* Civil War
railroads, Great Depression and 149
Randolph, Nancy 135
real estate: Brandonwood as gift to the Frederick McCormacks 129; for Emerson family 16; of George Vanderbilt III 155; IEE's gift of Russ Farm to Margaret 139; in IEE's will 148; land for Margaret to build at Arcadia 122–23; for Mar-

garet in Alfred's will 122; Margaret's maintenance of 151–52; on Waccamaw Neck, South Carolina 69–70; Whitehall, Narragansett 146; *see also* Arcadia; Brooklandwood property; The Emersonian; Eutaw Place mansion; Fayette Street building
Red Cross 131, 152
Reed, Michael P. 53
The Regulators 7
Reid, Mrs. Andrew Melville 45
Remington, Frederick 53
Remsen, J.S.S. 35
Reno, Nevada, divorce procedures in 81
Rhode Island Hospital Trust Company 143
rice plantations, Waccamaw Neck, South Carolina 69–70, 75–76
Richardson, J.A. 72
Ricketts, Robert 140
Ritchie, Albert 138
Rite Aid website, search for Bromo-Seltzer on 165
Robertson, A.B. 10
Robinson, William J. 63
Roche, Mrs. Arthur Somers 151
Rockefeller, John D., Jr. 148
Rogers, Will 66
Roizman Development Corporation 167
romances gone awry, Bromo-Seltzer and 65–66
Roosevelt, Theodore 32, 33, 61, 63
The Rosalind (private rail car) 49
Ruiz, Mary Agnes O'Brien 111–13, 121
Russ Farm, Worthington Valley, Maryland 139, 148; *see also* Sagamore Farm, Worthington Valley, Maryland
Rynwood Estate, on North Shore of Long Island 152

Sagamore Farm, Worthington Valley, Maryland 139, 148, 153, 155, 168
sailing and cruises: after Grant's Tomb dedication 30–31; Baltimore Yacht Club and 94–95; Emilie and 43; globe girdling adventure 47–49; to London 43; Margaret and Alfred's pre-nuptial agreement on 108; to Narragansett, Rhode Island (1900) 44; storm near Key West and 36; *see also* yachts
St. Louis Post-Dispatch 113, 180*n*50
St. Paul's School 168
Salignac, Eustase 45
San Francisco Chronicle 18–19, 104, 149
Sanders, Gil 85

Santee Gun Club, South Carolina 35
Sarazen, Gene 130
Sax, Sol 130
Schwarcz, Joe 12
Scientific American 65
sheet music, advertising on 21, **22–23**
Sherman, William T. 8
Shibusawa, Eiichi 49
Sinclair, Upton 61
Sixth Massachusetts Regiment 32–33
skipjacks, Chesapeake Bay 26
Slattery, George N. 66, 67
Smith, Daniel H. 97
Smith, John Walter 89
sodium bromide, in Bromo-Seltzer 16, 61
Southern Maryland Society 138
Spanish-American War (1898) 31–34, 42–43
Spanish Fly, FDA on 164
Sparrow, Edward 139
Speare, Dorothy 130
Sperry, Joseph Evans 85, 98, 124, 126
Stotler, J.H. (Bud) 153
Stuyvesant, Gerard 47
Stuyvesant, Minnie 47
sulfanilamide, elixir of, deaths due to 160
Supreme Court, U.S. 4, 96, 98, 163
Susquehanna (hunting yacht) 25
Swanson, Claude A. **128**
Swope, Herbert Bayard, Jr. 151

Taft, William Howard 63
Tally-Ho coach 24, 25, 30
theosophy 79
This Side of Paradise (Fitzgerald) 65
Thomas C. Basshor Co. 101–2
Tilden, Bill 130
Timonium Fair, IEE showing Guernsey cattle at 125–26
Tinsley, Linwood 157
Topping, Gloria Baker 152
Topping, Henry, Jr. 152
Totelli, Antonio F. 156
Tower Laboratories, Essex, Connecticut 165
trademarks 16, 159
Tumulty, Joseph P. 129
Twain, Mark 3
Tylenol 164
Tyron, William 7

U.S. Department of Agriculture 62
United States Pharmacopoeia 158–59
U.S. Senate's Pure Food Committee 61–62

University of North Carolina, Chapel Hill 10, 16, 44, 123, 140

Vanderbilt, Alfred G.: beneficiaries of will 122; Caroline Lorillard and 113; dressed to the nines *119*; family and fortune 108–9; lost aboard the *Lusitania* 119–21; marriage to Elsie French 111–12; marriage to Margaret 107–8, 113–14; Mary Agnes O'Brien and 112–13; at Narragansett (1913) 118; in open-air vehicle *110*; rumors of Margaret's relationship with 104
Vanderbilt, Alfred G., Jr.: to Arcadia after his father's death 122; arrives in Newport aboard *Adroit* 134; estate near Margaret's in Sands Point 151; at first Preakness, IEE and 137; as horseman, obituary on 153–54; IEE's bequest to 148; Margaret's entertaining in West Palm Beach and 151; marriages and divorces of 155; with mother at Belmont Park *154*; to Newport to stay with relatives 133; parents travel to New York without 114; Paris visit with his mother and siblings 132; rumors of potential marriage to Margaret 84–85
Vanderbilt, Alfred G., III 114, 121
Vanderbilt, Alice 119
Vanderbilt, Cornelius 14, 108
Vanderbilt, Cornelius, II 44, 108, 111
Vanderbilt, Elsie French 84, 111–12, 114, 122, 131
Vanderbilt, George Washington, III: to Arcadia after his father's death 122; arrives in Newport aboard *Adroit* 134; estate near Margaret's in Sands Point 151; father sailing on *Lusitania* and 120; IEE's bequest to 148; marriages and divorces 155; to Newport to stay with relatives 133; Paris visit with his mother and siblings 132
Vanderbilt, Louise "Lulu" Miriam Parsons 155
Vanderbilt, Louise Mitchell Paine 155
Vanderbilt, Lucille (Lulu) 155
Vanderbilt, Margaret Emerson McKim 107–8, 118, 120, 121–22, 127, *154*; *see also* Emerson, Margaret
Vanderbilt, Reginald 121–22
Vanderbilt, Mrs. Reginald 80
Vanderbilt, William Henry 108, 109, 122
Vanderbilt, William K. *see* horses and horse racing
Vanderbilt Hotel, New York 113

Vandiver, Murray 89
Vaughn, Guy 51
Venture (Alfred's coach) 109, 111
Vickers, James 10
Victoire 74
Vivian, Daniel J. 70, 75
Vogel, Dorothy 125

Waccamaw Neck, South Carolina 69–70, 71, 75; *see also* Arcadia
Waddell, A.M. 9
Waggaman, John F. 16, 17
Wakefield Trust Company 145
Waldorf-Astoria 89, 101
Walker, William H. 97
Walters, Henry 45
War College, Newport, Rhode Island 31
Ward, Bernard J. 51
Ware, Dr. 64
Warner, Charles Dudley 3
Warner-Lambert Pharmaceutical Company 164
Washington, Booker T. 27–28
Washington Evening Star 115
Washington Herald 129
Washington Opera Company festival (1927) 130–31
Washington Post 18, 21, 96, 180*n*50
Wayfarer (A. Vanderbilt's private rail car) 111, 114
Webb-Ware, Walter 85, 107, 112–13, 121
Weber, Henry 112
Wells, Ralph A. 142–43
West Palm Beach 151, 153
Western Pacific Railway's 1915 wine list 65
Westinghouse, George, Jr. 127
Wheeler, Wayne 66
White, J. Wesley 41
White, Lillie Dunn 133
White, Walter Woodward 42
white supremacy 9
Whitehall (IEE mansion), Narragansett *145*, 146, 149, 156
Whitney, Mrs. Harry Payne 121–22
Wickes, Dr. Walter F. 116
Wickes, Mrs. Walter F. 116
Wiley, Harvey W. 62–63, 64, **64**, 65
Williams, N. Winston 91
Williamson, Charles Spencer 62
Wilmington, North Carolina race riot (1899) 9
Wilson, Eleanor 117
Wilson, Ellen 117
Wilson, Jessie 117

Wilson, Penny 120
Wilson, Woodrow 93, 94, 116–17, 118, 129
Wilson Mirror 18
Winston, Harry 141
Women's Christian Temperance Union 67
women's rights, in Maryland (1890s) 41
Wood, Walter 119, 120
World War I 118–19, 131–32
World War II 132, 152, 155
World's Fair (1893) 21, 24–25
Worthington Valley property 139, 148
Wrigley, William, Jr. 148

yachts 31, 118, 150; see also *Adroit*; *The Eleanor*; *Gardenia*; *The Margaret*; *The Nydia*; *Queen Anne*; sailing and cruises; *Susquehanna*
Yantic (cruiser) 28–29

Zara (yacht) 150

www.ingramcontent.com/pod-product-compliance
Ingram Content Group UK Ltd.
Pitfield, Milton Keynes, MK11 3LW, UK
UKHW042002140426
5217IPUK00015B/929